Affections of the Mind

Affections
of the
Mind

The Politics of

Sacramental Marriage

in Late Medieval

English Literature

EMMA LIPTON

University of Notre Dame Press

Notre Dame, Indiana

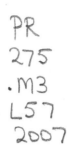
Designed by Wendy McMillen
Set in 11.2/14 Pavane by Four Star Books
Printed on 55# Nature's Recycled Paper by Versa Press

Library of Congress Cataloging-in-Publication Data

Lipton, Emma, 1964–
    Affections of the mind : the politics of sacramental marriage
in late medieval English literature / Emma Lipton.
        p.   cm.
    Includes bibliographical references and index.
    ISBN-13: 978-0-268-03405-4 (pbk. : alk. paper)
    ISBN-10: 0-268-03405-2 (pbk. : alk. paper)
    1. English literature—Middle English, 1100–1500—History
and criticism.   2. Marriage in literature.   3. Marriage—Political
aspects—England—History—To 1500   4. Marriage—Religious
aspects.   5. Authority in literature.   6. Social values in literature.
7. Social groups in literature.   8. Literature and society—England—
History—To 1500.   I. Title.
    PR275.M3L57   2007
    820.9'3543—dc22

                                                              2007020098

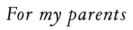

For my parents

CONTENTS

ACKNOWLEDGMENTS

Research for this book was generously supported by a Research Board fellowship from the University of Missouri, a Research Council Summer fellowship from the University of Missouri–Columbia, and by a Summer Research Fellowship and an Affirmative Action Research Grant from San Francisco State University. An early version of a portion of chapter 3 first appeared as "Performing Reform: The Marriage of Mary and Joseph in the N-Town Cycle" in *Studies in the Age of Chaucer* 22 (2001). I am grateful for permission to reprint that material here. A few pages of that same chapter are drawn from "Language on Trial: Performing the Law in the N-Town Trial Play" in *The Letter of the Law: Legal Practice and Literary Production in Medieval England,* edited by Candace Barrington and Emily Steiner (Ithaca: Cornell University Press, 2002).

I have many people to thank for their help in writing this book. Lee Patterson, Sarah Beckwith, Gail McMurray Gibson, Judith Ferster, and Stanley Fish shaped the initial project and my understanding of medieval literature and culture. Kathy Ashley, Frank Grady, and Emily Steiner read portions of the manuscript and made many helpful suggestions and comments. I am grateful for the engagement and support of my colleagues (and former colleagues) at University of Missouri, especially Martin Camargo, Ben Honeycutt, and Bill Kerwin. My book was significantly improved by the responses of the two anonymous readers for the University of Notre Dame Press. My thanks to Barbara Hanrahan for her wisdom and patience in guiding me through the publication process. My ideas about medieval marriage and medieval literature have been deepened and strengthened by many of my friends who are medieval scholars, especially Candace Barrington, Patricia DeMarco, Carroll Hilles, and Ethan Knapp. They offered an ideal blend of friendship and scholarly acumen; each offered invaluable suggestions and encouragement at key moments.

John Evelev read all of the manuscript multiple times. Without his in-tellectual engagement, love, and support, I might never have finished. The arrival of my daughter Margaret brought joy and distraction to the final stages of revision. This book is dedicated to my parents: to my mother, Alice Lipton, who first sparked my interest in the past, and to my father, Chuck Lipton, who always encouraged me to follow my passions.

Introduction

The Politics of Sacramental Marriage in Late Medieval Culture

Recent controversies over gay marriage have highlighted the important place of marriage in the complex nexus of civic and religious authority in modern life. We have suddenly been reminded that marriage is a deeply political institution. Although contemporary conservative voices have critiqued the political appropriation of marriage as a "perversion" of "traditional" values and of a "holy institution," my book argues that a similar politicized negotiation of social and religious authority can be found in late medieval England where an emergent lay middle strata of society used the sacramental model of marriage to exploit contradictions within medieval theology and social hierarchy. This model, derived from Saint Augustine and later codified in the twelfth century, defined marriage not as consummation but as the "affections of the mind," arguing that marriage was inherently virtuous.[1] According to the sacramental definition adopted by twelfth-century theologians and canonists, the substance of the sacrament of marriage was the mutual love between the two members of the couple; this love in turn was both the sign and substance of God's grace. *Affections of the Mind: The Politics of Sacramental Marriage in Late Medieval English Literature* traces the unprecedented popularity of the sacramental model of marriage as a literary topic in the late fourteenth and fifteenth centuries to its role as a contested category in the ideological conflicts between the laity and clergy, and between the members of the middle strata and the aristocracy. My book explores the ways that sacramental marriage was used to debate questions of authority in the period in a diverse group of late medieval texts, including the romance of Geoffrey Chaucer's *Franklin's Tale,* John Gower's lyric ballad sequence *Traitié pour Essampler les Amantz Marietz* (Treatise for Exemplifying Married Lovers), the autobiography of the bourgeois mystic Margery Kempe, and the N-Town plays.

I argue that the existence of a body of literature in late medieval England that was preoccupied with sacramental marriage can be linked to two key changes in the structure of contemporary society: the growth of lay piety, and the increased size and power of the middle sections of society. In late medieval England, the lay middle strata were a growing part of society whose members sought to share and appropriate the privileges of both the aristocrats and the clerics. Members of the middle strata began to encroach on aristocratic prerogatives: non-noble landowners acted as parliamentary representatives, merchants purchased country estates and coats of arms, and, while the knightly class declined, esquires were elevated to gentle status. These new political and social roles for the middle strata threatened the traditional hierarchical status of the aristocracy. Similarly, the growth of vernacular literature and lay devotional practices changed the relationship between lay and clerical authority. Clerical prerogatives became a subject of explicit debate in polemics exchanged between Lollard and orthodox proponents over such questions as the nature of the sacraments and the idea of a priesthood of all believers. It is the primary contention of this book that late medieval English literature presented sacramental marriage as a model for such values as lay spirituality and mutuality in social relations, and in doing so, helped both to express and create values for the members of the emergent middle strata, as well as helping them to construct an identity for themselves and understand themselves as a social group.

Sacramental marriage was one element of a wide range of complex, contradictory, and contested ideas about medieval marriage. Although there were many tensions within medieval marriage, two are especially important for my argument here.[2] Complicating the sacramental definition of marriage as consent, medieval theologians also taught the doctrine of the marital debt that required couples to engage in marital sex if the other partner required it. Another tension was between an understanding of marriage as a partnership based in love, a vision linked to the sacramental model, and a depiction of marriage as the rule of the husband over his wife. Robert of Brunne's early fourteenth-century *Handlyng Synne,* for example, paradoxically asserts that the husband is "No to be mayster, but felaw," only to continue a few lines later to instruct that the husband is "maystre, lorde & syre / To hys wyl [his wife] shall meke hyre."[3] This juxtaposition of conflicting marriage models without an acknowledgment of their seeming incompatibility is characteristic of late medieval marriage teachings.

These contradictions between defining marriage as love or sex, and as partnership or rulership, made it a particularly apt venue for negotiating tensions about shifting social and religious authority in late medieval England. Saint Augustine's consensual vision valorized a mutual model of marriage, assigning virtuous standing to horizontal relations, and thus potentially offering an alternative vision for broader social relations, one that shifted from the rigid hierarchy of the Three Estates to a more egalitarian vision. On the other hand, the hierarchical marriage model was sometimes deployed in late medieval writing as a metaphor for royal or local governance. It is arguably precisely because medieval marriage had a hierarchical model as well as a horizontal or partnership one that it was so useful in the articulation of middle strata values. Adopting the sacramental model, as I will show, was a way for the middle strata to reject a hierarchical vision of marriage that was associated with aristocratic or regal prerogative. Similarly, embracing a sacrament model of marriage based in love and mutual consent was a rejection of a model of marriage defined by sex which, at least since the twelfth-century ban on clerical marriage, was linked to the promotion of clerical prerogative. Adopting sacramental marriage could thus become a way to negotiate some of the traditional legitimizations of social hierarchy in late medieval English society, giving the middle strata its own discourse of legitimation.

Given the competing models of medieval marriage and their varying uses by different social groups, late medieval representations of marriage can be said to have the characteristics of "uneven development" that Mary Poovey has identified in a different context as describing the historical development of ideological shifts. Poovey argues that ideological formation can be

> uneven . . . in the sense of being articulated differently by different in-stitutions, discourses, and practices that it both constituted and was con-stituted by. . . . For some institutions or, for that matter, for some in-dividuals or groups within institutions, an ideological formation received one emphasis or was put to one use; while for other institutions, indi-viduals, or groups, the same ideological formation received a different emphasis and was used for another—even competing—goal.[4]

The sacramental marriage model was one possible "emphasis" in the over-determined "ideological formation" of late medieval marriage, which the members of the middle strata used to promote their own social values of lay authority and a horizontal vision of governance. Thus, my argument should not be understood as a comprehensive portrait of late medieval mar-riage or its politics, but as a claim that the lay middle strata were spe-cifically drawn to the sacramental model of marriage in contrast to the sexual model and the hierarchical model, embraced respectively by clergy and aristocracy.

Sacramental Marriage and the Promotion of Lay Authority

That the sacramental model of marriage supplied a vocabulary in late me-dieval texts for promoting the virtues of lay religious practice was in part the heritage of early twelfth-century legislation against clerical marriage which confirmed the status of celibacy as the truly pious life.[5] Making sexual status the defining line between clergy and laity, this legislation there-after tied the reputation of marriage directly to the status of the laity. In seeking to establish a clear hierarchy of the elite clergy over the lay masses, the laws against clerical marriage promoted the equation of marriage with sex, and sex with sin. Saint Paul's injunction that "it is better to marry than to burn" was often invoked to establish marriage as a last resort for those who could not maintain continence, and marriage was tolerated only as a remedy against carnal lust, a prophylactic measure against fornication and greater evils.[6] Even those who did not entirely reject marriage, and who saw procreation as one of the goods of marriage, nonetheless ranked it clearly below widowhood and far below celibacy. Despite the negative reputation of sex among theologians, the doctrine of the marital debt required spouses to have sexual intercourse if the other spouse requested it, and gave each spouse the right to request sex of the other partner.[7] Thus, while sex was thought to be sinful by medieval theologians, they nonetheless virtually required marital sex among the laity, an attitude that reinforced clerical authority and superiority.

On the other hand, by disassociating marriage from sex and defining it as love, sacramental marriage blurred the boundary between laity and clergy that reformers sought to impose and dignified marriage—and lay life generally—as a spiritual practice. The sacramental model of marriage had its roots in the writings of Augustine, who argued that marital affection instead of sexual relations defined marriage. In *De Bono Coniugali,* he argued that marriage was not just a relative virtue, in that it was better than fornication, but had three specific "goods," which became the substance of later medieval teachings on marriage: *proles, fides,* and *sacramentum.* In *De Nuptiis et Concupiscentia,* Augustine described the conjugal bond as a reflection of Saint Paul's exhortation: "Husbands, love your wives, even as Christ also loved the Church."[8] Augustine's writings on marriage were the basis of the sacramental definition adopted by twelfth-century theologians and canonists, who defined the substance of the sacrament of marriage as the mutual love between the two members of the couple; this love in turn was considered to be both the sign and substance of God's grace.[9] In the words of Hugh of Saint Victor:

> [T]he very association which is preserved externally in marriage by a compact is a sacrament and the substance of the sacrament itself is the mutual love of souls which is guarded in turn by the bond of conjugal society and agreement. And this very love again, by which male and female are united in the sanctity of marriage by their souls is a sacrament and the sign of that love by which God is joined to the rational soul internally through the infusion of His grace and the participation of His spirit.[10]

By linking conjugal love to God's grace, the sacramental definition clearly identified marriage as a spiritual practice. In the context of the laws against clerical marriage, the very fact that marriage, which defined the lay condition, could be a sacrament, suggested an elevation of lay status. Despite tensions between the sacramental and coital definitions of marriage, eventually, under Alexander III, consent between two legitimate parties, informed by marital affection, became the sole criterion of a fully legal and fully sacramental marriage.

The definition of marriage as based in love rather than consummation suggested that chaste marriage was an option for laypeople, a practice that seemed to blur the distinction between the continent clergy and the married laity which the reformers were so anxious to enforce. While chaste marriage was theoretically more admirable than procreative marriage, clerical authorities did not encourage this practice among the laity, and reasserted the centrality of sexual intercourse in marriage in pastoral manuals as a response to the adoption of marriage as a sacrament.[11] Nonetheless, a number of theologians recognized the possibility of chaste marriage, and the broad availability of this paradigm is evident in the many saints' lives portraying chaste marriage, which gained increasingly wide circulation in the course of the Middle Ages.[12] Chaucer's *Parson's Tale,* a compendium of conventional Church teaching, includes chaste marriage as a remedy for lechery. Furthermore, Dyan Elliott argues, "The impulse towards chastity was not an idiosyncratic fancy restricted to a handful of saints but was shared by 'ordinary' wives with pious leanings as well."[13] Chaste marriage narratives and practices were thus one way in which sacramental marriage promoted the spiritual authority of the laity.

Sacramental marriage not only made chaste marriage possible, it also led to practical issues of maintaining clerical control over weddings themselves. Since technically love was the substance of the marriage sacrament and the exchange of consent the sign of the sacrament, only the two consenting parties were necessary to make a valid and sacramental marriage.[14] Medieval weddings were potentially even more private than modern weddings. Unlike the modern ceremony in which a judge or religious officiant pronounces the couple husband and wife, according to medieval canon law, the words of the couple themselves had the performative function. Social and legal historians have shown that marriages consisting of a private exchange of vows, often referred to by critics as "clandestine marriages," were upheld by the Church courts.[15]

Furthermore, by making the sign of the marriage sacrament the exchange of vows, theologians ironically gave to laypeople crucial jurisdiction over one of the sacraments. With the exception of baptism and penance *in extremis,* no other sacrament could be performed without a priest. In the sacrament of the Eucharist, the words of the priest were performative in the sense that they caused what they signified, by transforming the bread and wine into the body and blood of Christ.[16] In the case of the marriage sacrament, by contrast, the words of consent spoken by the lay couple, rather than the words of the priest, were performative, and effectively transformed the two individuals into the one flesh that constituted the married state. This remained the case whether or not the wedding was performed in a church according to the proper liturgy and in the presence of a priest. The anomaly of the sacrament of marriage both presented a threat to clerical control over weddings and posed a potential challenge to the larger idea of priest-mediated sacraments.

This potential was realized in fifteenth-century East Anglia, when the Lollard heretics made marriage part of their challenge to clerical authority and the validity of the sacraments. Understanding that the hierarchy of virginity over marriage bolstered clerical monopoly and restricted lay claims to spiritual authority, the late medieval Lollards made an attack on clerical celibacy part of their challenge to clerical prerogative, and promoted marriage as a vocabulary for moral and religious life. According to the records of those prosecuted for heresy in the diocese of Norwich between 1428 and 1431, Edmund Archer of Lodne made the heretical claim that "chastite of monkes, chanons, freres, nonnes, prestes and of ony other persones is not commendable ne meritorie, but it is more commendable and more plesyng unto God al suche persones to be wedded and bringe forth frute of hare bodyes."[17] This deposition, like the many other similar ones in this court record, not only questioned the hierarchy of celibacy over marriage, but as a consequence also rejected the superiority of the clergy to the wedded laity. Just as the Norwich heretics systematically denied the need for other sacraments such as confirmation, confession, and baptism, and the transubstantiation of the Eucharist, so too they denied the need for "contract of wordis or solempnizacion in churche," claiming that only the consent of love between a man and a woman was necessary for marriage.[18] These depositions suggest that the accused did not understand that marriage was a uniquely lay sacrament that could be fully valid and fully sacramental according to orthodox definitions without the participation of the clergy. Nonetheless, they clearly did see the political importance of marriage, since they made their claim that marriage was superior to celibacy part of a broader attack on clerical prerogative.

Although the East Anglian Lollards used marriage explicitly to challenge clerical authority, marriage and the family also played an increased role in late medieval religious practices which was symptomatic of a broad-ranging growth in lay piety. Family pews were just beginning to be used in the late fifteenth century, and the growing presence of family tomb structures and marks of family ownership such as coats of arms in stained glass windows suggests that the family had become an important site for religious devotion in orthodox as well as heretical contexts.[19] Gail McMurray Gibson has shown that late medieval East Anglian parish churches often featured donor portraits with their families or married couples.[20] Marc Glasser has demonstrated that the number of married saints, including those with children and chaste saints, increased in the late Middle Ages.[21] For example, the increasingly popular cult of thrice-married Saint Anne was an overt celebration of family and kinship in religious practices, as the work of Kathleen Ashley, Pamela Sheingorn, and Gail McMurray Gibson has demonstrated.[22] Vernacular devotional books and religious objects were often found in the wills of wealthy merchants, and frequently a particular family member was named as the recipient.[23] Households supplied the bread for church services, encroaching on what had been the domain of the clergy.[24] Although laypeople were primarily spectators in Church liturgy, a new kind of private liturgy developed in books of hours, which were reformulated from old monastic rounds for consumption in the world and in the household.[25] Noblemen and wealthier merchants had private chapels in their homes, presided over by a family chaplain.[26] As these examples illustrate, in addition to the explicitly political uses of marriage made by fifteenth-century East Anglian Lollards, marriage and family were increasingly at the center of lay piety, subtly eroding the monopoly of clerical power.

Although the preceding account demonstrates several ways in which medieval marriage theology could promote lay piety, this perspective has not been emphasized in scholarly accounts of medieval theological history. Although the sacramental model of marriage was communicated to the laity through sermons, guidebooks, and penitentials, the fact that the marriage sacrament did not require a priest was deliberately avoided in these venues directed to a lay audience, which systematically described marriage as performed by a priest.[27] Works such as *The Book of Margery Kempe* and the N-Town Mary plays did political work by teaching this theology in vernacular forms that were available to a wider audience. As my readings will show, late medieval literature did not just repeat traditional marriage theology, but deployed it strategically to highlight its unorthodox implications.

Sacramental Marriage and the Social Authority of the Middle Strata

Late medieval English literature enlisted the sacramental model of marriage both to advocate for lay religious authority and to promote the social values of the emergent "middle strata" of society, an influential term coined in 1948 by Sylvia Thrupp to include "the lesser types of gentry, the merchant class, country yeomenry cherishing a tradition of free ancestry and perhaps also the more substantial semi-mercantile elements in London and other cities."[28] Although people like merchants, franklins, and lawyers may not have seen themselves as having the same interests, their absence from the traditional three estates model inevitably put them together. Even if they were not visible in the nostalgic and anachronistic three estates model still preached in the late Middle Ages, the growth of this sector of society was nonetheless evident from documents such as the poll taxes, sumptuary laws, and guild prayers. Furthermore, as Sylvia Thrupp and Paul Strohm have shown, the importance of this section of society was increasingly recognized in sermons, parliamentary documents, and other discursive accounts of late medieval English society.[29] Despite the fact that the middling sections of society were recognized in a variety of documents, as Sylvia Thrupp has argued, "there was obviously little cohesion among these assorted groups, not even a common theory of a middle class."[30] The members of the middle strata of society were in search of a social identity and a legitimizing ideology because they were a growing and newly powerful section of society that did not fit into conventional medieval theories of social formation. Sacramental marriage served an important role in the construction of an ideology for this emergent social group.

By depicting marriage as a partnership between husband and wife, the sacramental model favored a horizontal vision, and thus offered a microcosmic alternative vision for a broader social structure that worked to level the hierarchy of the three estates. That this more horizontal vision of society appealed to the members of the middle strata is not only logical, it is also evident from the social models present in documents such as contemporary records of guild ceremonies, and conduct books, which Kathleen Ashley, Mark Amos, and others have shown were consumed by both urban and rural elements of the middle strata of society.[31] For example, at the beginnings of meetings of the fraternity of Saint Christopher at Norwich, the members prayed for all of society. After enumerating the members of the "state of holy chirche," and then listing a range of aristocrats, the next group links urban and rural, noble and non-noble together, praying for "alle knyghtes, squyers, citeȝenis and Burgeys, fraunkeleyns and alle trewe tyliers and men of craft."[32] All three estates were grouped together in a fifteenth-century conduct book, *John Russell's Book of Nurture,* in the description for a possible seating plan for a feast. At the "table of good squyeris" the text proposes to seat religious figures (such as parsons, vicars, and parish priests), urban figures (such as city bailiffs, merchants, and "riche artyficeris"), middling landowners (such as "yeman of þe crowne" and "sargeaunt of arms") and a broader category of "gentilmen."[33] This description of the people to be seated at this table does not proceed by listing the members of each estate in turn, but instead moves randomly among the three estates as it progresses. In this way, this seating plan not only creates a group that cuts across the three estates, but demonstrates the extent to which the three orders could be integrated in fifteenth-century accounts of social status, especially those oriented to a middle strata audience.

This more horizontal method of viewing medieval society which traverses the conventional divisions of the three estates was also evident in a number of parliamentary documents that used income as a significant factor in determining social status. In the 1379 poll tax, for example, abbots, priors, and archdeacons are equated with barons and knights, while wealthy merchants are put on the same level as knights and esquires.[34] Similarly, the 1363 statute allowed merchants, citizens, burgesses, artificers, and handicraftsmen who made five hundred pounds per year to dress like esquires and gentlemen who made a hundred pounds per year.[35] Although the traditional model of society was not completely absent in this model, given that the nongentle urbanites had to make more money to garner the same privileges of dress as their gentle rural counterparts, these two statutes show a new recognition of the power and status of the middling sections of society and acknowledge horizontal models of society that challenge the hierarchy of traditional medieval political theory. In their emphasis on the role of income in defining social status, they also point to the increased social mobility of late medieval English society, especially for the middle sections.

This new social mobility can be linked to changing economic circumstances in the country and to the growth of professionalism and civil service. The economic conditions of late medieval England supported the advancement of smaller over larger landowners. In the mid-fourteenth century, revenues from aristocratic estates declined, and land values had dropped even more by the fifteenth century, although these factors were somewhat mitigated by the tendency of the size of landed estates to increase and by the addition of cash incomes to land resources.[36] On the other hand, economic conditions favored the advancement of smaller landowners, referred to in the poll tax as franklins, sergeants, *firmarii,* and esquires of lower means, who may have drawn a larger proportion of their income from rents.[37] This group was a prime target of the 1363 sumptuary legislation, reflecting an anxiety about the social mobility of this group in particular.[38] These smaller landowners played an increasingly important role in the administration of the shire, holding local offices and representing their localities in the House of Commons in Parliament, roles that had previously been held by knights. As E. W. Ives has shown, by the fifteenth century, the professionalization of legal practice provided an opportunity for social mobility, allowing a family to "rise within or into the ranks of the gentry."[39] A high-level lawyer like a sergeant-in-law could make enough to buy a significant estate, and in fact fifteenth-century English lawyers often showed their social aspirations by buying land and becoming country gentlemen. In addition to lawyers, a new class of civil servants also developed during this period, providing similar possibilities of social mobility for those wishing to enter or rise within the ranks of the gentry.[40] Wealthy merchants often intermarried with gentry, sent their sons to serve in gentle households, and even bought up land to become country landowners.

The middle strata's social mobility has been linked by scholars to a social vision in which virtue is defined by individual behavior rather than class status. Conduct literature promoted the idea that estate depends on behavior rather than birth, making instruction in aristocratic manners a venue for the development of an ideology of social mobility that appealed to the members of the middle strata. The "Lytylle Childrenes Lytil Boke," for example, decrees that having good manners makes people exclaim, "A gentylleman was heere."[41] Similarly, the fifteenth-century *Book of Nurture* presents profession as dependent on the capacity to learn:

> Now, son ʒiff y the teche, wiltow any thynge lere?
> wiltow be a seruaunde, plowʒman, or laborere?
> Courtyour or a clark, Merchaund, or masoun, or an artificere?[42]

This text articulates the very real promise that education could offer for social advancement in an age when law and civil service could provide entry into the gentry, linking social status to personal aptitude, while also suggesting that a failure to learn could lead to downward mobility.

This valuation of individual behavior and horizontally defined social relations which characterized the values of the middle strata correlates with the ideals of sacramental marriage outlined earlier. As we have seen, parliamentary documents, guild ceremonies, and conduct books all depicted a vision of society that made comparisons across the three estates, rejecting the traditional social hierarchy. Similarly, by defining marriage as mutual consent, the sacramental model depicted marriage as an equal partnership, in contrast to the hierarchical image of marriage simultaneously perpetuated in marriage sermons that instructed wives to obey their husbands. We have seen that the new social mobility of the middle strata correlated to the development of an ideology of virtue based in individual behavior rather than class status. Similarly, the sacramental model made marriage a matter of individual volition and private choice rather than an issue of family alliance or clerical control. Given this correlation between the social circumstances and values of the middle strata and the ideals of sacramental marriage, it is not surprising that a range of late medieval literature, from drama to romance, from lyrical ballads to mystical autobiography, showed an interest in sacramental marriage as a means of expressing the values and ideals of this emergent class.

The Literature of Sacramental Marriage

Aping aristocratic manners, dress, and pastimes and buying country estates and coats of arms were just some of the many ways that materials of aristocratic culture were appropriated and transformed by members of the middle strata to suit their own values and circumstances, as the work of Sylvia Thrupp and others has demonstrated.[43] In addition, the increased emphasis on the role of the family in religious practices, which I have described above, led to a similar appropriation and transformation of the materials of clerical culture as merchants became patrons of parish churches and owners of devotional texts and objects. The literature of sacramental marriage was another instance of this broader cultural appropriation and was accomplished through the revision of existing genres of writing and their accompanying models of love and marriage, demonstrating a process of cultural consumption of existing traditions.[44] As Michel de Certeau has argued, it is important to analyze the "manipulation" of representation by "those who are not its makers," since consumption manifests itself "through its ways of using the products imposed by the dominant order," making them "function in another register," which may entail making what one absorbs "one's own, appropriating or reappropriating it."[45] While the writers of this marriage literature in late medieval England are, of course, "makers" of representation, they are also notably appropriators, taking pre-existing forms and adapting them to their purposes in ways similar to de Certeau's imagining of the activism (rather than passivity) of modern consumers.

Late medieval marriage literature shows that its authors read or consumed existing genres and revised them to create new forms of marriage literature that often do not fit neatly into existing generic categories. The hybrid forms of late medieval sacramental marriage literature were a way both to appropriate the legitimation of traditional genres and to promote new social values. For example, in many vernacular works of the late Middle Ages, mystical marriage, traditionally used to glorify clerical celibacy and constructed by ecclesiastical interests, was depicted as part of the experience of lay spirituality, working to promote the virtues of earthly marriage. *Fin amor,* the literary expression of aristocratic honor and identity in ballads and romances, was transformed to create an image of mutual love in marriage that modeled a more horizontal model of social relations than could be found in the traditional three estates. By presenting marriage as a model for such values as lay spirituality and mutuality in social relations, the literature of sacramental marriage helped both to express and to create the values of the emergent middle strata, and assisted the members of the middle strata of society in constructing an identity for themselves and understanding themselves as a social group. The complex generic formulations of late medieval literature which depicted sacramental marriage showed an engagement with a new social and religious ideology in the period, illustrating Fredric Jameson's contention that "the mediatory function of a genre . . . allows the coordination of immanent formal analysis of the individual text and twin diachronic perspective of history of forms and the evolution of social life."[46] The prestige and authority of literary forms was eminently transferable, arguably far more so than the institutions and social positions of aristocrats and clerics.

I have chosen four texts as case studies which represent a range of genres demonstrating this "evolution of social life" through an engagement with aristocratic and clerical genres. By including the romance of the *Franklin's Tale,* the lyric ballad sequence of Gower's *Traitié,* the drama of the N-Town plays and the mystical autobiography of *The Book of Margery Kempe,* my book shows that the obsession with the discourse of sacramental marriage in late medieval English texts was not restricted to the literary history of a particular genre, but was instead a broad cultural phenomenon in which marriage was enlisted to perform ideological work for the middle strata. Each of my chosen texts can be identified as a recognizable genre and also as a hybrid (joining, for example, lyric ballad and treatise, or sermon and romance), showing the way that new generic formulations were necessary to express the emergent cultural values of the lay middle strata of society.

In addition to selecting examples from a range of genres, I have chosen to focus my analysis on works by authors and narrators representing the variety of social positions that composed the middle strata. Geoffrey Chaucer was the son of a vintner and became a civil servant (first a controller of customs from 1374 to 1387, and later a clerk of the king's works until 1391) and also an "esquire" who fought in the campaign of 1359–60, making him emblematic of those members of the middle strata whose social position was difficult to classify in traditional terms.[47] In contrast to Chaucer's own bureaucratic and mercantile experience, his rural landowner narrator, the Franklin, was representative of smaller non-noble landowners whose fortunes had risen in the fourteenth century in part due to their reliance on rents, at a moment when falling land values were hurting aristocrats with larger estates.[48] John Gower, who has been identified as an "esquire" and possibly as a lawyer, may have embodied a different aspect of the new professionalism of the period. Margery Kempe, herself a businesswoman, was the daughter of a wealthy merchant who was mayor of Lynn five times, and one of the town's two members of Parliament. Finally, the N-Town plays, possibly performed by guild members, may have found an audience in a broader cross section of urban society. The striking convergence of interest in sacramental marriage among these authors and narrators hints at the congruent religious and social goals within the diversity of late medieval English middle strata.

My work joins that of a number of scholars who have used the formulations of sacramental marriage to argue against the opposition of love and marriage in medieval culture as outlined in C. S. Lewis's landmark book *The Allegory of Love* (1936). Lewis saw the medieval literature of "courtly love" as fundamentally opposed to the predominant marital ideologies of the day, which he defined as the aristocratic vision, in which the woman was "little better than a piece of property," and the ecclesiastical vision, in which "passionate love itself was wicked," a depiction of marriage echoed in George Duby's widely cited *Medieval Marriage* (1978).[49] Henry Ansgar Kelly's important book, *Love and Marriage in the Age of Chaucer* (1975), sought to rectify this antimatrimonial vision of the Middle Ages by demonstrating the compatibility of love and marriage in a range of late medieval literature.[50] More recent book-length studies by Neil Cartlidge and Kathryn Jacobs have developed from Kelly's work, charting the theological and legal ramifications of the sacramental model of marriage backward into the twelfth and thirteenth centuries and forward into the Renaissance.[51] Although they engage with legal and theological history, all of these books focus on marriage as a domestic practice featuring the relationship of husbands and wives.

By contrast, my book argues for the public significance of this private institution. In this respect I follow a number of critics who have shown marriage to be crucial to the construction of late medieval sovereignty.[52] David Wallace, for example, argued in reference to the *Clerk's Tale* that "tyranny is . . . particularly for Chaucer, intimately connected with metaphors and flesh-and-blood practices of marriage."[53] Commenting on royal coronation rituals, Louise Fradenburg argued that the definition of marriage as consent was crucial to the construction of a positive image of royal power: "Marriage . . . is a powerful way of imagining the transformation of inequality into equality and thus assists sovereignty in the production of the experience of choice rather than coercion."[54] Lynn Staley has recently argued that "works of domestic economy and pastoral management" are "linked to a concept of nationhood," in which royal and familial figurations of authority are implicated in each other.[55] Following the work of these scholars, my book treats sacramental authority as deeply bound up with competing notions of society.

Rather than focusing on the marriage as an exploration of sovereignty, however, my book demonstrates how the literature of sacramental marriage engaged the mutually constituting realms of social and religious order by promoting the authority of the lay middle strata. Thus, the "politics" of my book title refers to social and religious rather than governmental politics.[56] In this connection, my work is influenced by the scholarship of Sarah Beckwith and Miri Rubin whose work on the Eucharist has demonstrated how Corpus Christi festivals and Corpus Christi drama mediated tensions between lay and clerical authority and staged issues of power and status within the lay urban community.[57] My argument that the literature of sacramental marriage promoted the values of the lay middle strata is indebted to Beckwith's and Rubin's understanding of sacramental representation as engaging with questions of both secular and religious authority. Beckwith's work has also shown that representations of the sacrament of the Eucharist were not enactments of a static set of established beliefs, but a staging of tensions and fissures within urban society.[58] Similarly, my argument suggests that literary representations of the sacramentalism of marriage do not so much convey conventional church teachings—although they draw on this discourse—but enact social tensions around the increasing power of the lay middle strata. Representations of the marriage sacrament were not deployed solely by the clergy, nor were representations of love the exclusive province of the aristocracy; they were also available to and appropriated by the lay middle strata. In looking at the relationship between literary representations of marital sacramentalism and the ambitions of the lay middle strata, I engage what Beckwith has termed the relationship between "social relation and symbolic act."

In arguing that sacramental marriage promoted the values of the lay middle strata, I understand marriage itself as a fluid and contested category rather than one with a fixed meaning. Drawing on Mikhail Bakhtin's and Homi Bhabha's notions of "hybridity," Glenn Burger has argued, "Medieval conjugality provides a conduit through which power relations flow, change and crystallize in hegemonic ways, working to resist and subvert authority."[59] The late medieval literature of sacramental marriage revised aristocratic and clerical traditions of writing on love and marriage in order to promote the values of the lay middle strata, subverting aristocratic and clerical prerogatives. The changing meanings of marriage in this period can be linked to a fluidity within the identity of the middle strata as its members began to understand themselves as a social group.

I begin with the *Franklin's Tale* from *The Canterbury Tales,* which has been central to discussions of late medieval marriage since 1912, when George Lyman Kittredge famously proclaimed it Geoffrey Chaucer's "solution" to the "problem" of gendered sovereignty raised in the tales of the "marriage group."[60] Unlike Kittredge, I will not make a broad argument about Chaucer's view of marriage, but will suggest that the *Franklin's Tale* is part of a larger cultural formation in which members of the lay middle strata used sacramental marriage to promote and formulate their social and cultural values. In making this claim, I build on the work of Lee Patterson and Glenn Burger, both of whom have argued that the depiction of marital relations in the *Canterbury Tales* is tied to the construction of bourgeois ideology.[61] By choosing to focus on one of the *Canterbury Tales,* I will necessarily not be saying all there is to say about marriage in the work of Chaucer, nor all there is to say about marriage and the construction of bourgeois ideology in the tales. Instead, my goal is to show how one specific marriage model—sacramental marriage—was appropriated and adapted by the middle strata and to demonstrate how Chaucer's *Franklin's Tale* is part of a larger body of writings drawn from disparate genres and authors to promote and formulate an ideology for the middle strata. Thus, I have chosen to focus on the *Franklin's Tale* not because it is Chaucer's answer to the marriage "problem," as Kittredge suggests, but because it is the tale most focused on the politics of the sacramental marriage model.[62]

Specifically, I argue that in the *Franklin's Tale,* Chaucer uses marriage to formulate a social ideology by revising the conventions of romance and secularizing an ecclesiastical tradition (as yet not properly recognized in the criticism of the tale) that drew on the vocabulary of the classical friendship tradition to describe mutuality in marriage. By the end of the tale these virtues of free will, generosity, and private value apply less to the married couple than to the homosocial bonds of friendship forged among the three men—the Knight, the Squire, and the Clerk—in their negotiations about the marriage. This exchange of marriage ideology among men becomes the basis for the idea that people of different social classes have equal claims to *gentillesse.* This political ideology would have appealed to a person like the Franklin, who as a "freeholder" was representative of the newly socially mobile middle strata of society, and as a civil servant was representative of the growth of government and civic ideology in the later Middle Ages. The Franklin's focus on male bonding at the end of the tale and his failure to address Arveragus's violence toward his wife suggest that he may be more invested in using marriage to articulate a horizontal ideology of equality than in constructing truly egalitarian gender relations. Thus, the tale is part of a new cultural formation of a political and social ideology for the Franklin and other members of the middle strata constructed from the discourse of marriage.

Just as Chaucer's *Canterbury Tales* has shaped discussions of late medieval marriage, John Gower's work, especially his *Confessio Amantis,* has been crucial to critical debates about medieval love and marriage. As Elizabeth Porter has shown, marriage functions as a miniature image of political community in the mirror for princes section of John Gower's *Confessio Amantis,* and Lynn Staley has recently demonstrated the importance of marriage to a number of Gower's other works.[63] I have chosen to focus on Gower's *Traitié pour Essampler les Amantz Marietz* in my second chapter because it is in this poem that Gower most thoroughly explores the sacramental model and here that Gower ties marriage not to the governance of the realm but to the values of his own social position. The *Traitié* appears exclusively domestic in subject but reveals its social politics by deliberately reworking the traditional genres of romance and sermons, creating a new ideology from the materials of aristocratic and clerical culture. In contrast to the paradigms of aristocratic romance, heroes such as Tristan and Ulysses are revealed to be domestic horrors, and it is the private world of sexual conduct, rather than the public world of military honor, that most determines masculine virtue. Revising medieval clichés of female virtue and vice familiar from clerical misogyny, the tales value marriage over chastity and shift moral responsibility for sexual practices from women to men. Gower replaces the three estates with the three grades of chastity and implies that anyone who is morally superior in marriage can be of the highest status. While presented as a classless secular model of male moral virtue, with the prologue addressed to "everyone in general" ("a tout le monde en general") and envoy "to the community of the whole world" ("Al université de tout le monde"), in fact the ballads of the *Traitié* participate in a new social vision for the emergent upper middle strata of society and reveal the ideological roots of the public voice of Ricardian poetry in a new masculinized vision of private life.[64]

My third chapter addresses the depiction of marriage in the N-Town plays through the context of the crucial role that Mary and Joseph played in the development of a sacramental definition of marriage. By staging the wedding of the holy couple, "The Marriage of Mary and Joseph" invites comparison between the marriage sacrament and the play's own dramatic form, calling attention to the way that defining a wedding as an exchange of vows made marriage a uniquely lay sacrament in which priestly participation was not essential. Similarly, in "The Trial of Mary and Joseph," marriage becomes a model for a sacramental drama sanctifying lay piety, as Mary is exonerated from accusations of adultery by the staging of a truth test, modeled on the linguistic sacrament of marriage. This chapter includes an analysis of "Joachim and Anna," which invokes contemporary controversy about the role of laypeople in religious practices by placing a married couple, rather than Church authority, at the center of religious practice, reflecting the lay pious sensibility of the guild members who probably staged the drama. These N-Town plays show that marriage was not only a domestic practice, but also a site of ideological contestation in late medieval England, marking complex fissures and tensions in the fabric of East Anglian religious life.

My fourth chapter argues that marriage is central to Margery Kempe's attempts to reconcile her spiritual ambitions with her lay bourgeois values. *The Book of Margery Kempe* both imagines a marriage ideology consistent with bourgeois values and uses marriage to formulate bourgeois ideology. I explore ways that *The Book* aspires to the genre of hagiography, depicting marital sex as horribly oppressive and unclean, a portrayal in conflict with the depiction of her marriage elsewhere in the text as conforming to companionate bourgeois norms. Behind this tension in the portrait of Kempe's marriage, I argue, is the split in theology between a definition of marriage based in sexual relations, which emphasized the marital debt, and a sacramental definition based in love, which had its roots in the politics of the conflict between the clerical and the lay authority. For Margery, marriage becomes linked to the construction of subjectivity and to the privacy oriented to a public audience typically seen to characterize the bourgeois values of a later period. Like the other texts in this study, from Chaucer's *Franklin's Tale* to the N-Town Mary plays, *The Book of Margery Kempe* appears to adapt marriage in unusual ways, but Margery's revision of mystical marriage is less the work of an eccentric individual than part of a larger body of writings, authored by and directed to the members of the emergent lay middle strata of society who appropriated clerical culture for their own ends.

CHAPTER ONE

Married Friendship

An Ideology for the Franklin

As with the other *Canterbury Tales,* criticism of the *Franklin's Tale* has been preoccupied with identifying the ways in which the tale reflects the social status of the teller. Early critics have seen in Chaucer's Franklin's hopes for his son and in his opulent hospitality evidence of social climbing.[1] On the other hand, Henrik Specht has argued that the Franklin is not a social climber because he may already be considered gentle, and thus an appropriate voice for gentle values.[2] More recently, Nigel Saul and Paul Strohm have identified the Franklin as a member of the middle strata, a wealthy freeholding landowner, a category of person who had not yet achieved gentility at the time *The Canterbury Tales* was written.[3] The figure of the Franklin was an effective representative of the new social mobility of late medieval society, because, as several historians have suggested, the forces for economic change at the end of the Middle Ages were to be found not so much in the urban as in the rural populations.[4] Franklins shared the freeborn status of gentlemen but were not themselves noble; however, as successful small landowners, they sometimes lived in a manner that resembled that of the lower ranks of gentle society. Thus, the Franklin was a crucial example of the members of the middle strata of society who did not fit comfortably into the conventional three estates model. In this tale, the Franklin formulates an ideology for his own emergent class through his portrait of marriage which becomes the basis for an egalitarian political vision at the end of the tale.

To derive a portrait of marriage that expresses the social values of the Franklin, the tale adopts and revises the conventions of romance and *fin amor,* mainstays of aristocratic literary ideology, by drawing on sacramental marriage. Although the *Franklin's Tale* is a romance, the tale critiques and transforms that genre's frequent association of marriage with knightly prowess and public display, replacing them with an emphasis on individual choice and mutual love characteristic of the sacramental marriage model. The tale not only draws on the broad ideas of sacramental marriage, but it also specifically invokes the classical friendship tradition, often used by medieval theologians and sermon writers to describe the mutuality of conjugal love. This language of marital friendship becomes a means of elaborating an ideal of marriage based in free will, private value, and choice, virtues, as we will see, that are particularly appropriate to the Franklin's social status in contrast to the aristocratic ideology commonly expressed by romance.

As Kathryn Jacobs has observed, although most of the tale focuses on the domestic relationship between husband and wife, Arveragus and Dorigen, by the end of the tale marriage has become the rubric for expressing a vision of an ideal society.[5] This is not a universal ideal, however, but one specifically suited to the Franklin's social politics. The values of mutuality, generosity, and free choice, initially used to depict the marital relationship, are associated at the end of the tale with the homosocial bonds of friendship forged among the three men—the Knight, the Squire, and the Clerk—in their negotiations about the marriage. This friendship, with its bonds of mutuality ranging across the estates, constructs a horizontal political model and a vision of society in which virtue is defined by personal merit rather than social status. Thus, the values of marital friendship, crucial to sacramental marriage, become the basis for an idealized middle strata political vision.

For many readers of the tale, the shift away from the domestic relationship at the end is surprising, and indeed Dorigen's absence from the end of the tale has been a conundrum for many critics. Her absence can be explained, however, if we see it as an indication that marriage has become a vocabulary for social politics. Although the shift to politics at the end is somewhat abrupt, the tale's appropriation of the aristocratic discourse of love to create a political model of marriage has a context in contemporary court poetry. As critics such as Lynn Staley, Lee Patterson, and others have demonstrated, love was recognized as a discourse of power by Chaucer and his contemporaries such as John Gower, Thomas Usk, and John Clanvowe.[6] C. Stephen Jaeger has shown that the social function of love as a political language has its origins in earlier Continental courtly discourse.[7] In the fourteenth and fifteenth centuries, the courtly discourse of love was used both explicitly and implicitly to comment on court and royal politics, often with references to specific events. Here, however, the discourse of aristocratic love is appropriated not for royal or court politics but to fashion marriage as a horizontal political model focused on personal merit and participatory governance which would have appealed to the members of the middle strata. This horizontal political model was of specific relevance to the Franklin, who is described in the Prologue as a member of Parliament and a sheriff. These offices make the Franklin emblematic of a representative ideal and a symbol of the new civic status accorded to members of the middle strata in the late Middle Ages. It is specifically the Franklin's role as a civil servant, I will argue, that explains the revision of romance to emphasize the values of free will, choice, and private value.

Rewriting Romance

It is logical for a socially mobile figure such as the Franklin to appropriate the language of love, because love was tied to public status and social standing in aristocratic literary tradition. As C. Stephen Jaeger has demonstrated, earlier Continental models established a courtly discourse in which feelings are seen as the province of nobles and love became a "form of aristocratic self-representation." Love asserted class privilege, stabilizing hierarchy in favor of an aristocratic elite, and conferred honor on those who practiced it by inspiring virtue, a construction indebted, Jaeger argues, to Ciceronian writings on the elitist honor of friendship.[8] A broad range of critics has shown that this paradigm of "ennobling love" was a commonplace in late medieval courtly literature.⁹ This idea that love was a source of chivalric virtue was both literary paradigm and aristocratic practice in the late medieval period, as this passage from the biography of Mareschal Bouicicault illustrates:

> [O]ne reads of Lancelot, of Tristan, and of many others whom Love made good and famous. Indeed, in our own time living now in France and elsewhere there are many such noble men . . . [O]ne speaks of Sir Otho de Graunson, of the good constable of Sancerre, and of many others whom it would be too long to name and whom love has made valiant and virtuous. O what a noble thing is love to him who knows how to use it!¹⁰

This association of love with nobility is acknowledged and transformed by the Franklin in his tale. He makes marriage and marital love the central vocabulary for defining virtue in the tale, appropriating some of the paradigms of *fin amor* and applying them to marriage and revising the portrait of marriage in romance. Virtue is tied not to aristocratic notions of martial prowess inspired by love but to civic values appropriate to the Franklin's social status and derived from sacramental marriage theology and teachings.

This familiar paradigm in which *fin amor* inspires a specifically knightly kind of virtue is invoked at the beginning of the *Franklin's Tale*:

> In Armorik, that called is Britayne,
> Ther was a knyght that loved and dide his payne
> To serve a lady in his beste wise;
> And many a labour, many a greet emprise,
> He for his lady wroghte er she were wonne.
>
> (729–33)¹¹

The Franklin calls to mind one familiar type of romance plot that recounts the narrative of an unmarried knight's famous deeds, the labors and enterprises inspired by the love of his lady, and ends with marriage, which Stephen Knight has referred to as "the knight-alone structure."¹² This passage alludes to the role marriage often plays in romance: as an apotheosis of battle, an ending that brings meaning to the tale by validating the prowess of a knight, while the meaning of marriage itself is taken to be self-evident. The passive verb form "she were wonne" suggests that the lady is a prize, an award that depends only on the great enterprise of the knight and not on her own volition. Furthermore, the generic quality of this passage and the substitution of "a knyght" and "a lady" for Dorigen and Arveragus's proper names suggests that Chaucer wanted to invoke this conventional equation of love and prowess.

Granting a woman in marriage to inspire or reward military prowess, as Margaret Adlum Gist has shown, was a familiar trope in medieval romance.[13] This convention is dramatized in the *Knight's Tale*, when Theseus establishes the tournament to determine whether Arcite or Palamon is to marry Emily. Just as the compressed opening lines of the *Franklin's Tale* elide any references to the lady's volition, Theseus claims to speak for Emily in proposing the tournament. Addressing the two rivals, he assures them that "Ech of you bothe is worthy, douteless, / To wedden whan tyme is" (1831–32), asserting, "I speke as for my suster Emelye" (1833). He goes on to say

> That wheither of yow bothe that hath might—
> This is to seyn, that wheither he or thow
> May with his hundred, as I spak of now,
> Sleen his contrarie, or out of the lystes dryve,
> Thanne sal I yeve Emelya to wyve . . .
>
> (1856–60)

In this passage Emily's agency, and her desire, are displaced by Theseus's in a conversation among the three men focused on resolving the conflict between Arcite and Palamon.[14] Before the marriage we hear only that "Bitwixen hem was maad anon the bond / That highte matrimoigne or mariage, / By al the conseil and the baronage" (3094–96). Her marriage is represented as an explicitly political act requiring the command of the king, the advice of Parliament and the participation of council and baronage. Her marriage is not her own but the embodiment and confirmation of the values of aristocratic society and its public world of honor, a public event as theatrical as the tournament that precedes it.

After its beginning passage, however, the *Franklin's Tale* begins to deviate from the conventions of *fin amor* by granting Dorigen agency and thus rejecting the values of romance in favor of the choice offered by marriage laws and derived from sacramental marriage theology. Unlike Emily, who, like a conventional romance heroine, is given in marriage by Theseus, Dorigen selects her marriage partner:

But atte laste she, for his worthynesse,
And namely for his meke obeysaunce,
Hath swich a pitee caught of his penaunce
That pryvely she fil of his accord
To take hym for hir housbonde and hir lord,
Of swich lordshipe as men han over hir wyves.

(738–43)

Although Dorigen is the subject of the passive verb "was wonne" in the opening lines, shortly thereafter she is given an active verb "she fil." As David Aers has observed, no mention is made of family, property, or money playing a role in her decision, often described by critics as determining factors in aristocratic marriage.[15] Indeed, the fact that she is said to have "comen of so heigh kynrede" (735) implies that she is of higher status than the knight and must have other reasons for marrying than social advancement. Her "pitee" is, by implication, less the generic expression of aristocratic identity than the motivation for a personal choice. Thus, by thematizing Dorigen's choice in marriage, the Franklin draws on a value derived from the sacramental marriage model to revise the terms of aristocratic romance.

Although Emily's marriage is represented as a public event, Dorigen's betrothal is accomplished not publicly but "pryvely." Despite the fact that the sacramental paradigm legalized private marriage, this trope of secrecy is characteristic not of betrothal but of the love vow in lais and romances, exemplified by the fairy lady's first command to her knight in Thomas Chestre's late fourteenth-century *Sir Launfal*:

But of o thyng, Syr Knyght, I warne the,
That thou make no bost of me
For no kennes mede!
And yf thou doost, I warny the before,
All my love thou hast forlore![16]

In this passage, the lady's words suggest that the very existence of her love depends on its secrecy and that it will be lost if forced into the social world. This association of *fin amor* and secrecy is also played out in other lais, romances, and courtly texts, such as *Sir Gawain and the Green Knight*, when the lady insists that Gawain keep her love token secret from her husband and the public sphere of her marriage, in the *Lai le Freine,* in which the private and tortured love of the heroine is transformed by a public and recuperative marriage at the end, and in the blunt assertion of Andreas Capellanus that "when made public love rarely endures."[17]

Although Dorigen's association of love with secrecy follows the generic expectations of romance, the application of this trope to marriage is unconventional. In response to Dorigen's agreement, Arveragus also makes a secret vow:

> And for to lede the moore in blisse hir lyves,
> Of his free wyl he swoor hire as a knyght
> That nevere in al his lyf he, day ne nyght,
> Ne sholde upon hym take no maistrie
> Agayn hir wyl, ne kithe hire jalousie,
> But hire obeye, and folwe hir wyl in al,
> As any lovere to his lady shal,
> Save that the name of soveraynetee,
> That wolde he have for shame of his degree.
>
> (744–52)

As with Dorigen's, Arveragus's vow does not completely break with the tradition of romance but shifts its terms. Like the good lovers of romance, he vows to obey his lady and to keep their love secret, but his vow applies to love within, not outside, marriage. According to Geoffroi de Charny's *Livre de Chevalerie,* secrecy in love is required by knightly honor:

> [L]ove a lady truly and honorably, for it is the right position to be in for those who desire to achieve honor. But make sure that the love and the loving are such that just as dearly as each of you should cherish your own honor and good standing, so should you guard the honor of your lady above all else and keep secret the love itself and all the benefit and the honorable rewards you derive from it.[18]

In contrast to de Charny's prescription, Arveragus's secrecy in love does not contribute to his honor as a knight, perhaps because his love is marital. Instead, his forbearance of mastery, with its private vow, is specifically identified as conflicting with his public knightly identity, since Arveragus feels compelled to maintain "the name of soveraynetee," while keeping the true nature of his relationship secret. This explicitly sets up the marriage as a private arrangement that is not only apart from the public world but in opposition to "his degree," the public social values of his aristocratic class.

Arveragus's decision to make this vow to Dorigen also differs from the public norms of aristocratic masculinity in its emphasis on his "free wyl." In contrast, many lais and romances portray love as a compulsion or sickness, beyond the individual's control.[19] Often the obligatory nature of love is linked to the vocabulary of feudal obligation, as in this passage from *Equitan,* a passage whose terms are endlessly repeated in the literature of *fin amor:*

> Love drafted him into his service:
> he shot an arrow at the king
> that opened a great wound in the heart,
> where Love had aimed and fixed it.
> Neither good sense nor understanding were of use to the king now;
> love for the woman so overcame him
> that he became sad and depressed.
> Now he has to give in to love completely;
> he can't defend himself at all.
>
> . . . .
>
> "I think I have no choice but to love her . . ."[20]

The word *service* implies that the king is a vassal of love, while the imagery of arrows and defense suggests the martial identity of an aristocrat. Love commands the man like a feudal lord, but this imagery becomes complex as the commanding figure turns his arrow toward his vassal instead of protecting his subject, and aggressively inflicts pain, while the lover is so overcome that he cannot defend himself. The opening lines of the *Franklin's Tale* briefly allude to the pain of love's rule when they describe the knight's hesitation to tell the lady of "his wo, his peyne, and his distresse," but instead of controlling him, Arveragus's love allows an acknowledgment of Dorigen's will and desires, and a willingness to forgo mastery over her. Arveragus's free will in love and his forgoing of mastery conflicts with his knightly identity, suggesting that he represents the interests of the Franklin telling the tale rather than his own aristocratic values.

This break with the code of aristocratic love is defined in the tale as an attempt to achieve happiness. In the above quotation, Arveragus makes this vow of obedience "for to lede the moore in blisse hir lyves." His promise is subsequently echoed by another vow by Dorigen, oriented toward a similar goal:

> She seyde, "Sire, sith of youre gentillesse
> Ye profre me to have so large a reyne,
> Ne wolde nevere God bitwixe us tweyne,
> As in my gilt, were outher werre or stryf.
> Sire, I wol be youre humble trewe wyf—
> Have heer my trouthe—til that myn herte breste."
>
> (754–59)

Dorigen's stated goal is to avoid strife in their marriage insofar as it is in her control. The diction of Dorigen's vow suggests that she is motivated by her admiration for Arveragus's more personal and civic virtue of *gentillesse*, rather than by his feats of battle, his "greet emprise." The fact that Dorigen's pledge comes after the Knight has already made his promise, and after she has been given "so large a reyne," makes her vow more than a mouthing of conventional female subservience; for this tale, true happiness and proper vows can only be made from a position of freedom, not obligation or servitude.

Dorigen's vow evokes the wording of vows in the English marriage formulas which expressed the mutual consent or free choice that was considered the sign of the love that was, in turn, the substance of sacramental marriage. In the Sarum Missal, the woman recites:

> I N. take te [*sic*] N. my weddyd husbonde, tho have et to holde for ths day for bettur, for wurs, for richere, for porer, in sykenesse and in helthe, to be bonowre et buxum, in bed et at bord, tyll deth vs departe, if holy chirche wol it ordeyne: et ther to I plyche te [*sic*] my throute.[21]

Similarly, Dorigen also pledges her "trouthe," and her vow "til that myne herte brest" suggests "tyll deth vs departe." By emphasizing the exchange of vows, the tale draws on sacramental law and teaching that represents mutual love as the basis of marriage. Furthermore, Chaucer softens the hierarchical implications of the wording of the marriage vow for women, by replacing the traditional vow to be "bonowre et buxum" with Dorigen's pledge to be "humble," and by pairing it with Arveragus's vow to "hym take no maistrie." In this way, the tale uses the ideals of sacramental marriage to revise the way that marriage is conventionally depicted in romance. Furthermore, by associating Dorigen and Arveragus's marriage with the secrecy usually reserved for *fin amor* in romance, the tale invokes the paradigm of private marriage made legal by the sacramental model.

This allusion to ecclesiastical discourse is marked by an abrupt shift in the pace of the tale immediately after the exchange of vows. Whereas the opening of the tale is recounted in a compressed style that parodies the parataxis of romance, after the exchange of vows between Dorigen and Arveragus discourse-time expands well beyond story-time, and the narrative dilation seems to resemble the expansive form of sermons as the Franklin temporarily takes on the discursive style of a preacher.[22] Not only does he specifically invoke the authority of clerics, "as thise clerkes seyn" (774), but his style is so evocative of clerical voicing that critics have commonly called this passage the "sermon on marriage." The Franklin begins his "sermon" by elaborating on the ideal of marital mutuality:

> For o thyng, sires, saufly dar I seye,
> That freendes everych oother moot obeye,
> If they wol longe holden compaignye.
> Love wol nat been constreyned by maistrye.
> (761–64)

In this passage, the Franklin depicts the marriage of Dorigen and Arveragus as based in a love that is made possible by their mutual obedience and the absence of hierarchical authoritarianism in their relationship. This depiction of marriage as grounded in loving mutuality echoes the logic of sacramental marriage as taught in popular sermons. In a characteristic example, Jacobus de Vitriaco (c. 1170–1240) derives his teachings from an exegesis of the formation of Adam and Eve:

> It is said in Genesis that the Lord took one of Adam's ribs, and formed woman from it. From this, we are to understand that the Lord wanted a wife to be her husband's partner, not his mistress, which is why she was not made out of man's feet. Therefore she should not be treated with

contempt or despised. Her husband should *love her as himself* since they are one flesh.[23] [My italics]

This exegesis of the formation of Adam and Eve was so common in marriage sermons that in their study of *ad status* sermons D. L. d'Avray and M. Tausche have named this recurring trope the "rib topos."[24] Since popular sermons were important sources through which theology reached the laity, we can safely assume that this paradigm of medieval marriage was widely known, and it was certainly familiar to Chaucer because he reproduced it in the *Parson's Tale* at the end of *The Canterbury Tales*.[25]

Concluding his "sermon," the Franklin shifts back to the courtly vocabulary of *fin amor,* demonstrating the difficulties of articulating the idea of marital mutuality using the terms of romance:

> Heere may men seen an humble, wys accord;
> Thus hath she take hir servant and hir lord—
> Servant in love, and lord in mariage.
> Thanne was he bothe in lordshipe and servage.
> Servage? Nay, but in lordshipe above,
> Sith he hath both his lady and his love;
> His lady, certes, and his wyf also,
> The which that lawe of love acordeth to.
>
> (791–98)

In this passage, marriage is represented as a hierarchy of husband over wife, and the opposite of the hierarchy of *fin amor,* in which the knight serves his lady. Although the ostensible goal of this passage is to praise the mutuality in the couple's marriage, the rhetorical form undermines this message, stressing instead a tension between mutuality and hierarchy. The double chiasmus (servant . . . lord . . . lordshipe . . . servage? . . . lordshipe) with the repetition of the terms *servant* and *lord* and the construction of an image of mutuality from a juxtaposition of contrasting hierarchies seems, as Susan Crane has observed, to show that the mutuality of Arveragus and Dorigen's agreement cannot readily be expressed using the aristocratic and feudal vocabulary of *fin amor*.[26]

The characterization of *fin amor* and marriage as antithetical hierarchies has its roots in a courtly tradition exemplified by the Friend's advice to the Lover in *Le Roman de la Rose,* when he argues against marriage:

Love cannot endure or live if it is not free and active in the heart. For this same reason we see that those who at first are accustomed to love each other *par amour* may, after they want to marry each other, find that love can hardly ever hold them together; for when the man loved *par amour* he would proclaim himself his sweetheart's sergeant, and she grew used to being his mistress. Now he calls himself lord and master over her whom he called his lady when she was loved *par amour*.[27]

Describing how marriage involves an inversion of the gender hierarchy present in love, this passage suggests that because the husband is "lord and master" in marriage, and love can exist only when "free and active in the heart," the attempt to achieve love in marriage is doomed to failure, since "love can hardly ever hold them together." This vision of love and marriage as contrasting hierarchies can be seen in the plot lines of many lais, such as *Guigemar,* in which a lover pledges obedience to his lady, who is in turn subject to her husband's control. The Franklin makes a similar assertion in a passage several lines before his exploration of the competing hierarchies of love and marriage:

> Love wol nat been constreyned by maistrye.
> Whan maistrie comth, the God of Love anon
> Beteth his wynges, and farewel, he is gon!
> Love is a thyng as any spirit free.
>
> (764–67)

Chaucer's Franklin repeats the Friend's association of love with equality, and he even uses the word *free* to describe mutuality in marriage. This similarity has led critics such as David Aers to read the Franklin's ideal of mutuality in marriage in the same context as the idealism of the *Le Roman de la Rose,* where freedom in love is associated with the lost golden age, and thus with an unachievable ideal.[28] Taking issue with G. L. Kittredge's famous reading of marital mutuality in the tale as Chaucer's answer to the problem of gendered sovereignty raised in the "marriage group," many critics view the Franklin's words and his vision of mutuality in marriage as a utopian ideal, divorced from the realities of medieval marriage practice and theory.[29] This reading is confirmed, these critics suggest, by the ending of the tale which shows conclusively that this goal of idealistic mutuality in marriage is doomed to failure.[30] Angela Weisl understood the hierarchical model of medieval marriage to be so predominant that she claimed, "As a public, political state, marriage's requirements are as conventional as those of romance."[31] As we have seen, however, the terms of marital mutuality were familiar from popular sermons based on sacramental marriage theology. Thus, the chiasmus of lordship and service which comes at the end of the sermon on marriage can be seen not as an effort to show the unavailability of the terms of mutuality in marriage in medieval society as a whole, but rather as a critique of their absence from the terms of romance, and perhaps from aristocratic society more generally.

The Franklin's rejection of romance paradigms in favor of the values of free choice and mutuality which are part of the sacramental marriage model is also achieved through the pacing of the text. As Judith Ferster has observed, the *Franklin's Tale* continually draws attention to its own textuality through an intrusive narrator obsessed with the timing of his storytelling who constantly calls attention to his own narrative acts.[32] One of the most dramatic shifts in pacing takes place in the opening five lines, discussed above, where the conventions of romance are articulated in radically compressed form. These five lines alone contain the entire plot line of many romances, in which a knight wins his lady, and can be seen as a formal parody of the compressed paratactic style typical of romances. There is a large gap between "discourse-time," the time it takes to peruse the text, and "story-time," the duration of the purported events of the narrative.[33] By contrast, in the portion of the narrative that leads up to and includes the exchange of vows between Dorigen and Arveragus, the pacing of the story slows down so that the time it takes to read the tale (discourse-time) and the time it takes for the actions to occur (story-time) become relatively equal. In the quoted dialogue of Dorigen's vow the time it takes to read that portion of the tale and the time it would have taken Dorigen to say the vow in the story are equivalent. In this way, the exchange of vows is recounted at a pace that makes them appear natural, while the pacing of the more conventional beginning of the romance calls attention to the artifice of its construction. This contrast in pacing works to validate the values of sacramental marriage embodied in the free and mutual exchange of vows, rather than the vision of marriage as the apotheosis of battle familiar from romance.[34] In this way, marriage is no longer associated with martial prowess, an aristocratic construction of virtue, but with the virtues of free will and mutuality, which, as we will see, are appropriate to the Franklin's social status.

Married Friendship and the Discourse of Mutuality

In developing a vision of marriage based on free will and mutuality, the Franklin not only adapts the terms of romance but also echoes the language of theologians and sermon writers who drew on the classical friendship tradition to depict sacramental marriage. Chaucer's Franklin draws on the friendship tradition explicitly at the beginning of his "sermon on marriage" in his meditation on the mutuality of the arrangement between Dorigen and Arveragus, in a passage we have already begun to analyze:

> For o thyng, sires, sauftly dar I seye,
> That *freendes everych oother moot obeye,*
> If they wol longe holden compaignye.
> Love wol nat been constreyned by maistrye.
>   (761–64; my italics)

We have seen that the phrase "Love wol nat been constreyned by maistrye," familiar from *Le Roman de la Rose*, could invoke the courtly tradition that warns against marriage by suggesting that love is not possible in the married state. The fact that this and other antimatrimonialist claims are often spoken by the figure of the Friend implies that marriage and friendship are seen as opposites in the courtly tradition. But Chaucer's narrator reverses the expectations of this genre by drawing on an opposing tradition of using friendship as an image of mutuality between spouses, when he asserts that "freendes everych oother moot obeye." Both marriage and friendship are placed under the broader rubric of love, and friendship in marriage is specifically linked to mutuality. This representation deviates from the conventions of romance but echoes the contemporary application of friendship vocabulary to marriage.

In using friendship to describe the marital mutuality of Dorigen and Arveragus's relationship, the Franklin's "sermon on marriage" echoes the language of popular sermons and theology which drew on the classical friendship tradition to depict sacramental marriage. Many classical writers included marriage as a type of friendship. Thomas Aquinas, for example, asserted in *Summa Contra Gentiles* that the greatest friendship was between marital partners because "they [also] unite themselves in the flesh by the copula [and not just spiritually]."[35] Aquinas's work on marriage was influenced by Aristotle's *Nicomachean Ethics,* a well-known text in the Middle Ages. In the *Ethics,* Aristotle argued that virtuous married partners were capable of achieving even the highest level of friendship:

> Between husband and wife a natural friendship seems to exist, for they are more inclined by nature to conjugal than political society. This is so because the home is older and more necessary than the state, and because generation is common to all animals. Only to this extent do other animals come together. Men, however, cohabit not only to procreate children but also to have whatever is needed for life. Indeed, from the beginning, family duties are distinct; some are proper to the husband, others to the wife. Thus mutual needs are provided for, when each contributes his own services to the common good. Therefore, friendship seems to possess both utility and pleasure. But it can exist for the sake of virtue if the husband and wife are virtuous, for each has his proper virtue and they can delight in it.[36]

According to Aristotle, friendships based on utility and pleasure were good, but only those based on virtue achieved the highest form of friendship. This passage suggests that the separation of duties, the difference between the roles of men and women, need not in and of itself preclude equality in difference. Aristotle explicitly stated that women are capable of the highest form of friendship, and that this kind of friendship could occur within marriage. Although *fin amor* was characteristically seen to promote virtue in courtly writings, in this passage Aristotle shows marital friendship to be a source of virtue.

Friendship was especially relevant to depicting sacramental marriage because for monastic writers, friendship was seen as a form of love, and as a great equalizer. As Saint Bernard explains, "Love neither looks up to nor looks down on anybody. It regards with an equal eye all who love each other truly, bringing together in itself the lofty and the lowly. It makes them not only equal but one."[37] In addressing this issue of loving the "unequal equal" in *De Spirituali Amicitia,* a book inspired by Cicero's *De Amicitia,* Aelred of Rievaulx used a familiar topos:

> [W]hen God created man, in order to commend more highly the good of society, he said: "It is not good for man to be alone; let us make for him

a helper like unto himself." It was from no similar, nor even from the same, material that divine Might formed this help mate, but as a clearer inspiration to charity and friendship he produced the woman from the very substance of the man. How beautiful it is that the second human being was taken from the side of the first, so that nature might teach that human beings are equal and, as it were, collateral, and that there is in human affairs neither a superior, nor an inferior, a characteristic of true friendship.[38]

The use of marriage as a vocabulary for explaining friendship, rather than vice versa, is striking, and demonstrates how thoroughly these vocabularies were entwined. Aelred of Rievaulx referred here to the description of the formation of Eve from the rib of Adam, which, as we have seen, was influential in the formation of a theology that promoted mutuality between the spouses. Echoing the terms of this passage, the vocabulary of friendship was often enlisted in popular marriage sermons to express the mutuality and love in marriage.[39] Thus, when Guibertus de Tornaco called husband and wife "equals and partners" (*pares . . . et socii*) in his *ad status* marriage sermon, he used the same terms used by Cicero to describe friendship.[40]

Although marriage sermons primarily enlisted the rhetoric of friendship to promote marital mutuality, the *Franklin's Tale* draws on other aspects of the friendship tradition to emphasize free will and choice. We have noted that Dorigen is given a more active role than conventional romance heroines in her selection of a marriage partner, and observed that the emphasis on Arveragus's "free wyl" in his decision to make his vow to Dorigen deviates from the conventions of romance in which love is characterized as compulsory, as a kind of sickness or feudal obligation. By contrast, friendship literature emphasizes the importance of choosing a partner. In his commentary on Aristotle's *Nicomachean Ethics,* Aquinas explains, "Friendship is a kind of virtue inasmuch as it is a habit of free choice."[41] The mutuality that constitutes friendship depends on free choice: "Mutual love—which belongs to the notion of friendship as we have indicated—is accompanied by deliberate choice, for this is found only in rational beings."[42] Aelred of Rievaulx also elaborates on the importance of volition in the formation of friendship: "The first essential is to choose someone whom you judge suitable."[43] These writers suggest that that intensity of the mutual emotion of friendship can exist only when friends have freely and deliberately chosen each other. In this context, the description of the marriage and the vows of Dorigen and Arveragus in the tale can be seen to draw on the friendship tradition. By elaborating on and emphasizing the choice and free will in Dorigen and Arveragus's vows, Chaucer revises the terms of romance and draws on the friendship tradition to theorize an aspect of sacramental marriage.

Dorigen and Arveragus's friendship-based marriage is tested when all the rocks appear to have vanished from the coast of Brittany, leaving Dorigen to choose between adultery and breaking her promise to Aurelius.[44] Although not generally part of the friendship tradition applied to marriage, accounts of friendship emphasize the need for friends in adversity, and the importance of misfortune in testing friendship. In *De Spirituali Amicitia,* Aelred explains that "the most important quality of all is loyalty, which is friendship's nurse and guardian. In good or ill fortune, in joy or sorrow, in happy times and bitter, loyalty shows itself steadfast and unchanging . . . ill fortune provides the best test of loyalty."[45] Reason makes a similar connection between friendship and misfortune in *Le Roman de la Rose*: "Contrary Fortune makes men understand and know, as soon as they have lost their possessions, the kind of love with which they were loved by those who were formerly their friends; for those friends whom good Fortune gives are so shocked by evil fortune that they all become enemies."[46] Testing each other's fidelity and discretion in marriage provides the plot for the *Franklin's Tale.*

Seldom demonstrated by the heroines of romance, Dorigen's confidence in her husband is one of the prerogatives of friendship, according to Cicero:

> What is sweeter than to have someone with whom you may dare discuss anything as if you were communing with yourself? . . . Adversity would indeed be hard to bear without him to whom the burden would be heavier even than to yourself . . . For Friendship adds a brighter radiance to prosperity and lessens the burden of adversity by dividing and sharing it.[47]

Thus, when Arveragus returns from his journey, she tells him, "Thus Have I seyd, . . . thus have I sworn" (1464), recounting the whole tale, she treats him as her friend, following the imperative in the friendship literature to open one's heart to one's friend and do his will.[48]

The diction of Arveragus's response to Dorigen also invokes the rhetoric of the friendship tradition. Friendship was believed to inspire virtue, as Cicero instructs: "Ask of friends only what is honorable; do for friends only what is honorable."[49] Arveragus explains that his actions are motivated by concern that Dorigen preserve her "trouthe":

"Ye, wyf," quod he, "lat slepen that is stille.
It may be wel, paraventure, yet to day.
Ye shul youre trouthe holden, by my fay!
For God so wisly have mercy upon me,
I hadde wel levere ystiked for to be
For verray love which that I to yow have,
But if ye sholde youre trouthe kepe and save.
Trouthe is the hyeste thyng that man may kepe"

(1472–79)

Instead of the standard of sexual purity often used to define female virtue in medieval writings, Arveragus makes Dorigen's inner integrity the issue, a characterization of honor in marriage absent from the romance tradition. The narrator's description of Arveragus's manner as in "freendly wyse" suggests that this trading in virtue is accomplished according to the friendship tradition. Arveragus's construction of his own behavior also redefines aristocratic masculine virtue. He suggests that by placing her integrity above his own honor he exhibits a virtuous selflessness, since he claims to be willing to die rather than jeopardize her word.

Despite Arveragus's use of the language of the friendship tradition, the violence of his threat to Dorigen at the end of his speech makes the narrator's characterization of his manner, "in freendly wyse," hard if not impossible to sustain. Although Arveragus agrees that Dorigen should keep her word and sleep with Aurelius, he threatens to kill her if she tells anyone what she has done (1481–83). The violence of Arveragus's threat is in direct contrast to the previous characterization of marriage as a friendship based in mutuality and free will. Drawing on the ecclesiastical use of the language of friendship to describe marriage, the tale had shown friendship to be possible between the sexes and within the institution of marriage.

In fact, the power disparity illustrated in this passage between husband and wife conflicts with the application of the paradigms of friendship to marriage, instead following the logic commonly used in both ecclesiastical and romance traditions to exclude women from friendship. In *De Amicitia*,

Cicero explains that *amicitia perfecta* is best cultivated by men of wealth, power, and rank, while those who do not possess a high degree of autonomy are poor candidates. He speaks disparagingly of the instances when friendship is "sought for the sake of the defense and aid they give and not goodwill and affection . . . and consequently, that helpless women, more than men, seek its shelter, the poor more than the rich."⁵⁰ Jerome compares wives unfavorably with friends, claiming that while "men marry so as to get someone to run the household, to solace weariness, to banish solitude; but a faithful slave makes a far better manager . . . than a wife . . . [F]riends and servants who are under the obligation of benefits received, are better able to wait upon us in sickness than a wife."⁵¹ Thus this scene in the *Franklin's Tale* dramatizes a tension between two aspects of the friendship tradition: one that argues that women can be friends and that marriage can be based in mutuality and friendship, the other that argues that women's lack of equality disqualifies them from friendship.

Not only is there a tension in this moment of the tale between the inclusion and exclusion of Dorigen from the friendship tradition, there is also a parallel tension between the embracing and rejection of the horizontal model of marriage. As we have seen, up to this point the tale has promoted a mutual model of marriage through the use of the friendship vocabulary, and although the squire and the clerk later admire and praise Arveragus's actions as promoting partnership marriage, in Arveragus's threat to kill Dorigen the ideal of mutuality seems to disappear in a violent resurgence of a hierarchical power. As we have seen in the introduction, there was a similar tension between these two models in medieval marriage sermons. An example can be found in a passage from a sermon by Honorius of Autun: "Let husbands love their wives with tender affection; let them keep faith with them in all things . . . In the same way, women should love their husbands deeply, fear them and keep faith with a pure heart."⁵² Here "fear" and "love," hierarchy and equality, are joined together in marriage without any acknowledgment that these terms are contradictory or paradoxical.

The tension between horizontal and hierarchical models of marriage in this scene is mapped onto social terms in the tale. Specifically, the horizontal model of marriage conflicts with Arveragus's public aristocratic identity. Arveragus's threat attempts to keep their arrangement secret or private and to guard against its public revelation. Weeping, he says to Dorigen,

> . . . I yow forbede, up peyne of deeth,
> That nevere, whil thee lasteth lyf ne breeth,
> To no wight telle thou of this aventure—
> As I may best, I wol my wo endure—
> Ne make no contenance of hevynesse,
> That folk of yow may demen harm or gesse.
>
>   (1481–86)

This passage shows that Arveragus believes his decision to preserve Dorigen's integrity, his participation in the friendship model of marriage, conflicts with the maintenance of his public reputation. Dorigen's "trouthe"—and by implication, the "trouthe" of their marriage—is defined as a private, internal condition, wholly specific to the individual and in contradiction to the public values of society.[33] This decision echoes the terms of their marriage contract in the beginning of the tale in the gap between their private arrangement and Arveragus's desire to preserve his public reputation, when Arveragus swears to obey her, "Save that the name of soveraynetee, / That wolde he have for shame of his degree" (751–52). As we have seen, this passage aligns the hierarchical model of marriage with his public aristocratic identity, and suggests that the private mutual arrangement he had with Dorigen conflicts with the values of his class. As we will see in the next section, these values of mutuality in marriage will be more explicitly tied to the social values of the middle strata and of the Franklin in the end of the tale. In this way, the conflict between horizontal and hierarchical models of marriage is clearly linked to social values and to the revision of romance.

Unlike the marriage sermons that do not acknowledge the ideological tension between horizontal and hierarchical models, the *Franklin's Tale* clearly recognizes the difficulties of seeing Arveragus's behavior—even the implementation of his friendship arrangement—as consistent with the horizontal model of marriage he has been promoting throughout the tale. As a result, the Franklin injects his own voice, instructing his listeners to withhold judgment until they hear the rest of the story:

> Paraventure an heep of yow, ywis,
> Wol holden hym a lewed man in this
> That he wol putte his wyf in jupartie.
> Herkneth the tale er ye upon hire crie.

She may have bettre fortune than yow semeth;
And whan that ye han herd the tale, demeth.

(1493–98)

In this passage, the Franklin seems to acknowledge the problematic nature of Arveragus's treatment of Dorigen and suggests that the solution to
her treatment, and by implication, to the handling of her marriage, will be
found in the later portion of the tale. As we will see in the next section, the
ending of the tale suggests that the Franklin finds the answer to the problems of Dorigen and Arveragus's marriage not in the domestic context but
in the social interactions of the three men from different social classes, in
which married friendship becomes a political model. Indeed, the Franklin's
focus on male bonding at the end of the tale, and his failure to address Arveragus's violence toward his wife suggests that he may be more invested in
using marriage to articulate a horizontal ideology of social equality than in
constructing egalitarian gender relations.

Marriage and Male Civic Identity

The use of the vocabulary of friendship to describe social relations becomes
overt at the end of the tale, as the language of friendship shifts from depicting the marriage of Dorigen and Arveragus to characterizing the relationship between the three men of disparate social status: the Knight, the
Squire, and the Clerk. Classical friendship literature was not only a source
for depicting sacramental marriage; writers such as Ambrose, Anselm, and
Aelred also transformed this discourse to articulate ideals for Christian monastic brotherhood.[54] At the same time, chivalric friendship between men
was an important part of the romance tradition. For example, in *Amis and
Amiloun* the male friends show their profound affection to each other, serve,
and fight for each other, in a relationship similar to the literary representations of love for women.[55] Unlike one element of the friendship tradition in
which marriage is seen as a threat to the bonds of male friendship, the exchange of the story of Dorigen and Arveragus's marriage becomes itself the
source of friendship between men. This exchange of values centered on marriage becomes the basis for a political model of social equality in which all
three men are capable of performing a *gentil* deed. By the end of the tale, the

values that had been associated with the friendship model of marriage, such as mutuality and free will, are more broadly identified as social values. Thus, the tale invokes a classical model in which friendship is associated with civic politics and thus constructs a model of social relations that would have appealed to a person of the Franklin's social status and civic identifications.

We have seen that in Arveragus's threats the mutual ideals of married friendship are called into question in the tale; it is at this juncture that the friendship vocabulary shifts from depicting marriage to describing the relationship among the three men, although it is marriage that provides the means of bonding among them. When Aurelius tells Dorigen to relay the following message to her husband he invokes the discourse of friendship:

> That sith I se his grete gentilesse
> To yow, and eek I se wel youre distresse,
> That him were levere han shame (and that were routhe)
> Than ye to me sholde breke thus youre trouthe,
> I have wel levere evere to suffre wo
> Than I departe the love bitwix yow two.
>
> (1527–32)

In this passage, Aurelius is generous toward Arveragus, demonstrating one of the key virtues of friendship. Arveragus's virtue inspires his own, enacting Cicero's dictum that "virtue . . . both creates the bond of friendship and preserves it."[56] Aurelius not only admires Arveragus and "his grete gentilesse," he also expresses his admiration for Dorigen's marital conduct, calling her "the treweste and the beste wyf" (1539) and is willing to sacrifice himself rather than harm their love. Similarly, after hearing Aurelius tell the tale of Dorigen and recount the "greet pitee" that he had of her in her plight, the Clerk makes his own bid for *gentillesse* by forgiving Aurelius the debt of a thousand pounds that he owes for the illusion of removing all the rocks from the coast of Brittany. Invoking the language of friendship, he calls Aurelius "Leeve brother," and tells him:

> Everich of yow dide gentilly til oother.
> Thou art a squier, and he is a knyght;
> But God forbede, for his blisful myght,

But if a clerk koude doon a gentil dede
As wel as any of yow, it is no drede!

(1608–12)

Just as Aurelius was inspired to virtue through the admiration of Arveragus, echoing the language of friendship, in turn the clerk is inspired to
virtue by the *gentillesse* of the other two. The Clerk's admiration for the actions of Arveragus and Aurelius leads him to value virtue over money and
material gain, specifically listed in the literature as a false motivation for
friendship.[57]

The bonds among these men in the *Franklin's Tale* show a shift in the
use of friendship discourse in the tale from the married couple to the three
men. In describing bonds of friendship among the men that inspire them to
virtue, the *Franklin's Tale* enlists a paradigm of "ennobling love" common in
both monastic and courtly traditions which drew on the classical discourse
of *amicitia* to describe profound attachments between men. Thus, the shift
in the *Franklin's Tale* of the terms initially associated with marital love to a
friendship among men should be seen in the context of C. Stephen Jaeger's
assertion that in the Continental tradition, "honoring love between men expressed itself in the gestures and language of passionate love."[58] This "ennobling love" was, to use Eve Kosofsky Sedgwick's term, "homosocial" because, although clearly erotic, it suggested but did not necessarily include
a sexual component.[59] The fluidity of the division between medieval con-
structions of love and friendship is illustrated by the fact that in Latin, the
language of much of the friendship texts read and written in the medieval
period, *amicus* (friend) and *amans* (lover) are derived from the same verb, *amo*
(to love), and were very often interchangeable, making it difficult to distinguish between them.[60] Given this context in which the word *friendship* is
applied to the emotional and erotic attachments between men as well as to
marriage, it is not surprising that we see the relationships among men at the
end of the tale described in the same terms used earlier to characterize the
marriage of Arveragus and Dorigen.

Despite the fact that chivalric friendship was a familiar romance paradigm, the language of friendship in the *Franklin's Tale,* as we have seen, is
first associated not with romance but with sacramental marriage, and it is
marital friendship that provides both the catalyst and the vocabulary for
the male friendships formed at the end of the tale. It is the commitment

shared by Arveragus, Aurelius, and the Clerk to heterosexual marriage which authorizes the homosocial bonds among the three men. By showing marriage facilitating the friendship among men, the end of the *Franklin's Tale* diverges from one strand of the medieval friendship tradition in which friendship and marriage are seen as antithetical. Advice against marrying was often voiced by the figure of the Friend in a range of popular medieval writings of both courtly and clerical origins, such as *La Roman de la Rose,* Eustache Deschamps' *Miroir de Mariage,* and the crude twelfth-century satiric poem of clerical provenance, "Against Marrying."[61] *De Amore,* addressed to a male friend, ends with a retraction that argues that loving women is not only inferior to male friendship but is actually dangerous to it: "It causes the development of ruptures between friends, and parlous enmities between men, attended by murder and numerous evils."[62] In contrast to Chaucer's *Knight's Tale,* in which the friendship of Arcite and Palamon is pulled apart by their rivalry for Emily, in the *Franklin's Tale* marriage becomes a means to create rather than destroy the bonds of friendship among men.

In the *Franklin's Tale,* marriage is not only the medium through which the bonds of male friendship are formed, it also is depicted as the source of the ideals of friendship in the tale. Free choice, which was so crucial to the description of Arveragus and Dorigen's marital vows at the beginning of the tale, becomes identified with the exchange of friendship among men at the end. Aurelius uses the term *free* to describe to the Clerk his decision to forgo his claim on Dorigen. He explains that after hearing her story, he "han of hire so greet pitee; / And right as frely as he sente hire me, / As frely sente I hire to hym ageyn" (1603–5). The term is also featured in the *demande d'amour* at the end of the tale: "Which was the mooste fre, as thynketh yow?" (1622). Unlike his Boccaccian source, Chaucer does not answer this question but instead ends the tale, suggesting that the ability to be "fre" is equally available to the Squire, the Knight, and the Clerk and is thus not socially determined.[63] The final question rephrases the Clerk's statement on *gentillesse* ("a clerk koude doon a gentil dede / As wel as any of yow" [1610–12]), articulating an ideology that defines virtue by character rather than status. Thus the squire's praise of the virtues of Dorigen, Arveragus, and their marriage is the occasion for the invocation of a social model in which men of different classes are equally capable of performing good deeds. These good deeds are defined in the terms of the friendship tradition, in which empathy, generosity, and good character are the basis of social vir-

tue. The shared values about marriage are not only the occasion for the
generation of bonds of affection between men, they are also the means of
breaking down boundaries among the Three Estates. Thus, the term *free,*
so crucially linked to marriage at the outset of the tale and to friendship
throughout, becomes at the end associated with a political vision. The values that have been associated with the friendship model of marriage earlier
in the tale, such as mutuality and free will, are in the end more broadly identified as social values.

The link between friendship and political theory was familiar from the
Nicomachean Ethics in which Aristotle compares kinds of friendship to
genres of political association. According to Aristotle, "Each form of government seems to involve a kind of friendship inasmuch as justice is present . . . On the other hand, as in corrupt forms of rule there is little justice, so there is little friendship."[64] Thus, Aristotle considers friendship a
marker of justice in any political system. He suggests that tyranny is antithetical to friendship, implying that friendship, and by implication justice,
is most fully present in more horizontal and inclusive forms of government:
"[Friendship] is minimal in the worst system, for in tyranny no friendship,
or very little, is found . . . In democracies, however, friendship is most fully
realized, for where all are equal there is much sharing."[65] This idea that
friendship and tyranny are opposites can also be found in the work of medieval political theorists such as John of Salisbury, who writes in the *Policraticus*: "In the secular literature there is even caution because one is to live
one way with a friend and another way with a tyrant. It is not permitted to
flatter a friend, but it is permitted to delight the ears of a tyrant."[66] By using
the vocabulary of friendship to imagine an inclusive political model in which
the estates share the same social values, the ending of the *Franklin's Tale*
draws on this tradition of the political use of *amicitia.*[67]

Friendship was also specifically associated with *civitas* by medieval writers, so that the rhetoric of friendship was seen not just as a commitment
to a specific individual but also as a broader readiness to help one's fel-
low citizens. Henry of Ghent, for example, defined the "disposition of the
civitas" as

the appropriate condition for men living in civil partnership and community; since that disposition could not exist unless bound together by
deepest friendship, by which each person is regarded by each other as

another self, and by the deepest charity, in which each of them loves the other as himself, and by the highest benevolence, by which each wills for the other what he wills for himself.[68]

This passage, in which society is bound together by "deepest friendship" and by "deepest charity" could describe the end of the *Franklin's Tale,* which, as we have seen, portrays an exchange of acts of charity and uses the bonds of friendship among the three male characters to create a vision of political society bound by mutual respect. Medieval understandings of terms like *community* and *civil partnership* are notoriously hard to pin down and were often used in the service of a wide variety of political interests, and so it is not entirely surprising that the details of the model of political organization presented at the end of the tale are not explicitly theorized.[69] Nonetheless, Henry of Ghent's description of civic society resembles the end of the *Franklin's Tale* in its emphasis on participation by various estates of society and on the values of free will and choice and its valuation of mutuality over hierarchy.

The values of free choice and participation would have appealed to a person like the Franklin who is depicted in the *General Prologue* as representative of a new civic identity and growth of government in the late Middle Ages. The Franklin is introduced as follows: "Ful ofte tyme he was knyght of the shire. / . . . / A shirreve hadde he been, and a contour. / Was nowher swich a worthy vavasour" (*GP,* 355–60). As a member of Parliament, a sheriff, and a *contour* (a pleader in county court), Chaucer's Franklin would certainly have cut an important figure in his locality. In fact, according to Nigel Saul, it was not typical for franklins to reach the level of sheriff or knight of the shire in the late fourteenth century, although a career of office-holding would have been typical, and they undoubtedly shared in the administrative work of the shire and were contours at county courts.[70] Chaucer may have chosen the offices of sheriff and member of Parliament for his Franklin not because they made him typical but because they *symbolized* the growth of government and the accompanying civic ideology in the later Middle Ages, and indeed the sheer number of offices held by the Franklin identifies him hyperbolically as a quintessential civil servant. According to Gerald Harriss, "The major development of the period from the thirteenth to fifteenth century was the emergence of a political society containing the middling landowners."[71] Government was no longer remote, but based on an elaborate network of rural and urban bureaucrats which involved all ranks of society in the activity of governing. As a contour, a professional man of law, the Franklin was specifically associated with the county court, itself instrumental in and emblematic of the growing importance of local communal civic government in late medieval England.[72] It is in this context of the Franklin's specifically civic identity that the emphasis on the political values of free will and choice should be understood.

The Franklin's offices of sheriff and member of Parliament also showed how the new civic roles for members of the middle strata contributed to their social mobility. The variety of civic offices held by Chaucer's Franklin is emblematic of the ways in which middling landowners began to take on important roles in the administration of local government which had previously been held by knights. The records for the poll tax of 1379 suggest that franklins were very numerous, with one in almost every English village, but resident manorial lords, whether magnates, knights, or esquires, were the exception rather than the rule. This may explain why, by the end of the fourteenth century, franklins and other middling landowners were playing, in the words of historian Rodney Hilton, "a substitute role for gentry."[73] Chaucer may have chosen the offices of sheriff and member of Parliament for his Franklin not only to symbolize his civic status but also to indicate the ways in which franklins and other middling landowners began to encroach on the prerogatives of knights. Sheriffs were supposed to be knights, but throughout the fourteenth century records suggest a continuing failure to appoint men of sufficient standing to this office. Although the majority of the sheriffs were knights, enough were of lesser standing to explain the recurring complaints by the Commons in Parliament.[74] A series of laws issued in close succession reiterated that the sheriff must be a substantial freeholder, indicating an ongoing problem. These land-owning qualifications for appointment as sheriff were repeated in the Provisions of Oxford, the Ordinances of 1311, the 1316 Statute of Lincoln, the Ordinance of 1326, the Statute of Northampton in 1328, the Parliaments of 1340, and the Parliament of 1371. Parliamentary representation in the county raised similar issues. Only half of the Gloucestershire "knights of the shire" in the fourteenth century were actually knights. Some may have been richer esquires who did not want the expense of knighthood, but two of the 102 men who represented the county in the fourteenth century were burgesses, while 27 were of humble enough origin to leave no record of holding manors at all.[75] By showing his Franklin holding the offices of sheriff and "knight of the realm," Chaucer referred to two civic offices that had been held by knights and were thus especially sensitive registers of the social mobility of the middling landowners. The idea at the end of the tale that virtue was defined by character rather than status would have appealed to a man of the Franklin's status who was a wealthy freeholding landowner, a kind of person on the cusp of gentility but who had not yet achieved gentle status at the time that *The Canterbury Tales* was written.[76]

The Franklin's identity as a member of Parliament makes him emblematic of the growth of parliamentary power and the accompanying development of theories of representation in the late Middle Ages. Unlike the members of the House of Lords, who represented themselves in Parliament, the members of the House of Commons ostensibly spoke for the community of the whole realm and came with sealed letters to authenticate their actions on behalf of their constituents in the late Middle Ages.[77] The standard formula in writs and documents after the Parliament of 1295 was for members to come with

> full and sufficient power [*plena potestas*] for themselves and *for the community of the county* aforesaid and the said citizens and burgesses for the communities of the cities and boroughs . . . to do what shall be ordained then *by common consent* in the aforementioned matters, so that for lack of the same power the business shall not remain undone in any way. [My italics][78]

According to J. R. Maddicott, "By the time of the Good Parliament of 1376 it was the parliamentary commons, and not the baronage, who had come to be regarded as defending the interests of town and country."[79] In the fourteenth-century treatise *Modus Tenendi Parliamentum,* the word *communitas* is used for both the Commons and the whole community of England, and by the fourteenth century the word was used consistently in legal statutes to represent the consent of the Commons.[80] Although members of the parliamentary Commons were not elected in the contemporary democratic sense, they were chosen by the county court with the supervision of the sheriff. According to Harriss, "Phrases such as 'by the assent of the aforesaid county court' or . . . 'the whole county court of Middlesex has elected . . .' are common enough on sheriffs' returns to imply that choosing of the country's members entailed consultation and not mere nomination."[81] In addition to being a member of Parliament, the Franklin, through his status as a sheriff, would also have been symbolically linked to the very process of parliamentary representation. Thus, as a member of the House of Commons, the Franklin would have participated in the most representational form of government available in England in the late Middle Ages, an organization whose very name was used interchangeably with *communitas*.

Chaucer's identification of the Franklin with parliamentary representation suggests an important context for interpreting the ending of the *Franklin's Tale* in which each of the three men demonstrates an equal claim to *gentillesse*. In doing so, the three men model a horizontal form of social organization that is depicted by the civic virtues of free will and mutuality expressed in the tale by the friendship tradition, which were understood in the period to have a political meaning. In fact, the implicit political model laid out at the end of the tale is similar to what David Wallace has argued is the new "associational ideology" instantiated in the group of Canterbury pilgrims at the opening of the *Tales,* an idea he believes was developed in trecento Florence in which "all inhabitants of the city-state share an equal footing on a lateral plane."[82] In an argument that more closely echoes my own, Glenn Burger has suggested that this notion of "associational ideology" finds parallels nearer to home in the idea of the "community of the realm" represented in the Commons, and is relevant to both the depiction of conjugality and the generation of middle strata identity in the *Canterbury Tales* as a whole.[83] More specifically, I suggest that the horizontal and participatory social model implicitly laid out at the end of the *Franklin's Tale* using the language of married friendship established earlier in the tale can be linked broadly to the interests of the middle strata of society and directly to the civic and representational identifications of the Franklin.

As Wallace reminds us, however, such communal ideology and its implied communities are "always to some extent imagined, exclusionary, and (between one group and the next) hierarchical."[84] Indeed, despite its rhetoric, the late medieval system of parliamentary representation was far from fully inclusive. Members of the House of Commons spoke for all but were not chosen by all (and notions of representation tended to exclude women and the unfree). In addition, as Judith Ferster has argued, the idea of representativeness was itself used to varying political purposes: "Different people and groups in different social strata were self-interestedly wielding the idea that everyone had some stake in the commonweal and thus some responsibility for protecting it. The idea was commandeered by those seeking to rule as well as those seeking to influence or resist their rulers"[85] In arguing that marriage is used in the *Franklin's Tale* to develop a horizontal social ideology that would have been appealing to the middle strata generally and specifically to a man of the Franklin's civic identifications, I am not suggesting that the social model promoted genuine democracy. After all, the Franklin would have been unlikely to champion the interests of peasants, and it should be noted that none of the three men at the end—the Knight, the Squire, and the Clerk—is a member of the third estate, nor is there such a figure in the tale. Thus the political vision outlined at the end of the tale corresponds both to the qualified notion of parliamentary representation current in the period and to the interests of the Franklin and of the middle strata more broadly. Even such qualified notions of parliamentary representation might seem idealistic after the brutal parliamentary politics of the 1380s, which culminated in the Merciless Parliament of 1388, when intimate members of Richard II's court were accused of treason and sentenced to death. Despite the fact that the *Franklin's Tale* is generally believed to have been written in the 1390s, the social model at the end of the tale does not reflect the grim proceedings of contemporary Parliament, but is rather an idealized vision that used the vocabulary of sacramental marriage and marital friendship to promote the social and political values of the Franklin.[86]

Despite the overdetermined description and context for the political and social status of Chaucer's Franklin, he does not tell an overtly political tale. And yet, the Franklin expresses his politics through the depiction of marriage, finding in married friendship a vocabulary for promoting the civic values appropriate to his social position. The Franklin uses marriage as the basis for his social vision because, counter to the assertions of some scholars of the tale, sacramental marriage and the language of married friendship offered a well-developed discourse of mutuality. The Franklin transfers the values of married friendship to the context of an egalitarian social vision and representative politics because these middle strata values lacked the legitimizing logic already afforded by marriage. As we have seen, the Franklin also revises the discourse of aristocratic romance and its accompanying paradigm of ennobling love to validate not aristocratic but middle strata values. Thus, the tale does not so much outline Chaucer's ideal of marriage, as Kittredge argues, as it uses marriage to articulate the Franklin's political and social ideals.

CHAPTER TWO

Public Voice, Private Life

Marriage and Masculinity in John Gower's Traitié

Despite medievalists' ongoing interest in the subject of marriage, John Gower's Anglo-Norman ballad sequence, *Traitié pour Essampler les Amantz Marietz,* which features a sequence of tales about the misfortunes of lovers who fail to respect the institution of marriage, has received little scholarly attention.[1] The poem was written after the *Confessio Amantis* and is appended to it in seven out of ten manuscripts. The connection between the two poems is reinforced by an allusion to the *Confessio* in the prose proem:[2]

> Puisqu'il ad dit ci devant en Englois par voie d'essample la sotie de cellui qui par amours aime par especial, dirra ore apres en François a tout le monde en general un traitié selonc les auctours pour essampler les amantz marietz. . . .

> [Because he spoke here above in English to illustrate the foolishness of those who love especially for love, he will now write below in French

51

for the entire world generally a treatise according to the authorities to exemplify married lovers. . . .][3]

This description of a shift in Gower's attention from love to marriage is substantiated by the abbreviated use in the *Traitié* of many of the tales in the *Confessio,* included not as in that longer poem to illustrate the seven deadly sins with tales about love, but to convey a more unitary message promoting the value of marriage.

With its identification of a shift in subject matter from love in the *Confessio* to marriage in the *Traitié,* as the proem to the ballad sequence suggests, this latter poem revises the tradition of aristocratic writings on love to produce a new model of marriage. Written in Anglo-Norman, the poem takes the form of a series of eighteen ballads composed of three stanzas each, all in rhyme royal, perhaps the most popular of lyric forms of the fourteenth century and a favorite of such well-known French court poets as Guillaume de Machaut, Eustache Deschamps, and Oton de Granson.[4] Through his use of the courtly ballad format and repeated references to the heroes and paradigms of romance, Gower seems determined to link adultery to aristocratic love. In addition to criticizing adultery, the *Traitié* also invokes and overturns the chivalric paradigm that love is equivalent to military might. The repetitively patterned tales that constitute the central portion of the ballad sequence feature the heroes of romance, but in contrast to romance paradigms, central figures such as Tristan and Ulysses are revealed to be domestic horrors, and it is the private world of sexual conduct, rather than the public world of military honor, that most determines masculine virtue in the *Traitié.*

The poem's advocacy of marriage as a moral practice echoes contemporary conventional Church teachings, but the poem revises clerical convention to make marriage a male rather than female concern and to promote lay authority. The tales of the *Traitié* revise medieval clichés of female virtue and vice familiar from clerical misogyny, shifting moral responsibility for sexual practices from women to men. The ballads' central message that marriage is a form of self-regulation is familiar from contemporary sermons and confessors' handbooks, as is the use of brief exemplary tales; learned ecclesiastical discourse is invoked by marginal Latin glosses that explain the morals of the various ballads.[5] The fact that the *Traitié* echoes the language and content of contemporary confessors' handbooks and sermons for the laity is not surprising given the well-documented influence of these materials on Gower's *Confessio Amantis*.[6] The *Traitié*, however, not only invokes but also revises clerical conventions by valuing marriage over chastity, reversing a hierarchy that promotes clerical over lay authority, and by depicting justice as secular and lay rather than divine or ecclesiastical.

Whereas the early ballads of the *Traitié* enlist the tropes of marriage sermons, most of the rest of the ballads, which tell the repetitive tales of heroes whose marital failures caused them to suffer bad ends, recall the tradition of the "fall of princes," familiar from Boccaccio's *De Casibus* and book 7 of Gower's own *Confessio Amantis*, invoking the language of exemplary history. In this way, the *Traitié* initially seems to address the subject that George R. Coffman long ago deemed the unifying project of Gower's poetry, his "most significant role": articulating the ideals and responsibilities of kingship.[7] Critics such as Elizabeth Porter and Russell Peck have emphasized the ways in which Gower's poetry explores the ethical and moral principles of rulership, whereas others, such as Frank Grady, Judith Ferster, Andrew Galloway, Lynn Staley, and Steven Justice, have shown that Gower's *Confessio Amantis*, *Vox Clamantis*, *Cronica Tripertita*, and "In Praise of Peace" responded to a range of specific events in the turbulent reign of Richard II and in the subsequent reign of Henry Bolingbroke, including the Merciless Parliament, the actions of the Appellants, and the Rising of 1381.[8]

Despite its invocation of the conventions of the "fall of princes," and concomitantly the broader mirror for princes (*Fürstenspiegel*) tradition, the poem is neither addressed to nor primarily concerned with princes. Unlike the *Confessio*, which was dedicated first to Richard II and later to Henry of Derby (later Bolingbroke), the prologue of the *Traitié* is addressed not to a ruler but to "everyone in general" ("a tout le monde en general") and the envoy "to the community of the entire world" ("Al université de tout le monde"), making the poem not so much a mirror for magistrates but a mirror for all. For readers familiar with Gower's poetry of kingship, the *Traitié* is striking in its lack of topicality and the absence of a clear relationship to the landscape of contemporary political events, such as the dramas of king and Parliament that so dominated much of Gower's other poetry. In place of historical specificity, the final ballad of the *Traitié*, which functions as an envoy for the whole sequence, supplies autobiographical detail in an act of dedication:

Al université de tout le monde
Johan Gower ceste Balade envoie;
Et si jeo n'ai de François le faconde,
Pardonetz moi qe jeo de ceo forsvoie:
Jeo sui Englois, si quier par tiele voie
Estre excusé . . .

[To the community of the entire world
John Gower sends this ballad;
And if I do not have eloquence in French,
Forgive me if I go astray:
I am English, thus I seek in this manner
To be excused . . .]

(XVIII.4.22 – 27)

A similar gesture occurs at the end of the Latin passage that follows the ballads, when after summarizing the moral message of the poem ("Ordo maritorum caput est et finis amorum" [the estate of marriage is the chief end of love]) Gower ends the *Traitié* with reference to his own marriage: "Hinc vetus annorum Gower sub spe meritorum / Ordine sponsorum tutus abhibo thorum" [Thus I Gower, prudent and aged in years, in hope of merit / Undertake the ordinance of marriage], referring to his marriage to Agnes Groundolf in the year 1398, and suggesting that Gower wrote the *Traitié* as an occasional rather than a topical work.[9] This turn to the autobiographical invites us to read the *Traitié* not as an ideology of marriage for all but rather as a marital ideology specifically for Gower's own subject position.

Although not much is known for certain about Gower, existing evidence suggests that he was a country landowner from an arms-bearing family and probably a lawyer.[10] John Gower's tomb in Saint Mary Overeys Priory Church includes a coat of arms, and the inscription identifies him as "arm," an abbreviation for *armigier,* but elsewhere he is referred to in documents as "esquire."[11] As N. Denholm-Young and Nigel Saul have shown, esquires had assumed the status of (nonaristocratic) gentility by the mid-fourteenth century, parting company with the franklins, sergeants, and *valetti* with whom they had been grouped in the thirteenth century.[12] In this way, the complications of the esquire's social status mark the social mobility of the upper ranks of the middle strata in the period. Thus, while the poem appears to speak of and to "the community of the entire world," this ideal is traceable to Gower's own position and social standing.

The poem's claim for a universal audience in the envoy is also mitigated by the complexity of style and language of the poem as a whole. This elaborately rhymed poem is written both in French and Latin, a guarantee that only the very literate will be able to read and understand it. Furthermore, Gower's exempla are so abbreviated that they almost require previous knowledge of the stories to be intelligible. Thus, while presented as a classless secular model of male moral virtue, in fact, the ballads of the *Traitié* reveal a new masculinized vision of marriage and private life that participates in a new ideology for the emergent upper middle strata of society. As with Chaucer's *Franklin's Tale,* Gower revises *fin amor* and ecclesiastical language to formulate a model of marriage appropriate for his own position as a layman, lawyer, and landowner, straddling the lower ranks of the gentry and the upper ranks of the professional classes. The hybridity of genres invoked by the *Traitié*—courtly ballad, sermon, catalogue of wicked wives, fall of princes—signals the emergent nature of its ideology of marriage.

Revising Romance, Privatizing Masculine Virtue

Gower's *Confessio Amantis* has long played a central role in revisions to the classic formulation of "courtly love," challenging the idea that it was necessarily adulterous by emphasizing the compatibility of marriage and *fin amor.* In a 1966 volume of essays dedicated to C. S. Lewis, for example, J. A. W. Bennett argued that in the *Confessio,* Gower commends "honest love" and shows marriage to be "'courtois' sentiment at its highest."[13] Similarly, in *Love and Marriage in the Age of Chaucer,* Henry Ansgar Kelly used the *Confessio* in his argument that "there was never a seriously or generally held opinion that love was impossible within marriage."[14] The *Traitié,* however, is not so much concerned with demonstrating the compatibility of *fin amor* and marriage as it is with critiquing *fin amor* in favor of marriage.[15] The short tales of *Traitié* feature some of the best-known lovers from courtly lyric, and also famous heroes from the *Roman de Troie* and Ovid, presented in the martial terms of romance. The military paradigms of epic and romance are invoked and then rejected in the ballad sequence in favor of an emphasis on the private realm of sexual behavior. In contrast to the paradigms of aristocratic romance, in the *Traitié* heroes such as Tristan, Lancelot, and Ulysses are revealed to be bad husbands, and it is the private world of conjugal conduct rather than the public world of military prowess which most determines masculine virtue. Thus, instead of the public world determining the private sphere, as is often the case in romance, this trajectory is reversed in the *Traitié,* and it is the private world that determines the public. Conjugal virtue comes to define masculine identity.

The heroes Lancelot, Tristan, and Gawain are often present in courtly poems in the temple of Venus, but these paradigmatically great lovers are directly criticized for courtly practices of love in the *Traitié.* For example, in the single ballad devoted to him in the poem, Gawain is condemned for being changeable:

> N'est pas compaigns q'est comun a chascune;
> Au soule amie ert un ami soulain:
> Mais cil qui toutdis change sa fortune,
> Et ne voet estre en un soul lieu certain,
> Om le poet bien resembler a Gawain,
> Courtois d'amour, mais il fuist trop volage:
> A un est une assetz en mariage.

> [He is not a lover who is common to many women;
> A lover should be with only one woman:
> But he who constantly changes his fortune,
> And is unable to stay in one place,
> That man resembles Gawain,
> Courteous in love, but too fickle:
> One woman is enough for one man in marriage.]
>
> (XVII.2.8–14)

The peripatetic habits condemned in this passage refer to the journeys and quests that Gawain must make according to chivalric convention to prove himself as a knight, adventures that are often designed to win the heart of a lady. Thus, the quintessential knightly journey and quest are reduced to wanderlust and detached from the higher goals with which they are usually associated, such as the protection of honor. The phrase *courtois d'amour* (courteous in love) invokes the reputation of Gawain as famous for love talking and manners, which are here discounted; knightly courtesy to all ladies is reduced to fickleness and, by implication, to infidelity.[16] Whereas in romance marriage is often seen as destructive to chivalric values, in this passage Gower suggests the reverse: that courtly behavior is damaging to marriage.[17] Similarly, both Lancelot and Tristan are lumped together in a nearby stanza and condemned for their adultery, as the Latin gloss for that stanza illustrates:

> Qualiter ob hoc quod Lanceolotus Miles probatissimus Gunnoram regis Arthuri vxorem fatue peramauit, eciam et quia Tristram simili modo Isoldam regis Marci auunculi sui vxorem violare non timuit, Amantes ambo predicti magno infortunii dolore dies suos extremos clauserunt.

> [How therefore because the most excellent knight Lancelot foolishly persevered in love for Guenevere the wife of King Arthur, and also because Tristram in a similar way did not fear to dishonor Isolde the wife of his uncle King Marc, both of the aforesaid lovers ended their last days with great affliction of misfortune.] (XV.1)[18]

The tales of these famous knights are reduced to the facts of their adultery, a topic so repetitively and relentlessly emphasized that Gervase Mathew has charged that it is given "too much space" in the poem.[19] This insistent emphasis on the adultery of the famous lovers of romance and the minimal presence of other detail show that Gower wanted to stress the dangers of *fin amor* and omit any features that would identify them as heroes.

In addition to critiquing the famous lovers of romance, the *Traitié* also invokes famous martial heroes of romance and shows them to be bad husbands. The story of Hercules is paradigmatic of the repetitively patterned brief tales that constitute the central portion of the *Traitié,* and the description of Hercules' marriage is a clear invocation of the romance paradigm that equates military might with love. The first stanza of this ballad encapsulates this topos in its compressed narrative:

> Danz Hercules, prist femme a son honour
> Qe file au roi de Calidoine estoit;
> Contre Achelons en armes conquestoit
> La belle Deianire par bataille.

[Master Hercules took a wife honorably
Who was the daughter of the king of Caledonia;
Against Achelous in arms
He won fair Deianira in battle by force of arms.]
                                        (VII.1.3–6)

One of the few descriptive details in the stanza identifies Deianira as "Qe
file au roi de Calidoine" (the daughter of the king of Caledonia), locating
the tale in the high social echelons of the aristocratic world. Furthermore,
the use of the word *honour* invokes the public world of chivalric reputation,
an association confirmed by its gloss in the subsequent phrase "en armes
conquestoit" (conquered by force of arms), which implies that honor is
equivalent to military might. The idea that marriage is the prize for successful battle depends, as we have seen in our discussion of the opening
lines of the *Franklin's Tale*, on the reciprocal construction of love and
military prowess, as Geoffroi de Charny's commentary on chivalric love
exemplifies:

> [J]ust as one should want to protect the honor of one's lady concerning
> one's relationship with her for the sake of the love one has for her, one
> should also protect one's own honor for the sake of the honor of one's
> lady and for the love she shows to oneself. That means that by your man-
> ners, your behavior and your personal bearing you should so present your-
> self that your renown may be so good, so noble, and so honorable that
> you and your great deeds are held in high esteem in your quarters and on
> the field, especially in feats of arms in peace and in feats of arms in war
> where great honor wins recognition. Thus your ladies will and should be
> more greatly honored when they have made a good knight or man-at-arms
> of you.[20]

The repetition of the term *honor* five times in this short passage suggests
its importance for defining aristocratic identity. Furthermore, the lady, her
love, and the private world with which they are associated are presented
not as inherently important but only as the motivation for deeds of arms
in the public sphere which bring the knight public acclaim.

Love follows from and encourages military prowess in the conventions
of romance, but in Gower's version of the tale of Hercules and elsewhere
in the *Traitié,* the private world of sexual behavior rather than the public

world of military honor determines masculine virtue. The famous feats of
this epic hero are reduced to one brief line, even an epithet ("Cil qui d'arein
les deux pilers fichoit" [He who firmly planted the two pillars]), while the
rest of the tale is devoted to his indictment for adultery, reading his downfall as the inevitable result of his destruction of his marriage. The moral of
the refrain, "C'est grant peril de freindre l'espousaile" (It is a great peril to
break a marriage; VII.1.7), an ominous indictment of our hero, intrudes at
the end of stanza one before we have even heard about his failings. This
pattern runs through the ballad sequence, in which Gower shifts the terms
for evaluating masculine virtue from public to private, rejecting the aristocratic valuation of knighthood.

The *Traitié*'s critique of aristocratic love becomes even more overt in a
subsequent passage that is explicitly didactic. A later ballad confirms that
we are to read the tale of Hercules as a broader lesson about male identity
and male virtue:

> Om truist plusours es vieles escriptures
> Prus et vailantz, q'ont d'armes le renoun,
> Mais poi furont q'entre les envoisures
> Guarderont chaste lour condicion.

> [One finds many brave and valiant men in old writings
> Who have renown in arms,
> But there are few who
> Guard their chaste condition from snares.]

$$(XVI.1.1-4)$$

In this passage, all tales of bravery are lumped together, and feats of arms are
made secondary to maintaining sexual virtue. The tale of Alboin also critiques the assumption that military success is linked to success in love and
marriage. This tale recounts how this "prince bataillous" (warlike prince)
killed King "Gurmond" and married his beautiful daughter, Rosamund, an
act that the ballad characterizes not as an honorable proof of military talent
but with the following ominous refrain: "Cil qui mal fait, falt qu'il au mal
responde" (He who does evil will be answered in kind; XI). The tale overtly
criticizes the idea that marital success can necessarily follow from martial
victory. The ballad ascribes the blame for Alboin's death by poisoning not to
his adulterous wife or her lover, but to his own cruel act of killing his wife's

father, explaining that "La dame, q'estoit pleine de corous / A cause de son piere, n'ama mie / Son droit mari, ainz est ailours amie" (The lady, who was full of anger / Because of her father, did not love / Her rightful husband at all, but loved another instead; XI.2.10–12). Not only does this ballad separate martial prowess from love, it even shows military success to be antithetical to married happiness and marital virtue. In the *Confessio*, by contrast, Alboin's crime is not his killing of Rosamund's father so much as his pride and his grotesque flaunting of his conquest by having Rosamund unknowingly drink from her father's skull: "Thenkende on thilke unkynde Pride, / Of that hire lord so nyh hire side / Avanteth him that he hath slain / And piked out hire fader brain, / And of the Skulle had mad a Cuppe" (I.2565–69). The *Confessio*'s tale ends by recapitulating standard chivalric terms in a discussion of Alboin's honor: "His lose tunge he mot restreigne, / Which berth of his honour the keie" (I.2660–61), whereas the *Traitié*'s focus is on the damage suffered by Alboin and Rosamund's marriage.[21]

The vocabulary of military exploits is consistently appropriated and reapplied to the private sphere and to internal struggle:

> Honest amour, q'ove loialté s'aqueinte,
> Fait qe les noeces serront gloriouses;
> Et qui son coer ad mis par tiele empeinte,
> N'esteot doubter les changes perilouses.
> Om dist qe noeces sont adventurouses;

> [Honest love, which acquaints itself with loyalty,
> Makes weddings glorious;
> And he who has given his heart in this way
> Need not fear dangerous changes of fortune.
> Men say that weddings are risky exploits;]
>   (IV.3.15–20)

Familiar martial terms like *gloriouses, perilouses,* and *adventurouses* are applied here to the private sphere of weddings and love. Furthermore, the term *adventure* can apply to both conquests of arms and pursuit of love, indicating the extent to which these ideas are intertwined in Old French and Anglo-Norman writings, a connection that the *Traitié* is at pains to sever. The displacement of the honor of battle from public to private becomes even more overt later in the text:

Qui d'armes veint les fieres aventures,
Du siecle en doit avoir le reguerdoun;
Mais qui du char poet veintre les pointures,
Le ciel avera trestout a sa bandoun.
Agardetz ore la comparisoun,
Le quell valt plus, le monde ou Paradis:
Qui sa char veint, sur toutz doit porter pris.

[He who overcomes terrible dangers by means of arms,
Will have the world's reward;
But he who is able to overcome the pricks of the flesh,
Will have Heaven at his disposal.
Now look at the comparison,
Which is worth more, the world or paradise:
He who conquers his flesh, will above all carry the reward.]

(XVI.2.8–14)

Instead of the knight working to protect God's works on earth, as the
Knight's role is characterized in the three estates model, martial prowess
is deliberately separated from heaven in Gower's ballad. Here the battle is
waged not with an opponent on the field of battle but within the individual;
the true adversary, the true foe, is one's own flesh. This parallel between
the conquests of arms and of the flesh is emphasized by the repetition of the
same word *veintro/veint* (overcomes/conquers), applied both to arms and
to the internal fight against the seductions of the body. In short, the battle
becomes an internal one of self-regulation.

Like the tale of Hercules, the tale of Ulysses is paradigmatic not only of
the way the ideal of military or epic heroism is replaced by the promotion
of sexual morality, but also of the replacement of public history by marital
history in the *Traitié*. The following is the sole stanza devoted to Ulysses:

Rois Uluxes pour plaire a sa caroigne
Falsoit sa foi devers Penolopé;
Avoec Circes fist mesme la busoigne,
Du quoi son fils Thelogonus fuist née,
Q'ad puis son propre piere auci tué.
Q'il n'est plesant a dieu tiele engendrure,
Le fin demoustre toute l'aventure.

[To please his body, King Ulysses
Betrayed his vow to Penelope;
With Circe he did the same thing,
From which union his son Telegonus was born,
Who later also killed his own father.
We can see that such engendering is not pleasing to God since
The end reveals the whole story.]

(VI.3.15–21)

The heroic military achievements of Ulysses are not mentioned, because Gower deals only with his infidelity and its consequences. "Pour plaire a sa caroigne" (To please his body) becomes a kind of Homeric epithet that labels the hero as ruled by his body, not his reason. Ulysses is described solely by his lust and even associated with "engendrure" (engendering), and thus with the process of procreation. In this way, even Ulysses, a great classical military hero, is judged by standards of behavior focused on sexuality, and his legacy is counted as an act of reproduction, rather than in terms of cultural or national heritage. As an epic hero, Ulysses is a figure for the power of Greece, but in Gower's version, Ulysses' actions have their effect not on his nation but on his family. In contrast to the epic genre, history is constructed in the *Traitié* not as public event but as the history of individuals and their marriages. History is replaced by a genealogy in which behavioral patterns as well as genes are passed along. The implication here is that Ulysses not only "engendered" a son, Telegonus, but he also passed down to him the legacy of his sinful marital behavior.

The *Traitié*'s appropriation of the story of Troy from the *Roman de Troie* and other contemporary sources shows the extent to which the epic, public, and national Trojan story is privatized and subsumed to marital history in the ballads. In this respect, Gower's ballad sequence resembles the works of courtly writers who detached the Trojan protagonists entirely from history by treating them as wholly amorous figures, in works such as Machaut's *La Fonteinne Amoureuse* and Jean Froissart's *Paradys d'Amours,* and, to some extent, in Gower's own *Confessio Amantis.*[22] In the *Traitié,* however, these figures represent not just lovers, as in these other courtly poems, but specifically husbands whose marital failings seal the fate of a city and a nation. In one passage, the poem refers directly to the chronicle genre, which typically addressed public and political events, only to focus instead on the domestic arena. The speaker of the poem reports: "Du quoi jeo trieus une

Cronique escrite / Pour essampler . . . Horribles sonts les mals d'avolterie"
(I have found a chronicle written / To illustrate this subject . . . Horrible
are the sins of adultery; IX.1.4–5, 7). Immediately following this stanza
are the tales of Agamemnon, Helen, and Paris, suggesting that perhaps
the "cronique" that Gower has in mind is either Guido delle Colonne's or
Benoît de Sainte-More's romance of Troy. These books identify adultery
as the central cause for the fall of Troy, reworking the story of the *Iliad* to
make it a more private and less public story, and converting it from epic to
romance.[23] The *Traitié* takes this process of privatizing Trojan history even
further. Unlike the expansive attention given to battles in these lengthy
narratives, the single stanza devoted to Helen in the poem gives most of its
attention to her courtship, and only one line to the fall of Troy:

La tresplus belle q'unqes fuist humeine,
L'espouse a roi de Grece Menelai,
C'estoit la fole peccheresse Heleine,
Pour qui Paris primer se faisoit gai;
Mais puis tornoit toute sa joie en wai,
Qant Troie fuist destruite et mis en cendre:
Si haut pecché covient en bass descendre.

[The most beautiful woman who ever lived,
The wife of Menelaus, the king of Greece,
Was the foolish sinner Helen,
Whom Paris first courted gaily;
But afterwards all his joy turned to woe,
When Troy was destroyed and burnt to ash:
Such a great sin brings such utter downfall.]
(X.1.1–7)

The destruction of this great city is framed as the explanation for the change
in Paris's mental state from joy to woe, and public history is displaced into
individual consciousness. Even as the poem consistently invokes the past
through repeated references to well-known epic heroes and old tales, it
suppresses public historical consciousness and replaces it with individual
emotion.

The fatality that destroys Troy locates causality not at the level of divine
will but of human action. The tales of the *Traitié* repeatedly suggest that an

individual man's lack of self-control in marriage is the cause of his fate. In this respect the poem is notably different from the *Roman de Troie* in which the death of each hero is followed by "com dure destinee!" or a similar phrase that invokes the determining force of destiny or fortune.[24] Although in the *Confessio,* Ulysses' betrayal of Penelope is attributed to the whims of fortune (VI.1509–17), Gower's *Traitié* consistently subordinates any notion of fortune to a kind of marital individual determinism, in which each character's fate is presented as the natural outcome of his conjugal behavior. We are told that he who bestows honest love "N'esteot doubter les changes perilouses" (Need not fear dangerous changes of fortune; IV.3.20), suggesting that fortune is not a transcendent force beyond human control, but a function of the individual's inner state of mind about his marriage. Even though God is often presented in the tales as the agent of punishment, it is most often human sins rather than God's mysterious ways that are the determining and motivating factors. The tale of Jason omits all reference to God or divine agency, save for the refrain that punctuates the three stanzas of the tale: "Friente espousaile dieux le vengera" (God will revenge broken wedlock; VIII). In fact, in the *Traitié*'s ballads, fortune is not presented as a universal presence or transcendent force but as a characteristic of love:

> As uns est blanche, as uns fortune est noire;
> Amour se torne trop diversement,
> Ore est en joie, ore est purgatoire,
> Sanz point, sanz reule et sanz governement:
> Mais sur toutz autres il fait sagement,
> Q'en fol amour ne se delite mie . . .

> [To some fortune is white, to others it is black;
> Love is extremely changeable:
> Now it is joy, now purgatory,
> Without limit, without rule, without government:
> But he is wiser than all others,
> Who does not delight himself at all in foolish love . . .]
>
> (XV.3.15–20)

Fortune is represented as an attribute of love that can be avoided by the individual's choice of marital affection over the instabilities of love. This is one of many examples in the ballads in which the transcendent forces of history and destiny are reframed as dramas of individual consciousness. Rather than men being a pawn of fortune, fortune itself is virtually subject to the rule of individual will.

Gower's tales of heroes turned into adulterers who are inevitably punished transform the narrative conventions of aristocratic romance. The lessons of national and epic history are retold as marital dramas, and chronicles are replaced by genealogy. Motivation for major historical events is explained not by the workings of fortune or of God but by individual marital conduct. Unlike the aristocratic romance model, public and private worlds are no longer presented as equivalent. On the contrary, masculine honor is defined not by public military achievement but by the private world of sexual conduct. Thus, Gower transforms the conventions of romance narrative to make marriage central to masculine identity.

Regendering Marriage

By reworking romance paradigms, the short tales that compose the *Traitié* give the moral responsibility for sexual practices to men, in contrast to the more common ascription to women in the Middle Ages. Whereas traditional medieval antimatrimonialism was tied to misogyny, in this ballad sequence Gower defends marriage without defending women. In contrast to the antimatrimonial voices of the misogynist tradition, which take the failure of marriages as evidence that it is better not to marry at all, Gower converts tales about the failures of marriages into a defense of the institution by claiming that the bad ends of the heroes in the tales are the fault of these individuals and not of the institution of marriage. In this way, the *Traitié* revises the misogynist traditions of both aristocratic and clerical writing, constructing marriage as a model for masculine identity and self-control.

In its short tales about marriages gone wrong and in its cast of characters, the *Traitié* invokes the antifeminist tradition of the "wikked wives" catalogue.[25] Almost all the female characters who appear in the tales in the *Traitié*—Eve, Deianira, Medea, Clytemnestra, Helen, Lucretia, Penelope, Sarah, Bathsheba—were virtual clichés in medieval discussions of the virtues and vices of women. A parodic representative of the genre is Jankyn's "Book of Wicked Wives" from Chaucer's *Wife of Bath's Tale*. The Wife

explains that Jankyn read to her not only about Eve, who "for hir wikked-
nesse, / Was al mankynde broght to wrecchednesse," but also "Of Hercules
and of his Dianyre, / That caused hym to sette hymself afyre" and "Of
Clitermystra, for hire lecherye, / That falsly made hire housbonde for to
dye, / He redde it with ful good devocioun."[26] The abbreviated and nota-
tional form of this passage, which is only slightly briefer than the accounts
of these figures in Gower's ballads, suggests that Chaucer expected his audience to be familiar both with these particular misogynist examples and
with the genre of the antifeminist catalogue, perhaps reflecting the fashion
for vernacular misogynist texts in the fourteenth century.[27]

As the example of antifeminist catalogues illustrates, medieval writers
routinely enlisted antimatrimonialism in the service of misogyny.[28] In *Le
Roman de la Rose,* an important source for Gower's *Confessio Amantis,* Jean
de Meun draws on Jerome's retelling of Theophrastus for the Friend's antimatrimonial tirade:

> If I had believed Theophrastus, I would never have married a wife. He
> considers no man wise who takes a wife in marriage, whether she is beau-
> tiful or ugly, poor or rich, for he says, and affirms it as true in his noble
> book, *Aureolus* (a good one to study in school), that married life is very
> disagreeable, full of toil and trouble, of quarrels and fights that result
> from the pride of foolish women, full, too, of their opposition and the
> reproaches that they make and utter with their mouths, full of the de-
> mands and the complaints that they find on many occasions.[29]

This passage is paradigmatic of the way misogynist logic was routinely em-
ployed in support of antimatrimonialism by medieval writers. The problem
with marriage, their logic goes, is that one is permanently saddled with the
wickedness and unpleasantness of women, whose actions inevitably bring
unhappiness. In misogynist texts, marriage is also often seen as a drain on
the husband's wealth, on his physical and emotional well-being, and on his
ability to concentrate.[30]

Marriage is not only disagreeable but antithetical to *fin amor* in the convention of aristocratic misogyny. A classic, perhaps even notorious, version
of this assertion is the statement by Andreas Capellanus, ostensibly from a
letter by Marie of Champagne, that "[w]e state and affirm unambiguously
that love cannot extend its sway over a married couple."[31] In the *Miroir de
Mariage,* Deschamps articulates this perceived antipathy between marriage

and love in terms that provide a striking echo for the *Traitié*'s ballad on Gawain, discussed above:

Et si vault mieulx vie commune
Que un seulz en veuille avoir une
Seulement, qui n'avenra mie.
Pis vault avoir femme qu'amie.

(*Miroir,* 2933–36)

[And thus a communal life is better than for one man alone to want to possess one woman, which will never happen anyway. It is worse to have a wife than a lover.][32]

Far from Gower's assertion that "a un est une assetz en mariage" (one woman is enough for one man in marriage; XVII.2.14), here a variety of lovers is explicitly recommended. Furthermore, the *Traitié*'s assertion that "N'est pas compaigns q'est comun a chascune" (He is not a lover who keeps the company of many women; XVII.2.8) is virtually a direct refutation of this advocation of the "vie commune." In another passage, Deschamps defends lawful marriage in language notably similar to that of the *Traitié,* but places that defense in the mouth of the obviously unreliable character Folie. "Now do it," he advises, "and see to it that you have in marriage a humble, beautiful, good and virtuous woman, as the law commands" (Or fay donc et si te delivre / Que tu aies par mariaige / Femme humble, belle, bonne et saige / Ainsis que la loy le commande).[33] By putting these words into the mouth of Folie, Descamps makes it clear that in the convention of *fin amor* the imagination of such positive traits in a woman was an impossibility. Instead of rejecting marriage in favor of *fin amor,* Gower's *Traitié* rejects *fin amor* in favor of marriage.

Despite the resemblance of the *Traitié* to the antifeminist catalogue in both its form and cast of characters, Gower neither adopts these antimatrimonial lines nor rewrites these tales to defend women, as Chaucer does in *The Legend of Good Women* and Christine de Pizan does in *The Book of the City of Ladies.* Instead Gower de-emphasizes the role of women entirely, focusing instead on the role of their husbands. If the Friend from *Le Roman de la Rose* is careful to enumerate the various actions women can undertake to make men's lives disagreeable (quarrels, demands, reproaches, and so on), Gower's women are passive and his focus, and the blame, is all on male sexual conduct in marriage.[34] Gower's lack of interest in criticizing women is illustrated in the tale of Hercules that we have been discussing, where Hercules is presented as the hero while Deianira makes only a cameo appearance. In the first stanza that introduces the two characters, Hercules is given all the active verbs: he "fastened" (fichoit) the two pillars, he "took a wife honorably" (prist femme a son honour). Deianira remains passive and occupies the grammatical position of an object. She is the "wife" (femme) that he "took" (prist) and the prize that he "won" (conquestoit) in battle (VII.1.1–6).

The lack of attention paid to Deianira in Gower's text is especially notable in view of the fact that she is usually a favorite illustration of the evils of female behavior in medieval misogynist writing. Again, the discourse of the Friend in *Le Roman de la Rose* is paradigmatic:

> According to the author Solinus, this Hercules was seven feet tall, and no man, as he said, could ever attain a greater height. Hercules had many struggles: he conquered twelve horrible monsters, and when he had overcome the twelfth he could never finish with the thirteenth, his sweetheart Deianeira, who, with her poisonous shirt, lacerated his flesh, all enflamed by the poison. His heart had already been made mad with love for Iole. Thus Hercules, who had so many virtues, was subdued by woman.[35]

In the Friend's version, Deianira is blamed for her husband's death; she is given the active verb (she "lacerated his flesh"), and the shirt is clearly identified as hers. On the other hand, in the source for this tale, Ovid's *Metamorphoses,* Deianira does not fully understand the nature of the magic robe she gives to her husband. The text describes her as "not knowing what she is giving, the cause of her own sorrow." Because it was given to her by Nessus the Centaur "to help make her love him," she mistakenly believes that it will make her husband love her.[36] In contrast to Ovid, the Friend explicitly names Deianira "the thirteenth monster," likening Hercules' wife to his enemies. No responsibility is ascribed here to Hercules for his passion for Iole, for he retains his "many virtues" in the very next sentence and Deianira's blame remains unqualified.

While the Friend's discourse revises Ovid to emphasize Deianira's guilt in Hercules' death, Gower downplays Deianira's role so completely that it is not clear that she has any part in it at all:

Unqes ne fuist ne ja serra null jour,
Qe tiel pecché de dieu vengé ne soit:
Car Hercules, ensi com dist l'auctour,
D'une chemise, dont il se vestoit,
Fuist tant deceu, qu'il soi mesmes ardoit.
De son mesfait porta le contretaille;
C'est grant peril de freindre l'espousaile.

[There was never a time nor will there ever be one when
Such a sin will not be avenged by God:
For Hercules, as the author says,
Was so deceived that he burnt himself from a shirt,
Which he put on.
He bore the retribution of his misdeed;
It is a great peril to break a marriage.]

(VII.3.15–21)

The agent of Hercules' deception remains mysterious, and instead Hercules himself appears the direct cause of his destruction, as indicated by the reflexive verb in the phrase "qu'il soi mesmes ardoit" (he burnt himself). His fate is not attributed to the evil of Deianira, but to the "contretaille" de "son mesfait" (retribution of his misdeed), and the burning shirt was presumably the means by which the "pecché" (sin) of his infidelity was "de dieu vengé" (avenged by God).[37]

For Gower, not Deianira's actions but Hercules' own marital infidelity is the source of his bad end:

Bein tost apres tout changea cell amour
Pour Eolen, dont il s'espouse haoit:
Celle Eolen fuist file a l'emperour
D'Eurice, et Herculem tant assotoit,
Q'elle ot de lui tout ceo q'avoir voloit.
N'ert pas le fin semblable au comensaile;
C'est grant peril de freindre l'espousaile.

[Quite soon thereafter this love changed completely
So that he hated his wife, and loved Iole:
This Iole was the daughter of the Emperor

Of Eurice, and Hercules was so fond [of her]
That she had of him whatever she wanted.
It was not in the end like the beginning;
It is a great peril to break a marriage.]
                                        (VII.2.8–14)

The addition of the detail of Hercules hating his wife directs the reader's
attention toward Hercules' marriage rather than to his love affair. This detail is not in the Ovidian source nor in the longer version of this tale in the
Confessio Amantis where the tale is used to illustrate Nessus's envy in love.[38]
While the Friend and other misogynist voices of the antimatrimonial tradition take the failure of this and other marriages as evidence that it is better not to marry at all, Gower converts a tale about the failure of marriage
into a defense of the institution by claiming that Hercules' bad end is the
direct result of his abandonment of marriage.

Even in cases where his text recognizes the fault of women, Gower still
focuses on male behavior and defends marriage. Gower's de-emphasis of the
faults of Helen of Troy, Procne, and others is remarkable, especially when
compared to the allusions to these same figures in the following notorious
misogynist passage from Jerome. Here he ascribes the fault for major wars
and national tragedies to women:

> [I]n all the bombast of tragedy and the overthrow of houses, cities and
> kingdoms, it is the wives and concubines who stir up strife. Parents take
> up arms against their children; unspeakable banquets are served; and
> on account of the rape of one wretched woman Europe and Asia are in-
> volved in a ten years' war.[39]

We have already seen that Gower gives Paris rather than Helen the primary responsibility for the fall of Troy. He also blames Tereus rather than
his wife Procne for the "unspeakable banquet" of his young son alluded to
by Jerome, describing him as "motivated by false delight, against reason"
(De foldelit contraire a sa reson), and acting "against his vow" (Contre sa
foi) of marriage "to seize the flower of virginity from Philomena," concluding, "a treacherous lover receives his just desserts" (De Philomene
en sa proteccion / Ravist la flour de sa virginité / . . . / Malvois amant
reprent malvois loer; XII.2.8–12, 14). Thus, even in cases where the woman

is the direct agent of destruction, the responsibility for marital conduct is given to men and presented as crucial to their identity.

Not only does Gower fail to indict the usual misogynist suspects, underplaying the roles of such traditional villainesses as Deianira, Medea, and Clytemnestra, but he also treats good wives the same way. Penelope and Lucretia, famous symbols of wifely virtue, potentially could have provided evidence in support of marriage. Indeed, they are used in just this way in the *Confessio Amantis,* where they appear in Venus's court and are praised as wives, indicating a compatibility between courtly love and marriage.[40] In the *Traitié,* however, they also almost disappear behind their spouses. Even misogynist writers generally felt that they needed to address the subject of these two virtuous wives in order to make their attacks on women and marriage convincing. For the most part, these writers emphasized the anomaly of these women, as the following passage from Walter Map illustrates:

> The very best woman, who is rarer than the phoenix, cannot be loved without the bitterness of fear and care and frequent disaster . . . The banner of chastity was won by Lucretia and Penelope and the Sabine women, and it was a very small troop that brought the trophy home. My friend, there are no Lucretias, Penelopes or Sabine women now: beware of them all.[41]

Map's assertion that the best of women are rarer than phoenixes—a claim that recurs in other misogynist classics—corresponds to the paucity of exempla of virtuous married women in hagiography and other medieval writings.

Clearly Gower did not feel that his defense of marriage required an engagement in the dispute over the virtue of women, or the relative commonality or rarity of good wives. Although Lucretia was one of the few examples of female married virtue in medieval writing, in Gower's poem she takes a minor role compared with Tarquin, the villain of the tale:

> Tarquins auci, q'ot la pensé vileine,
> Q'avoit pourgeu Lucrece a son essai,
> Sanz null retour d'exil receust la peine;
> Et la dolente estoit en tiel esmai,

Qe d'un cotell s'occist sanz null deslai:
Ceo fuist pité, mais l'en doit bien entendre,
Si haut pecché covient en bass descendre.

[Tarquin, who also had villainous thoughts,
Had tried to seduce Lucretia,
Received the penalty of exile without return.
And the suffering Lucretia was in such pain and dismay,
That she killed herself with a knife without any delay:
That was piteous, but one should well understand that,
Such a great sin brings such utter downfall.]

(X.2.8–14)

While Lucretia is commonly seen as an emblem of a good wife, because she
so loved her married chastity that she killed herself rather than live with
her defilement, no mention is made of her virtue in this passage. Instead,
the ballad focuses on her pain and the means of her suicide, remarking "ceo
fuist pité," a phrase that hardly connotes heroism or virtue. There is no description of her motives or of her sexual virtue, usually a central concern in
representations of women in medieval writings.[42] In the *Traitié,* Lucretia's
pain and death are merely casualties of Tarquin's "low descent" and the result of his sin. In the same way, Gower's story of Ulysses, the protagonist
of an earlier tale, turns his virtuous wife, Penelope, into merely the passive
object of a preposition: "Rois Uluxes pour plaire a sa caroigne / Falsoit sa
foi devers Penolopé" (To please his body, King Ulysses / Betrayed his vow
to Penelope; VI.3.15–16). Thus, the tales of Penelope and Lucretia become
instead the tales of Tarquin and Ulysses, and the tales of virtuous wives become the stories of men who come to a bad end because they fail to uphold
their marriages by restraining their desires.

Gower's failure to accord Lucretia and Penelope their usual accolades
for moral virtue is part of a larger pattern in the *Traitié,* which shifts moral
responsibility for sexual practices from women to men. This shift is especially evident in Gower's treatment of the biblical tale of Bathsheba,
which differs from her representation in a whole range of medieval literature. Conventionally she was held accountable for David's seduction, even
though she is consistently acknowledged as an object of desire and not the
desiring subject, illustrating the extent to which women were cultural sym-

bols of lust.[43] Strikingly similar commentaries on Bathsheba can be found in religious texts such as the *Ancrene Wisse,* in courtly texts such as Deschamps's *Miroir de Mariage,* and Walter Map's *De Nugis Curialium,* and in later secular texts such as Caxton's *Book of the Knight of the Tower,* suggesting the extent to which this example became standardized; the idea that this example illustrates—that sexual morality is primarily the wife's obligation—was even more widespread.[44]

Instead of blaming Bathsheba for uncovering herself, the *Traitié* holds King David responsible for his lack of control over his fleshly desire:

> Trop est humaine char frele et vileine;
> Sanz grace nulls se poet contretenir:
> Ceo parust bien, sicom le bible enseine,
> Qant roi David Urie fist moertrir
> Pour Bersabée, don't il ot son plesir

> [So frail and base is the human flesh,
> Without grace no one can resist [temptation]:
> That is apparent, as the Bible teaches,
> When King David murdered Uriah
> For Bathsheba, from whom he had his pleasure]
>   (XIV.1.1–5)

In this passage, David's lack of control is responsible both for his "pleasure" and for the murder that inevitably results. Later in the same ballad Gower explains the source of David's downfall:

> La bealté q'il veoit ensi lui meine,
> Qu'il n'ot poair de son corps abstenir,
> Maisqu'il chaoit d'amour en celle peine,
> Dont chastes ne se poait contenir:
> L'un mal causoit un autre mal venir,
> L'avolterie a l'omicide esguarde

> [The beauty that he beheld led him
> Not to have power over his own body
> But he fell into such distress from love

That he could not keep his chastity:
One evil causes another evil to happen,
Adultery leads to homicide]

(XIV.2.8–13)

Bathsheba virtually disappears and is replaced by the abstraction "bealté." Instead of tracing the homicide to the seduction by Bathsheba, Gower shows the death of Uriah to be the result of David's adultery, which itself stems from David's lack of self-control. As illustrated in a more solemn idiom by the tale of Bathsheba and more extravagantly and humorously by Chaucer's *Wife of Bath's Tale,* often in medieval literature women are associated with the body and with lust. In Gower's *Traitié,* by contrast, men are held responsible for governing their own lust.

In addition to shifting attention and responsibility from female to male characters in these tales of adultery and self-destruction, Gower regenders conventional marriage teaching about restraint, avoiding the familiar association of male with soul and female with body.[45] The association of the body with woman and the soul with man is one of the conventional reasons for the rulership of husband over wife. An *ad coniugatos* sermon by Alan de Lille demonstrates this analogy: "Let a man maintain a spiritual marriage between flesh and spirit, so that the flesh, like a woman, obeys the spirit, and the spirit, like the husband, rules the flesh as its wife."[46] De Lille uses marriage not only to discuss the hierarchical relationship between the sexes but also as a metaphor for a gendered hierarchy within the individual self. The subject matter of the first ballads of the *Traitié,* where Gower describes the rule of the soul over the body, provides a perfect opportunity to enact traditional divides, matching body with female, and soul with male, but nothing of this nature occurs. Instead, not only the soul but also the body appear to be gendered masculine: "Li corps par naturele experience / Quiert femme avoir, dont soit multipliant" (The body by natural experience / Desires to have a wife in order to multiply; II.1.3–4). It could be argued that this is a natural consequence of the gendering of the French language, which happens to have assigned a male gender to the noun *corps,* but Gower's choice of *femme* in this stanza, instead of the ambiguously gendered *espouse,* which he uses in much of the sequence, deliberately emphasizes the female nature of body's marriage partner, and thus, by implication, the body's own masculinity. By gendering the body male, and making the male protagonists of the tales responsible for their own desire, Gower shows that, for him, lust and its regulation through marriage are not solely or especially a female concern. Furthermore, marriage is presented here not just as a hierarchy of man over women, but as a hierarchy of attributes within the self that function as a model for male self-control.

Promoting Marriage and Lay Authority

Although the poem's central message that marriage is a form of self-regulation echoes contemporary conventional Church teachings, the *Traitié* goes further in its promotion of marriage over chastity, implicitly endorsing lay over clerical authority.[47] This implicit embrace of lay authority is also evident in the *Traitié*'s shift from engaging the tropes of marriage sermons in the early ballads to invoking the "fall of princes" genre in a series of ballads that takes up the majority of the sequences. In these later ballads, as in the *De Casibus* tradition, ecclesiastical authority is replaced by a secular vision of justice. Combining this political genre of writing with ecclesiastical conventions about marriage, Gower's poem revises traditional teaching to imagine a secular and civic vision of marriage not just for princes but as a broader model for male identity.

Central to the poem's rejection of courtly values is its lesson that marriage is a means of self-regulation. The first stanza, for example, teaches the reader that God "l'alme d'omme ad fait a son ymage, / Par quoi le corps de reson et nature / soit attempré per jouste governage" (made the soul of man in His image, / So that the body by reason and nature / Would be tempered by just governance; I.1.2–4).[48] A few lines later Gower expands on the regulatory function of the soul over the body, by explaining, "En l'alme gist et raison et mesure" (In the soul lie both reason and measure; I.3.15). He promotes a similar message in the *Confessio Amantis* when he explains that the philosopher teaches Alisandre "that he schal mesure / His bodi, so that no mesure / Of fleisshly lust he scholde excede."[49] In both poems, Gower's didacticism echoes the tone and content of discussions of the sin of lechery in confessors' handbooks. The fourteenth-century *Fasciculus Morum,* for example, cites the following definition: "Lechery is the desire to have sex which rises beyond reason and against measure."[50]

Like contemporary marriage sermons, the *Traitié* also defends marriage on the grounds that it originated in paradise. One of the early ballads in the sequence reads as follows:

Primerement qant mesmes dieus crea
Adam et Eve en son saint paradis,
L'omme ove la femme ensemble maria

. . . .

Et puisque dieus qui la loi ordina
En une char ad deux persones mis,
Droitz est qe l'omme et femme pourcela
Tout un soul coer eiont par tiel devis

[In the beginning when God created
Adam and Eve in His holy paradise
They were married

. . . .

Because God who ordained the law
United two people in one flesh,
It is proper that man and woman
Should share one heart in this way.]

(III.2–3.8–10 and 14–17)

This justification comes from Augustine's defense of marriage in his famous treatise *De Bono Coniugali,* often quoted or paraphrased in late medieval *ad status* sermons. Both Guibertus de Tornaco and Jacobus de Vitriaco, for example, defend the honor of marriage in the same terms, arguing that the goodness of marriage may be seen from the fact that the Lord instituted the married state (*ordinem coniugalem*) Himself, and in paradise, whereas the other orders (*ordines*) were founded outside paradise and by men.[51] Confessors' handbooks, such as *Fasciculus Morum,* also defend marriage on the grounds that the Virgin was married when she gave birth to Christ: "Christ himself in his sinlessness deigned to be born in wedlock—not only in the purity of virginity but also in the honorable state of matrimony—that he might show how eminently worthy this sacrament is."[52] The *Traitié* also uses the fact that Christ was born to the Virgin Mary while she was married to condemn adultery and defend marriage:

De l'espousailes la profession
Valt plus d'assetz qe jeo ne puiss descrire:
Soubtz cell habit prist incarnacion
De la virgine cil q'est nostre Sire

[Marriages are more worthy than
I can describe:
In marriage, our Lord
Was made Incarnate through a virgin]
(V.2.8–11)

The exegetical method of Gower's defense of marriage, his choice of biblical evidence, and his reading of these examples all echo theological and popular defenses of marriage.

Although Gower defends marriage on conventional theological grounds, he goes further than convention in his valuation of marriage over chastity. Whereas Gower's *Traitié* begins by acknowledging the conventional hierarchy in which marriage is ranked below virginity in the three grades of sexual status, as the poem develops, marriage takes on the highest rank. Early in the sequence, in ballad two, Gower describes the superiority of spiritual love and chastity:

De l'espirit l'amour quiert continence,
Et vivre chaste en soul dieu contemplant;
Li corps par naturele experience
Quiert femme avoir, dont soit multipliant;

. . . .

Si l'un est bon, l'autre est assetz meilour.

[Love seeks continence from the soul,
To live chaste, contemplating God alone;
The body by natural experience
Desires to have a wife in order to multiply;

. . . .

If the one is good, the other is even better.]
(II.1.1–4 and 7)

Gower gives the usual explanation for the hierarchy of virginity over marriage: whereas marriage is good, virginity is better because it does not involve the flesh and is thus more spiritual. In an exaggerated form, this logic is used in antimatrimonial writings, as we have seen, which Gower invokes by his choice of tales but studiously avoids in his retelling of them. By ballad eighteen, however, Gower has more explicitly rejected this logic by turning this earlier hierarchy on its head: "Des trois estatz benoitz c'est le seconde, / Q'au mariage en droit amour se ploie" (Of the three estates, most blessed is the second, / Which submits itself to marriage according to proper love; XVIII.2.8–9). By calling marriage the second estate, instead of widowhood, Gower changes the usual order of the "three grades of chastity" (virginity, widowhood, marriage), and by suggesting that marriage is the "most blessed" of the three, he upsets the hierarchy of celibacy over marriage. Since marriage was the sign and state of lay life, and celibacy was the distinguishing feature of the clergy and the sign of their superior purity and moral virtue, upsetting the hierarchy of sexual status can be read as an implicit challenge to the moral superiority of the clergy.[53]

Whereas the early ballads of the *Traitié* invoke the language of marriage sermons, later ballads present the exempla of fallen heroes who suffer for their crimes against marriage which resemble the more secular model of Boccaccio's *De Casibus*.[54] As Boccaccio says in his preface, his book is "a succinct account of fallen leaders and of the falls of other famous persons, both men and women from the beginning of the world up to our own age."[55] Like Boccaccio's text, Gower's ballads focus on the fall of important figures of the past, but his focus, as we have seen, is exclusively on men rather than on both men and women, as in Boccaccio's text, or on women, as in the misogynist tradition. Furthermore, although lust is one of the evils illustrated by Boccaccio, there are many others exemplified in the *De Casibus*, including pride and tyranny. In the *Traitié*, on the other hand, the focus is relentlessly on the subject of marital failings. The *Traitié* clearly shares, however, the didactic purpose of the *De Casibus* as stated in the preface: to persuade wicked people to reform themselves, by showing what has happened to those who did not. As Boccaccio says, "I intend to tell them what God (or, to use their expression, Fortune) can do to those who are in high places."[56] In contrast to Boethius's *Consolation of Philosophy* and the beginning of Chaucer's *Monk's Tale*, Boccaccio's and Gower's tales are intended to illustrate not the capriciousness and instability of Fortune, but rather falls that are deserved.[57] Fortune becomes the providential agent of moral justice on earth which punishes the wicked for their evil deeds. Far from showing men subject to fate, Gower's text shows fate subject to man's actions. Gower's story of Nectabus, for example, is glossed as follows: "Cil q'est de pecché pres sa grace esloigne: / Ceo parust bien, car tiele destinée / Avint depuis, qe sanz nulle autre essoine / Le fils occist le pere tout de grée" (This happens to he who with sins removes his salvation: / For such a fate / Followed, that without any other motivation / The son willingly killed his father; VI.2.1–4). Instead of being haphazard, fortune is depicted here as the agent of retribution that men bring on themselves by choosing evil actions.

Although Gower's ballads invoke a providential model and use the language of sin, as in *De Casibus,* ecclesiastical authority is notably absent, and justice operates through lay agency. God is mentioned in the *Traitié*'s tale of Nectabus, but He functions primarily through narrative logic: "Q'il n'est plesant a dieu tiele engendrure, / Le fin demoustre toute l'aventure" (We can see that such engendering is not pleasing to God since / The end reveals the whole story; VI.3.20–21). Similarly, in the story of Hercules, God's will is represented as functioning on earth without ecclesiastical intermediaries or other authorities. The final stanza of this ballad explains that there will never be a time when "tiel pecché de dieu vengé ne soit" (such a sin will not be avenged by God; VII.3.16), but the punishment in this case involves only the sinner's own agency. Hercules is described as "tant deceu, qu'il soi mesmes ardoit" (so deceived that he burnt himself from a shirt; VII.3.19). Similarly, many of the refrains represent justice as taking place on earth almost without agency at all: for example, "Cil qui mal fait, falt qu'il au mal responde" (He who does evil will be answered in kind; XI), and "Malvois amant reprent malvois loer" (A treacherous lover receives his just desserts; XII). Sometimes evil itself seems to have the power to act: "L'un mal causoit un autre mal venir" (One evil causes another evil to happen; XIV.2). Not only is ecclesiastical authority notably absent, but unlike hagiography, there is generally no separation between earthly and secular realms of justice in these tales.[58] Most of the punishments described are endured in life and on earth, rather than in hell after death. In their use of a language of sin that relies on narrative rather than explicitly clerical authority, the tales of the *Traitié* promote lay rather than ecclesiastical authority.

Some of the tales of the *Traitié* depict secular rather than ecclesiastical justice at work repaying those who commit marital and sexual crimes. The denouement of the tale of Agamemnon and Clytemnestra appears in the final stanza of ballad nine:

Son propre fils Horestes l'ad despite,
Dont de sa main receust la mort subite;

Egiste as fourches puis rendist sa vie:
Horribles sont les mals d'avolterie.

[Her own son Orestes despised her,
And from his hand she received sudden death;
Later Aegisthus surrendered his life on the gallows.
Horrible are the evils of adultery.]

(IX.3.18–21)

Although adultery is described as a "mal," no mention of God or divine justice occurs in this passage. Instead, divine retribution is replaced by a secular legal punishment, as Aegisthus dies by hanging. Clytemnestra's death at the hands of her son is presented as a parallel fate that is the inevitable consequence of her adultery, despite the lack of legal mechanism. Similarly, only human justice operates in Gower's account of the fate of Alboin's adulterous wife and her lover, Helemechis:

Elmeges ove sa dame lecherous
Estoient arsz pour lour grant felonie;
Le duc q'ot lors Ravenne en sa baillie
En son paleis lour jugement exponde:
Cil qui mal fait, falt qu'il au mal responde.

[Helemechis and his lecherous lady
Were burnt for their great wickedness;
The duke who had the area near Ravenna in his jurisdiction
Set forth their judgment in his palace:
The one who does evil will be answered in kind.]

(XI.3.17–21)

Although adultery is represented as a moral crime, the secular jurisdiction over adultery is clear in this passage since the punishment for adultery is enacted by the duke, a secular authority, in his palace.

This subtle shift of jurisdiction over crimes against marriage from heavenly or ecclesiastical authority to a more earthly and secular economy of justice also occurs in the diction of the poem. In the description of Helemechis and his lover in the passage above, explicitly moral vocabulary,

such as the term *mal,* is blended with secular diction drawn from legal ter-
minology, such as the description of the sexual crime as a "felonie." Not only
sexual but also sacred phenomena are described in civil legal terms. In the
first ballad of the *Traitié,* Gower concludes his description of God's creation
of man in His image, and His creation of the soul and the body, with the
following refrain: "Dont sur le corps raison ert conestable." My translation,
"Wherefore reason will be guardian over the body," is consistent with the
tone and content of the stanza, but the term *conestable,* which I have translated as "guardian," clearly has a more specific meaning as an official of the
secular courts.[59] This use of secular legal vocabulary to describe God's work
in creation suggests that Gower saw heavenly and earthly economies of justice as coextensive. The blending of the religious and secular language
of justice culminates in the final portion of the Latin coda, which asserts,
"Hec est nuptorum carnis quasi regula morum" (Marriage is to the body as
regulation is to custom). While this depiction of marriage as a regulation of
the body was familiar from confessors' handbooks, the comparison of marriage to law itself is unusual. In this passage, Gower implies that both the
individual and the social body require external control: marriage controls
the body, while laws shape the habits of the social body. Thus, this analogy
locates marriage squarely on earth, not, as theologians would have it, in a
liminal space between secular and spiritual, physical and sacramental.

Gower's poem also represents the secularization of the sexual realm
by focusing on adultery and rape rather than fornication. Fornication was
solely the province of the confessional and the ecclesiastical courts, but the
jurisdiction for adultery and rape was shared between civil and ecclesiastical courts. In addition to being a moral crime, adultery was thought to be
an appropriation of another man's rights, and thus was considered a crime
that involved property; in addition to other penalties, punishments for adultery were often financial.[60] Similarly, rape was considered a civil as well as
a moral crime, and a particularly social crime because it was understood to
be the seizure of another man's property.[61] Almost all of the tales in the
Traitié concern adultery, and two of them—Procne and Philomena, Tarquin
and Lucretia—depict rape. The beginning of the *Traitié* might have led the
reader to expect a more religious poem, and an emphasis on fornication
would have been equally appropriate for illustrating the lesson that marriage was a form of self-regulation. The focus on adultery and rape in the
tales of the *Traitié,* however, suggests that a more secular notion of justice is

at work in the poem. This subtle emphasis on lay over clerical authority in the administration of justice in marital crimes is consistent with the poem's promotion of marriage over celibacy, a move that shifts power to the lay realm. As we will see in the next section, Gower not only revises and critiques clerical teaching, as he had revised and critiqued conventional forms of aristocratic writings on love, he also uses marriage to articulate an identity particularly meaningful for people like himself: men of the upper middle strata in late medieval England who are neither aristocratic nor clerical in their affiliations.

Marriage as Social Politics

In addition to enacting a subtle shift from clerical to lay authority over moral behavior in marriage, the *Traitié* also presents a larger political vision of social regulation and order. On first impression, the *Traitié* appears not to be a political poem, especially compared with Gower's overtly political *Vox Clamantis* and *Cronica Tripertita,* and the more conspicuously political *Confessio Amantis,* with its shifting dedications to Richard II and Henry Bolingbroke and its mirror for princes section. The *Traitié* engages not in the governmental politics of kingship and Parliament, however, but in social politics, by using the vocabulary of class and estate to apply to marriage. As we saw previously, Gower presents marriage as an estate: "Des trois estatz benoitz c'est le seconde, / Q'au mariage en droit amour se ploie" (Of the three estates, most blessed is the second / Which submits itself to marriage according to proper love; XVIII.2.8–9). Here Gower replaces categories of the three estates that are based in work—those who pray, those who fight, those who labor—with the sexual categories of the three grades of chastity—virginity, widowhood, and marriage—that are traditionally applied to women. This not only shifts the categories of male identity from work to sexual status, but also implies that anyone who behaves properly in marriage can potentially be morally superior, even in comparison to those of a higher class, thus presenting a potentially equalizing vision of social order. The model of society depicted here is not a hierarchy but an aggregate of individual self-controlled subjects. Envisioning a society structured by what might be called "marital individualism," Gower constructs an ideology for his own middle strata identity.

This idea that marital behavior trumps social status is also provided by the examples illustrating the poem's message of self-governance. By choosing great heroes and kings as examples of adulterers who met unpleasant ends in the portion of the poem that invokes the "fall of princes" genre, the *Traitié* conveys an impression of potential equality among all ranks of men. Elizabeth Porter has argued of the *Confessio* that the applicability of the advice offered to kings to "every member of the body politic" is a general characteristic of mirrors for princes, because of the "stress on individual ethics" in these works.[62] Diane Watt has recently made a similar point about the *Confessio,* arguing that "the consistent juxtaposition of political macrocosm and social microcosm in the poem makes it clear that at some levels at least the figure of the prince or king is an everyman."[63] This tendency of the *Confessio* becomes considerably more overt in the *Traitié,* as a comparison between passages in the two poems illustrates. For example, a discussion of lust in book 7 of the *Confessio* offers a message of sexual self-control that echoes the terms of the *Traitié,* but this is framed as wisdom for princes:

> So as the Philosophre techeth
> To Alisandre, and him betecheth
> The lore hou that he schal mesure
> His bodi, so that no mesure
> Of fleshly lust he scholde exceed.

Only a few lines later the elite nature of the audience for this advice is emphasized:

> He mot be more magnified
> For dignete of his corone,
> Than scholde an other low persone,
> Which is nought of so hih emprise.[64]

In this second passage control of lust corresponds to higher social standing, to kingly status. In the *Traitié,* by contrast, a similar lesson about the importance of self-control is framed with a more inclusive message. We have seen that the *Traitié*'s account of King David's desire for Bathsheba is directly preceded by the admonition that "Trop est humaine char frele et vileine; / Sanz grace nulls se poet contretenir" (So frail and base is the human flesh that / Without grace no one can resist; XIV.1.1–2); it is also concluded with the moral that "N'ert pas segeur de soi qui dieus ne guarde" (No man is master of himself unless God watches over him; XIV.1.7). Thus, the story of this king is overtly identified as the story of everyman, and the potentially equalizing aspects of the *Traitié*'s marital ideology are made clear.

Gower's recognition of the political implications of marital behavior is also evident in his use of the term *treson* to refer to the adulterous act, further demonstrating this intimate connection between the private and public spheres. After describing the "crazy love" (fol amour) that Aegisthus had for Agamemnon's wife, Clytemnestra, the last stanza of the ballad asserts: "Agamemnon de mort suffrist penance / Par treson qe sa femme avoit confite" (Agamemnon suffered the punishment of death / Because of the treason that his wife had committed; IX.3.15–16). By associating treason with private relations, the poem reflects the definition of treason in the law of 1352, which referred to insubordination both against the king by his people and against a husband by his wife. A portion of the law reads as follows:

> And in addition there is another kind of treason, that is to say when a servant kills his master, a woman kills her husband ["une femme qe tue son baron"], when a secular man or man in religious orders kills his prelate, to whom he owes faith and obedience ["a qi il doit foi & obedience"].[65]

Echoing the legal definition in its account of Clytemnestra's killing of Agamemnon, the *Traitié* implies that the sexual behavior of an individual has a larger effect on the social body as a whole.

Whereas the treason law clearly suggests that only women can commit treason in the household, in the *Traitié* both male and female infidelity is considered "treson," as the poem's tale of Tereus and Philomena illustrates. Gower describes how, after marrying Procne, Tereus conspires against her sister: "Cil Tereüs par treson pourpensée / De Philomene en sa proteccion / Ravist la flour de sa virginité" (This Tereus conspired by treason / To seize the flower of her virginity / From Philomena who was in his protection; XII.2.9–11). In this case, it is Tereus rather than Philomena who is guilty of treason, and thus treason in the household is detached from its usual patriarchal content. The use of treason to apply to both genders suggests that although Gower understood marriage as a political category, he avoided making it a model for hierarchical rule.

The *Traitié*'s application of "treson" to both genders is consistent with the image of marital mutuality promoted throughout the ballad sequence. The exegesis of the story of Adam and Eve at the beginning of the poem promotes an ideal far from the hierarchical Pauline model:

Droitz est qe l'omme et femme pourcela
Tout un soul coer eiont par tiel devis,
Loiale amie avoec loials amis:
C'est en amour trop belle retenue
Selonc la loi de seinte eglise due.

[It is proper that man and woman
Should share one heart in this way,
Loyal friend with loyal friend:
In a love beautifully sustained
According to the law of holy church.]
                              (III.3.17–21)

As in Chaucer's *Franklin's Tale,* here Gower describes marriage as an equal and mutual relationship based in friendship. This equality is reinforced syntactically by the symmetrical repetition of words in the phrase "Loiale amie avoec loials amis" (Loyal friend with loyal friend). Thus, like the end of Chaucer's *Franklin's Tale,* the ideals of marital mutuality and fidelity become a means of promoting a more inclusive model of social relations. But unlike the end of the *Franklin's Tale,* in which marriage presents the vocabulary for a new social vision but excludes Dorigen and thus marriage itself, in the *Traitié* marital practices are themselves the basis for a new vision of society.

This emphasis on mutuality in marriage is consistent with the inclusivity of the *Traitié*'s address in the prologue "a tout le monde en general" (to everyone in general) and in the envoy "Al université de tout le monde" (to the community of the entire world). The poem's universalizing address corresponds to what Anne Middleton has identified as the unique "public poetry" that developed in the Ricardian period. According to Middleton, this poetry is "defined by a constant relation of speaker to audience within an ideally conceived worldly community." Although speaking in a "common voice," this "public poetry" is nonetheless marked with the values of the middle strata: "It speaks for bourgeois moderation, a course between the rigorous absolutes of religious rule on the one hand, and, on the other, the rhetorical hyperboles and emotional vanities of the courtly style."[66] The *Traitié*'s "bourgeois" or middle strata "moderation" can be seen in its negotiation of ecclesiastical teachings about marriage and courtly writings on love.

Despite the poem's initial and final invocations of "common voice," the specifically middle strata values of the *Traitié* are evident in the complexity of style and language of the poem as a whole. Gower's elaborately rhymed ballad sequence excludes all but the literary elite through its use of exempla that are so abbreviated that they almost require previous knowledge of the stories to be intelligible, and by the fact that it is written in Anglo-Norman and Latin. Steven Justice and David Aers have both made a similar argument about Gower's *Vox Clamantis,* arguing that although it claims to speak for the common people, its use of Latin distances the narrator from the masses and the rebels.[67] This exclusion of lower and peasant classes becomes overt when the narrator excoriates them in book 1 of the *Vox,* representing them as domestic animals turned wild predators that speak with cacophonous cries. Such negative portrayals of the lower classes—or indeed any portrayals at all—are notably missing from the *Traitié,* as they are also absent from Chaucer's *Franklin's Tale.* Instead, the *Traitié* excludes them implicitly both by its use of language and by its turn to autobiography at the end. Although the final ballad is addressed "Al université de tout le monde," the last words of the *Traitié* in the Latin coda that follows the ballads identify Gower by name. Whereas the first time Gower names himself in the final ballad he belittles his skills as an author, apologizing for a lack of eloquence in French that he attributes to his English identity, in this final Latin passage, as we have seen, Gower refers to his own impending marriage, identifying himself with the subject matter of the poem.[68] Thus, the marital ideals of the *Traitié* are traceable to Gower's own subject-position and social standing.

This final self-revelation in the *Traitié* resembles the surprise ending of the *Confessio* (XIII.2908–31), in which Amans is revealed to be an aged John Gower.[69] In this passage of the *Confessio,* Gower appears as a subject within the poem, not just as an authorial figure. Venus turns Gower away from her court, and by implication from *fin amor,* a model of love making that is explicitly rewritten in the *Traitié.* The aged John Gower who leaves the court of Venus in the *Confessio* thus finds a home in the *Traitié*'s marital ideology, suggesting that Gower identified himself with marriage rather than *fin amor*. In this way, the *Traitié* may function as an appendix to the *Confessio*, containing his latest thinking on the subject of marriage, much the way the *Cronica Tripertita* functioned for the *Vox Clamantis,* supplying Gower's latest comments on the volatile world of royal and parliamentary politics. Reading *Traitié* and the end of the *Confessio* together suggests that Gower turned simultaneously toward autobiography and marriage and that he saw marital ideology as particularly relevant to his own situation. This is consistent with Diane Watt's recent argument that by the time Gower wrote the *Confessio,* he was writing "not for the king and the higher court, or the realm of England as a whole but . . . primarily for an audience of near social-equals."[70] Thus, the *Traitié*'s turn to marriage and autobiography may be seen as part of a larger shift in focus at the end of Gower's poetic career.

Marriage is not only essential to Gower's personal identity in the *Traitié,* it is part of the poem's development of an ideology that values individual behavior over social status. This valuation of private behavior over class status makes the depiction of marriage in the poem similar to the representation of manners in conduct literature: as a venue for the development of an ideology of social mobility. The *Traitié*'s very identification of marriage as a classless secular model of moral virtue marks this ballad sequence as part of an emergent ideology for the expanding upper-middle strata of society. As we have seen, the tension between the poem's ostensible direction to a universal audience and the implicit elitism of the poem is consistent with the ambiguous social positioning characteristic of those in the growing middle ranks of late medieval society who benefited from the increased fluidity of social categories but sought to consolidate their social gains by differentiating themselves from those further down the social scale. The *Traitié*'s invocation of "common voice" is itself a mark of the poem's middle strata values, revealing the roots of the public voice of Ricardian poetry in a new masculinized vision of private life.

CHAPTER THREE

Performing Reform

Marriage, Lay Piety, and Sacramental Theater
in the N-Town Mary Plays

Although the cult of the Virgin Mary was popular in the late Middle Ages, with the life of the Virgin told in many texts and new feasts of the Virgin added to the ecclesiastical calendar, there was no feast for her marriage and curiously little attention was given to the subject of her marriage in late medieval English lives of the Virgin.[1] This lack of emphasis is particularly odd given the important role the Virgin played in the development of the theology of sacramental marriage, which was the basis for the canon law practiced in the courts of England throughout the Middle Ages. Compared with other play collections and other late medieval English lives of the Virgin, however, the subject of her marriage is given unusual emphasis in the late fifteenth-century N-Town manuscript (BL MS Cotton Vespasian D. 8); it devotes an entire play to the subject, "The Marriage of Mary and Joseph," which contains within it a wedding ceremony enacted according to contemporary liturgy.[2] The preoccupation with the marriage in the N-Town plays is also evident in "Joachim and Anna," in which the strength of the marriage of the Virgin's parents is tested by their infertility, and in "The Trial of Mary and Joseph," in which a conspicuously pregnant Mary and her husband are tried for adultery. In this chapter, I argue that the focus on marriage in the Mary plays of the N-Town manuscript should be understood in the context of the controversial role played by the holy couple in the development of sacramental marriage theology and in the context of contemporary fifteenth-century East Anglian disputes about the validity of the sacraments. I will show that these N-Town plays mobilize orthodox marriage theology for reformist purposes, reinforcing the values of lay piety and questioning clerical authority.

The manuscript of the East Anglian N-Town plays is a unique late fifteenth-century compilation of pageants from a number of earlier sources arranged in cycle form. Even when compared with other medieval dramatic texts, notorious for the complexity of their textual and performance histories, the N-Town manuscript is exceptional since there are no references to the place of performance and no extant records of performance have been positively linked to it. In the absence of concrete evidence, theories for the location of the manuscript have proliferated, although speculation has centered on East Anglia and dialectologists agree that the language of the plays is from that region. Recent accounts of the manuscript have argued that at least some of the plays were intended for touring rather than for performance in one specific city, which explains the indication in the banns that the plays will be performed in "N-Town."[3] Unlike the York cycle, which has arguably become a dominant paradigm for late medieval drama, the N-Town plays were probably not performed as part of the Corpus Christi celebration, since their stage directions indicate a place and scaffold format of performance and the banns refer to their performance on a Sunday.[4] The N-Town manuscript was compiled from pre-existing texts, including a "Proclamation Play," a "Mary Play," a "Passion Play," and an "Assumption Play." "The Trial of Mary and Joseph" is listed in the banns and is thus believed to have been part of the "Proclamation Play," whereas "Joachim and Anna" was most likely added to the manuscript from the "Mary Play" material, and "The Marriage of Mary and Joseph" combines two pageants from the "Proclamation Play" with material from the "Mary Play," resulting in a blended text.[5] The text's complications are best explained by the medieval theory of *compilatio,* or communal authorship, by which the scribe-compiler rearranged and combined his materials into a single text that could be used according to the needs of various playing communities.[6]

This notion of *compilatio* justifies a consideration of these three Mary plays together in this chapter despite their origins in different sources for the manuscript.[7] As Alan Fletcher has argued, the scribe-compiler would have seen the text as "common property," since he did not privilege his source texts and felt free to dismantle their structure as necessary, nor did he emphasize the integrity of his own text, instead providing his work with an *accessus,* a means to open its contents for selective use as required.[8] In this chapter I read plays from different sources for the manuscript, not only on the grounds that they were combined in the only surviving manuscript of the plays, but because they share cultural contexts and concerns. Thus, it is possible to argue for cultural continuity without assuming a dramatic continuity, since there is no evidence that the plays were ever performed (or intended to be performed) together.[9] Nonetheless, I address the theatricality of individual plays, since evidence suggests both that the sources for the N-Town compilation were intended for performance and that the manuscript presented itself—and was in fact used—as a sourcebook for performance.[10]

Gail McMurray Gibson has argued that the "hybrid blend of monastic and lay spirituality" that is the "signature" of East Anglian piety is an important context for understanding the N-Town manuscript, and she has suggested that East Anglian drama helped to make the monastery "a visible sign of an invisible contemplative ideal relevant to every Christian life."[11] For example, although Gibson argues that the N-Town play of "Mary in the Temple" demonstrates the "monastic preoccupations of the compilation," linking Mary's dedication in the temple to monastic virtues, she also demonstrates that the play's childlike characterization of the Virgin and its embroidering of an emotional scene of separation from her doting parents makes the Virgin an "emulatable model for lay piety."[12] Thus, Gibson's well-known case for the origins of the N-Town compilation in the monastic borough of Bury St. Edmunds, an important dramatic center and home to the prolific author and monk John Lydgate, should not be used to overemphasize the compilation's ecclesiastical allegiances, especially since Gibson takes Bury St. Edmunds as a "case in point" that, "as lay and monastic piety increasingly overlapped in late medieval culture, the dividing line between parish and monastic devotional spectacle grew ever more blurred."[13]

Critical consensus has since grown to see the Mary material from the N-Town manuscript as reflecting a lay pious sensibility and perhaps deriving from or embodying the interests of a lay guild. Ruth Nisse and Theresa Coletti have both recently argued that the depiction of Mary in the N-Town plays celebrates female spiritual authority in the framework of salvation history.[14] Kathleen Ashley's identification of a "cosmology of purity" in the N-Town's plays led her to argue that they "might have belonged to an East Anglian religious guild with both lay and clerical membership and strong ecclesiastical ties."[15] Peter Meredith argues that the text "fits well with a devotional audience of the kind that a gild or parish could provide," and, more concretely, he has suggested that the repetition of an error in a marginal genealogy of the Holy Family in the "Joachim and Anna" portion of the N-Town manuscript and in Robert Reynes's commonplace book (which contains a series of texts for recitation at guild festivities) indicates that the "Mary Play" may have been the property of a Saint Anne guild.[16] These arguments for the potential lay origins of the "Mary Play" and the possibility that the manuscript was compiled from a mixture of lay and monastic material are consistent with my argument that the N-Town Mary plays demonstrate the reformist implications of orthodox marriage theology.

The depiction of marriage in the N-Town plays should be understood in the context of the controversial role it played in contemporary East Anglian religious politics, where the growth of lay piety exerted gentle pressure on clerical authority and where Lollard heretics made more direct challenges to clerical hierarchy.[17] Records of the heresy trials conducted by Bishop Alnwich in Norwich from 1428 to 1431 consistently show that the accused used marriage as part of their attack on clerical authority, claiming that it was superior to celibacy.[18] The plays' theatrical promotion of marriage would have appealed not only to Lollard extremists but also to moderate constituencies, such as the wealthy merchant patrons of the numerous parish churches in East Anglia and the members of East Anglia's many religious guilds. As both Gail McMurray Gibson and Norman Tanner have demonstrated, fifteenth-century East Anglian religious culture was tolerant of unorthodox religious attitudes and both clergy and laymen explored a range of religious options.[19] Similarly, Anne Hudson's claim that "Lollardy and orthodoxy were not in every regard mutually exclusive creeds" and Sarah Beckwith's warning against understanding religious drama or other aspects of "sacramental culture" as "merely orthodox or dissentient" set the context for my reading of marriage in the N-Town plays.[20] The N-Town plays are not merely heretical, nor do they simply reflect religious commonplaces, although they draw on orthodox marriage theology and liturgy. They perform cultural work by mediating religious political tensions around the relationship between clerical and lay prerogatives in East Anglia. In doing so, the plays both reflect and help to create religious and social ideologies that promote lay spiritual authority. Thus my reading of marriage in the N-Town plays participates in what Theresa Coletti has recently termed "an emergent consensus" among critics who see medieval religious drama not as an invocation of static orthodox commonplaces, as an earlier scholarly model would have it, but as a vernacular religious discourse that "symbolically mediates tensions within late medieval religious beliefs, politics and practice."[21]

"Joachim and Anna": Marriage at the Center of Religious Practice

"Joachim and Anna" explores the religious meaning of marital affection, posing the initially infertile future parents of Mary against the clerical definition of the purpose of marriage as procreation. The play begins when the priest Ysakar summons "all tribus in my cure" to the temple to make sacrifices, and Joachim expresses concern to Anne that their lack of children will make the priest despise them. His fears are realized when Ysakar ousts him from the temple on the grounds that he and his wife are barren. Exiled from the community and from Anne, Joachim goes to live among the shepherds, and it is here that the angel comes to him to prophesy the end to Anne's barrenness. The fact that the prophecy is delivered among the shepherds rather than in the temple presents the shepherds as an alternative to priestly Ysakar. Meanwhile, a parallel prophesy is delivered to Anne, and the couple is reunited at the end of the play, suggesting that the married couple is a locus for pious practice. By staging the mutual love of Anne and Joachim and demonstrating the limits of clerical spirituality, the play offers a notable validation of the piety of laypeople.

In this play, the priest Ysakar sees fertility or having children as the definition of the pious life. He summons "all þe kynredys" to Jerusalem to "do
sacryfyse" (36–37), but in practice he is not so inclusive.[22] He claims that
"ʒe þat to do sacryfice worthy are" but bars Joachim from participation:

> Abyde a qwyle, sere; whedyr wytte þu?
> Þu and þi wyff arn barrany and bare;
> Neyther of ʒow fruteful nevyr ʒett ware.
> Whow durste þu amonge fruteful presume and abuse?
> It is a tokyn þu art cursyd þare.
> Whereffore with grett indynacyon þin offeryng I refuse!
> (100–105)

Seeing barrenness as a "tokyn" of cursedness, Ysakar equates the production of children with spiritual purity. Thus, the couple's infertility is not
innocuous in his view but the grounds for excluding Joachim from the
temple and from the community of worshipers. In this passage Ysakar digni-
fies the sexual aspect of marriage along the lines promoted by Saint Augustine. In a lesson often repeated in late medieval sermons, Augustine made
proles one of the three "goods" of marriage, by which he meant not only the
physical reproduction of children, but also the reproduction of believers
dedicated to God through the education of children and their introduction
into the Church.[23] Even at this early moment of the play, Ysakar is discredited in the eyes of the audience members who know the story and recognize
the piety of Anne and Joachim. Through the example of this holy couple, the
audience knows that it is possible to be both infertile and pious, and yet the
equation of holiness with procreation is affirmed later in the play. An angel
appears first to Joachim and then to Anne, to give the "good tydynge" that
Anne will bear a child, so that the confirmation of Anne and Joachim's piety
takes the form of a cure for their barrenness. Thus, although Ysakar's authority is discredited in the play, his equation of piety with procreation is
not, and the play reinforces the lesson of Augustinian marriage theology
that makes *proles* one of the three "goods" of marriage. In this way, the play
dramatizes the equation of piety with married procreation.

This emphasis on Anne's procreative married piety in the play is consistent with her familiar role as a patron of marriage in late medieval sermons and vernacular devotional culture.[24] A characteristic example is a

passage from the *Liber Celestis* in which Saint Bridget recounts a vision of Anne. The saint introduces herself:

> I ame Anne, ladi of all weddid folke þat were byfor þe lawe. Doghtir, wirshepe God of þis manere: "Blissed be þou Jesu Criste, þe son of God þat chesid þe one modir of þe weddinge of Joachim and Anne. And, þerfor, for þe praiers of Anne, haue merci of all þame þat are in wedeloke or þinkes to be weddid, þat þai mai bringe furth froite to þe wirshipe of Gode."[25]

In this passage, Anne represents herself as the patron saint of married people and invites laypeople to identify with her, an invitation facilitated by the use of direct address to her listener. A similar passage can be found in a sermon in *Mirk's Festial*, which invites the listener to pray to Saint Anne for "grace to kepe your ordyr of wedlok, and gete such chyldyrn þat byn plesant and trew seruandys to God."[26] Saint Anne dignified the reproductive aspects of marriage because the doctrine of the Immaculate Conception presented the possibility that marital sex could be not only sinless, but actually a positive good.[27] Saint Anne also sanctified married procreation since she had been married three times, and she played a crucial role in the genealogy of the Holy Family, one version of which, as we have seen, was inscribed on the margins of the N-Town manuscript.[28]

Although the holy kinship was appealing to nobility and clergy, it was especially attractive to the members of the prosperous middling classes because it provided them with a means to acquire a worthy lineage that helped in their social aspirations.[29] Burgher families often decorated tombs and altars with family trees, sometimes painting themselves as the holy kinship.[30] Indeed, as Ton Brandenbarg has argued, the popular cult of Saint Anne, and its "regulation of sexual intercourse within a legally concluded marriage," fit "in well with the burgher's profit economy society . . . in which self-control, reliability, diligence, profit making and achievement were important values."[31] That fifteenth-century East Anglian guilds were drawn to the married piety of Saint Anne is clear in the fact that there were dozens of Saint Anne guilds in East Anglian towns, including Lynn and Bury St. Edmunds.[32] As Gibson has observed, in the Acle poem (linked by Meredith to the N-Town manuscript), Joachim and Anne are described as "ryght ryche folk," and generally depicted as "merchant's saints par excellence."[33]

Like the Acle poem and other contemporary East Anglian versions of the legend, the N-Town "Joachim and Anna" presents Joachim as a respected guildman or merchant.[34] When Joachim first introduces himself, he says, "My name is Joachym, a man in godys substancyall" (46). The proximity of his assertion of his wealth to his act of self-naming suggests the centrality of his goods to his identity. Furthermore, this identification of his wealth as coming from "goods" clearly identifies Joachim as a merchant rather than an aristocrat. Only after his economic and class status have been clarified does Joachim further gloss his name as "He þat to God is redy" (47), so that Joachim's piety is immediately identified as mercantile in the play. He explains that he is "clepyd rightful" (50) because of his charity with his goods, which he divides by giving part of them to the temple, part to pilgrims and poor men, and keeping only part for himself. After Joachim's sacrifice is rejected by Ysakar and he is among the shepherds, Joachim laments his unworthiness, "I am nott wurthy, Lord, to loke up to hefne" (149), but also sees his wealth as a sign of his holiness: "I thank þe more herefore þan for all my prosperité. / Þis is a tokyn þu lovyst me, now to the I am bounde" (154–55). Joachim's pious almsgiving is validated later in the play by the angel who comes to him to give the news that Anne will bear a child, saying that "God is plesyd with þin helmes" (176).

This same passage suggests that Joachim's mercantile religious practice should be a model for the clergy instead of the other way around. Just as Joachim describes his division of goods, he says,

> So xulde euery curat in þis werde wyde
> Ʒeve a part to his chauncel, iwys,
> A part to his parochonerys þat to povert slyde,
> The thyrd part to kepe for hym and his.
>
> (54–57)

The idea that a merchant would offer advice to the clergy and present himself as a model for a "curat" to follow is an implicit challenge to clerical authority. This depiction of Joachim was consistent with the role that the powerful merchant elite played in local religious practices in contemporary East Anglia, providing patronage for the decoration and construction of vast numbers of parish churches in the fifteenth century, giving Norfolk and Suffolk the greatest density of churches of any counties in England.[35]

Since the laity paid the clergy for their services, and important townspeople could influence clerical careers, priests were required to meet lay demands, making the relationship between lay and clerical power reciprocal and not merely hierarchical.[36] By depicting Joachim offering recommendations for clerical behavior, the play demonstrates the power of mercantile lay spirituality in East Anglian religious culture.

Clerical authority is challenged more directly in the play when the priest Ysakar is compared unfavorably with shepherds. Rejected by Ysakar, Joachim finds solace among the shepherds, and it is in their company that the angel delivers the prophecy of Mary's birth. The shepherd's offer, "we xal for ȝow pray" (144), provides exactly what Ysakar refused, and his consoling prediction that "Aftere grett sorwe, mayster, ever gret grace growyht" (143) establishes his credentials as a humble preacher. Virtually the same words are repeated by the angel to Anne later in the play when he delivers news of the Incarnation:

> . . . þu xalt conseyve and bere a childe
> Which xal hyght Mary; and Mary xal bere Jesus,
> Which xal be Savyour of all þe werd and us.
> Aftere grett sorwe evyr grett gladnes is had.
>
> (223–26)

The fact that the shepherd's words are also repeated by the angel in this last line suggests that he literally speaks the words of God, and validates the superiority of his piety over Ysakar's. Further confirmation of the shepherds' holiness is provided symbolically by the fertility of their sheep, which are "lusty and fayr, and grettly multyply," and which they pasture "ful wyde" (135–36).

The inclusion of the shepherds and this dialogue in the story of the conception of Mary is unusual; they are found neither in the recognized sources for the N-Town play nor in other contemporary versions of the story, but the shepherds were nonetheless commonly present in both orthodox and heterodox sermons and in commentaries on the Nativity, where they were frequently used to discuss the corruption of the clergy.[37] For example, in the *Mirror of the Blessed Life of Jesus Christ*, a probable source for the N-Town plays, Nicholas Love alludes to a Nativity sermon by Saint Bernard when he explains why the angel appeared to shepherds:

Wherfore cristes innocens & childhode conforteþ not iangeleres & gret
spekers, cristes wepyng and teres conforteþ not dissolute lagheres. His
simple cloþing conforteþ not hem þat gone in proude clothing, & his
stable & crache conforteþ not hem þat louen first setes & worldly wir-
chipes. And also þe angeles in cristes Natiuite apperyng to þe wakyng shep-
herdes conforten none oþere bot þe pore trauaileres, & to hem tellen þei
þe ioy of new liȝt & not to þe rich men, þat haue hir ioy & confort here.[38]

Love's account follows Franciscan tradition by describing the shepherds'
poverty as a sign of virtue, contrasting Christ's "simple cloþing" with the
"proude cloþing" of others. Joachim's greeting of the shepherds in the
N-Town play invokes the depiction of the shepherds in this sermon when
he says, "In ȝow is lytel pryde" (133), and a few lines later, "The meke God
lyftyth up, þe proude overthrowyth" (141). In this passage Love contrasts the
shepherds not merely with the wealthy and the proud, but also with false
preachers.

The association of the shepherds with true understanding, in contrast to
the corruption of false clergy, becomes more explicit in a contemporary Lollard sermon that explained the role of the shepherds in the Nativity. After
explaining, like Love, why God chose to reveal the news of his son's birth to
poor rather than rich men, the sermon explains "þat God ofte tymes scheweþ
his priuetees of Scripture to semple men and of esi lettere whiche beþ meke,
and hideþ it fro grete clerkis and hiȝe litterid men þat beþ proude of her kun-
nynge."[39] In this passage, the shepherds are distinguished not only by their
poverty but also by their status as "semple men" who nonetheless surpass
more educated clerics in their understanding of Scripture. The second shepherd in the N-Town play invokes the terms of this sermon and others like it
when he prefaces his offer of prayer with this qualification: "Sympyl as we
kan" (144). By calling into question the superiority of clergy to speak the
word of God, this sermon and the N-Town play invoke Lollard arguments for
a priesthood of all believers.[40] The N-Town play's unusual inclusion of the
shepherds in the story of Mary's conception thus promotes lay piety at the
expense of clerical authority, an idea that would have appealed not only to
East Anglian Lollards but also to the sensibility of the more mainstream
guild members.

As the play progresses, Anne and Joachim join the shepherds as the
agents of worship privileged over Church authority, and married life be-

comes the center of religious practice. Although the shepherds represent a kind of lay piety and speak the word of God, it is Anne and Joachim who receive His word directly. After his ejection from the temple, when Joachim goes to live among the shepherds, he exiles himself from Anne, who remains at home alone. The angel appears to each of them in turn and specifically says to each that God has heard their prayers and their tears. To Joachim the angel says, "God is pleasyd with þin helmes and hath herd þi prayere; / He seyth þi shame, þi repreff, and þi teyrs cler" (176–77). To Anne he responds in similar terms, saying that "God hath herd þi preyour and þi wepynge" (220). In spite of their geographical separation, parallel prophecies are delivered simultaneously to Joachim while he is among the shepherds and to Anne at home. Whereas contemporary accounts of Mary's conception consistently include the angelic delivery of the prophecy to both Anne and Joachim, the full and parallel revelations are unusual, and emphasize their marital love.[41] In the script they speak directly after one another and each tries to protect the other by taking the blame for their infertility. Joachim asks, "Punchyth me, Lorde, and spare my blyssyd wyff Anne / Þat syttyth and sorwyth ful sore of myn absens" (159–60), and Anne asks, "Why do ȝe thus to myn husbond, Lord? Why? Why? Why? / For my barynes?" (167–68), her emotionally wrought state signaled by the staccato series of rhetorical questions. The fact that the angel delivers the prophecy to the couple when they are concerned for each other, rather than in the public space of the temple, indicates that it is their marital love that makes them an alternative to the priestly Ysakar.

Anne and Joachim's mutual affection is expressed throughout the play in many parallel lines, and by the fact that they continually talk either to or about each other, often using the collective pronouns *us* and *we*.[42] As their grief gives way to the joy of togetherness, the couple fulfills the shepherds' prediction of immanent grace. Anne says, "Þer can no tounge telle what joye in me is! / I to bere a childe þat xal bere all mannys blys, / And haue my hosbonde ageyn! Ho myth haue joys more?" (232–34). In this passage, her pleasure at the prospect of rejoining her husband is given almost equal semantic weight to her joy in giving birth to the mother of the Savior. Similarly, Joachim exclaims, "A, gracyous wyff Anne, now fruteful xal ȝe be. / For joy of þis metynge in my sowle I wepe" (239–40). His joy in learning of Anne's role as the indirect bearer of the Savior is equal to his joy at the prospect of regaining her company. The joy of New Dispensation is expressed as marital affection.

The linking of grace with marital affection has a theological basis, since, in the words of Hugh of Saint Victor, "the substance of the sacrament itself is the mutual love of souls . . . And this very love again . . . is a sacrament and the sign of that love by which God is joined to the rational soul internally through the infusion of His grace. . . ."[43] This grace, and indeed the sacraments in general, were made possible by the birth of Christ, who was, as the N-Town angel explains, in turn made possible by the miraculous Immaculate Conception of Mary. The shepherd's words to Joachim similarly tell salvation history as marital drama in the phrase discussed previously: "Aftere grett sorwe, mayster, ever gret grace growyht" (143). His words predict the plot of the play, in which Joachim and Anne become happy after hearing the words of the angel. As we have seen, the angel makes a similar statement to Anne, when he articulates a theological understanding of the consolation made possible by Christ, whose birth Anne's conception of Mary facilitates. The shepherd's words are addressed to Joachim, and the angel's words are addressed to Anne, but these statements are applicable to each member of the audience, and of the fallen human world. The expression of theology as a narrative of marital affection demonstrates the ways in which earthly married life can contain grace.

This passage is paradigmatic of the way the deceptively simple narratives of the Mary plays function as theology, often with surprisingly complex content. The resolution of the play shows that abstract theology can manifest itself as social and earthly, and that theoretical doctrine can become lived experience. Gibson has argued that this "tendency to transform the abstract and theological to the personal and the concrete was . . . [part of] . . . a growing tendency to see the world saturated with sacramental possibility and meaning and to celebrate it."[44] In the N-Town play of "Anne and Joachim" it is specifically the marriage sacrament that makes everyday life an opportunity for devotion. As we have seen, marital affection is the substance of the marriage sacrament, and can be represented or enacted in the ordinary actions of laypeople.

By staging the marital affections of Joachim and Anna, and demonstrating their relevance to the doctrine of the New Dispensation, the play makes a claim for the piety of all married people. By contrasting the couple's religiosity with the dubious clerical authority of Ysakar, the play uses marriage

to make an argument for the piety of laypeople more generally. In the last
lines of the play, Anne says:

> Now homward, husbond, I rede we gon,
> Ryth hom al to oure place,
> To thank God þat sytt in tron,
> Þat þus hath sent us his grace.
>
> (250–53)

In this final passage the house is privileged over the temple as a place of
worship, and the piety of this lay married couple favored over the clerical
authority of Ysakar.

"The Marriage of Mary and Joseph": Theology for Lay Piety

In contrast to the spirituality embodied in marriage in "Joachim and Anna,"
"The Marriage of Mary and Joseph" begins by dramatizing in contemporary form the trouble that Mary's marriage had historically posed to clerical authority, because it raised questions about the relative merits of virginity and marriage which were understood as early as Augustine to threaten
the hierarchy of clergy over laity. In this play, Mary's parents bring her to
the temple in accordance with a law that requires that every virgin should
appear at the age of fourteen to be married:

> Þe lawe of God byddyth þis sawe:
> Þat at xiiij ȝere of age
> Euery damesel, whatso sche be,
> To þe encrese of more plenté,
> Xulde be browght in good degré
> Onto here spowsage.
>
> (8–13)

This law articulates the view that women should be married in order to
procreate, a position consistent with the equation of marriage with worldly
existence. Mary resists, on the grounds that she has already been dedicated
to God and to a life of chastity, committed from the time of her parents'

prayer to God in the temple that ended their barrenness. She argues her case forcefully:

> Such clene lyff xuld ȝe nouht
> In no maner wyse reprove.
> To þis clennesse I me take.
> This is þe cawse, as I ȝow tell,
> Þat I with man wyll nevyr mell!
> In þe servyse of God wyll I evyr dwell—
> I wyl nevyr haue other make.
>
> (72–78)

Mary's definition of the contemplative life as a choice of the "servyse of God" over an earthly spouse ("other make") is a conventional trope found in guides addressed to nuns. An example is *Holy Maidenhood,* written to encourage girls to enter into religious life, in which a lurid picture of "what the wedded endure" is contrasted with a vision of "the blessed maiden who has entirely escaped from such slavery, as God's free daughter and his Son's spouse, need not suffer such things in any way" and is given "immeasurable reward" instead.[45] Whereas in most late medieval accounts of the life of the Virgin it is clear that the law that requires Mary to marry at fourteen applies only to the virgins of the temple, making the law appear unproblematic, in the N-Town version this is not specified, and thus the law takes on a broader meaning, seeming to challenge the traditional hierarchy of virginity over marriage by requiring that Mary, like other women, marry.[46] Mary's words remind the audience of the familiar association of the "clene lyff" with virginity, but this argument is surprisingly situated in the play in opposition to the authoritative figure of the bishop and the law. "I am þat lord þat made þis lawe" (4), says the bishop.

Although neither contemporary versions of the story nor the apocryphal source treat this law as problematic, it is troubling to the N-Town bishop, whose concerns highlight tensions within Church teachings about the relative merits of marriage and celibacy.[47] When the bishop asks Mary why she does not want to marry, his reasonable approach underlines and contrasts with the conflict of values inherent in his own law. For if virginity is superior to marriage, then why should the Virgin marry? In a quandary, the bishop muses,

In clennes to levyn in Godys servise
No man here blame, non here tene.
And ȝit in lawe þus it lyce,
Þat such weddyd xulde bene.

                    (83–86)

Unable to reason his way out of this paradox, he calls on his ministers, who, in turn, cannot advise him. When human reason is insufficient to solve the conundrum, at the advice of his counsel, the bishop prays to God, who sends an angel down to confirm that Mary should be married, and to arrange that the selection of her marriage partner should be accomplished through a divinely sanctioned test. All the men of the town are to come to the temple with rods, and the man whose rod blooms is to be Mary's husband. By emphasizing the dilemma of the bishop and his ministers and the need for divine intervention, the play calls attention to the awkwardness caused by the Virgin's marriage, an awkwardness created by the ambivalent status accorded to marriage by theology and Church teachings that simultaneously grant marriage spiritual significance yet rank it below chastity in virtue.

Joseph also initially resists the marriage. First he tries to avoid going to the temple, and when he reluctantly arrives he lags behind, unwilling to participate in the rod test, pleading age and infirmity: "I am so agyd and so olde / Þat both myn leggys gyn to folde— / I am ny almost lame!" (226–28). After he finally participates in the test and is miraculously selected to be Mary's spouse, his response is not joy but consternation, even horror:

What! Xuld I wedde? God forbede!
I am an old man, so God me spede!
And with a wyff now to levyn in drede,
It wore neyther sport nere game!

· · · · · · · · · · · ·

An old man may nevyr thryff
With a ȝonge wyff, so God me saue.

                    (268–71, 278–79)

Joseph fears he will be cast in the role of the *senex amans* of fabliau, and, like January in Chaucer's *Merchant's Tale,* become the dupe of a young wife. Through Mary and Joseph's resistance to the marriage, the N-Town play poses the following questions: if marriage consists primarily of sex (as Joseph assumes) and is thus inferior to the virginity that both Mary and Joseph clearly prefer, then how is the merit of Mary and Joseph's marriage to be explained? Why is marriage dictated for Mary when virginity would allow her to live a holy life in the temple?

The play's answer is that by the sacramental definition marriage is endowed with a purely spiritual content and consummation is deemed inessential. The spirituality of marriage is emphasized by the angel, whose intervention and proposal of the rod test in the play shows that the holy couple's marriage is divinely sanctioned. The rod test presents a theoretical as well as logistical answer to the bishop's problem by emphasizing that marital fecundity need not be understood as purely sexual. The spectacle of the actors holding up rods to see whose will bloom would have been a graphic image of phallic sexuality, but this sexuality, and the attendant genre of fabliau, is invoked only to be denied. Although Joseph's physical impotence is emphasized aggressively in the dialogue (when summoned to the test, he complains, "I kannot my rodde fynd" [235]), it is Joseph's rod that miraculously blooms instead of the rods of the other younger, presumably more vigorous men present. This shows, in the words of the bishop, that "blyssyd of God we se art thou" (258), underlining the fact that Joseph's fertility—and the fertility of his marriage—while materially represented, is not sexual but spiritual.

More than dramatic stagecraft, this moment stages in the vernacular a controversial Latin debate between Jerome and Augustine about the marriage of Mary and Joseph which played a crucial role in the later development of a sacramental definition of marriage. Joseph's objections to marrying invoke Saint Jerome's rejection of the claim that Mary and Joseph had been married. In the play, Joseph's resistance to the marriage with Mary stems from his belief that marriage is about sexuality, not spirituality or companionship; similarly, in *Adversus Helvidium,* Jerome based his claim that the Virgin could not have been married on an understanding of marriage as equivalent to sex. Denying the Virgin's marriage was, for Jerome, a way "to guard the sacred lodging of the womb in which He abode for ten months from all suspicion of sexual intercourse," and to protect the Virgin Mary from the horrors of the flesh, particularly pregnancy, which he considered one of the "humiliations of nature."[48] For Jerome, the hierarchy of virginity over marriage was absolute and indisputable: marriage entailed sex, and sex and piety were incompatible. He even went so far as to claim, in *Adversus Jovinianum,* that "the defilement of marriage is not washed away by the blood of martyrdom."[49] On the other hand, the use of the imagery of the blooming rod to emphasize that Joseph's suitability for marriage is his spiritual rather than his physical potency echoes the arguments of Saint Augustine, who refuted Saint Jerome by arguing that although Mary and Joseph remained celibate, they had a true marriage. In *De Consensu Evangelistarum,* Augustine argues that because Mary and Joseph were married, intercourse did not define marriage:

> [I]t was not held allowable to consider [Joseph] dissociated from the married state which was entered into with Mary, on the ground that she gave birth to Christ, not as the wedded wife of Joseph, but as a virgin. For by this example an illustrious recommendation is made to faithful married persons of the principle, that even when by common consent they maintain their continence, the relation will still remain, and can still be called that of wedlock, in as much as, although there is no connection between the sexes of the body, there is the keeping of the affections of the mind.[50]

As this passage illustrates, in Augustine's exegesis, the biblical example of the holy couple's marriage, although seemingly exceptional, defined all marriages as based in the affections, rather than in carnal knowledge.

As we have seen in the introduction, Augustine's definition of marriage as a spiritual practice, which he derived from the example of Mary and Joseph, both rescued marriage from the vituperations of Jerome, and was central to the development of the sacramental definition by Hugh of Saint Victor and others which became the legal definition of marriage throughout the later Middle Ages.[51] Hugh of Saint Victor also developed his definition of the marriage sacrament in the course of defending Mary's virginity in his treatise *De Beatae Mariae Virginitate* and in *On the Sacraments,* which he wrote about the same time. In the latter, Hugh cites Augustine's analysis of Mary and Joseph's marriage in support of the claim that "the sacrament of marriage is accomplished in marital consent."[52] The wording of Hugh's definition echoes the language of Augustine's exegesis of the holy couple's marriage; he defines marriage as "a legitimate consent, that is, between legitimate persons . . . to observe an individual association in life. In this consent, indeed, the commerce of carnal copulation by equal vow is not forbidden to be nor is it praised when not about to be."[53] In the N-Town play, the holy couple voices the words of consent, which their own marriage made central to the wedding liturgy and to the legal definition of marriage; in this way, the play effectively retraces the argumentative logic of theologians such as Augustine and Hugh of St. Victor.

The origin of the doctrine of marital consent in Mary and Joseph's marriage seems unremarkable if one has read the work of these theologians, but, as few scholars have emphasized, such theological logic and history would not have been so easily accessible to the laypeople of East Anglia who constituted the play's audience. Indeed, lay sermons tended to emphasize not the marriage of Mary and Joseph but the procreative couple Adam and Eve.[54] In addition, as we have seen, there was no feast of the marriage of the Virgin, and late medieval English lives of the Virgin do not emphasize the subject.[55] While the legal definition of marriage as an exchange of vows may have been based on the example of the holy couple, the courts were hardly a forum for theological instruction.

The relative absence of the example of Mary and Joseph's marriage from sermons, feasts, and books designed for a lay audience is arguably the heritage of the anxieties this story raised for theologians and canonists. We have seen that at the beginning of the play, the bishop was puzzled by the prospect of forcing the Virgin to marry because doing so seemed to challenge the hierarchy of virginity over marriage. In this respect, the N-Town bishop is part of a long line of ecclesiastical authorities for whom the marriage of the Virgin was troubling because it dignified marriage as a spiritual practice, and thus made it difficult to distinguish from celibacy, the exclusive province of the clergy.

Even the theologians responsible for developing the sacramental definition of marriage from Mary and Joseph's marriage were not anxious to make the holy couple's marriage paradigmatic. While they clearly saw chaste marriage as holier than ordinary marriage, they did not wish to promote it as an example for laypeople to emulate. Augustine used Mary and Joseph's marriage to develop a spiritual understanding of marriage, but he was careful not to advocate chaste marriage as a model for laypeople, a concept that would confuse clerical and lay identities organized by sexual activity and abstinence.[56] Although Hugh of Saint Victor argued that "true marriage and the true sacrament of marriage can exist, even if carnal commerce has not followed," he described a twofold institution of marriage: the office of marriage, based in consummation, and the compact of love, which entailed only consent.[57] Similarly, Peter Lombard described one sacrament that signified the union of Christ and the Church but had two aspects, will and nature, the one spiritual and the other physical, asserting that Mary and Joseph's marriage lacked the aspect that pertained to nature.[58] Both of these twelfth-century thinkers were trying to maintain the theological centrality of the Virgin's marriage but to remove it as a viable mode of life for the laity. By contrast, as we shall see, the N-Town play both celebrates the Virgin's marriage as the basis for marital sacramentality and posits her marriage as a model for all laypeople.

In comparison to Peter Lombard, Hugh of Saint Victor, and other supporters of sacramental marriage, twelfth-century theologians who maintained that sex was essential to marriage found the Virgin's marriage even more problematic, as they sought clearly to distinguish marriage from celibacy and thus defend the moral superiority of the clerical elite over the lay majority. The complexity of marital definitions on the part of these theologians demonstrates the extent to which they were loath to relinquish the identification between the laity and sexual practices, despite the obvious difficulties of imagining a sacrament based on something so unholy as the carnal act. In the influential twelfth-century *Decretum,* the canon lawyer Gratian attempted to reconcile the coital and consensual theories found in his sources by positing that marriage was begun by consent but ratified only by sexual intercourse. He distinguished between the initiation of marriage, when both parties exchanged words of consent to marry each other, and the completion of marriage in sexual consummation, both of which, he claimed, were required to make a marriage.[59] But even with this complex two-part definition, it was difficult to reconcile the example of Mary's marriage with the conviction that sexual consummation was a necessary component of complete marriage. Thus, the Virgin's marriage threatened the use of sexual status as a marker between laity and clergy, causing consternation among theologians that echoed the troubles of the N-Town bishop.

The Virgin Mary's presumed vow of chastity was sufficiently problematic for Gratian in his attempts to keep clear boundaries between married laity and celibate clergy that it inspired an especially convoluted passage in which he argued that the Virgin had consented to fulfilling the marital debt, while remaining true to her vow of chastity:

Blessed Mary intended to keep her vow of virginity in her heart, but she did not express that vow of virginity with her mouth; she subjected herself to the divine disposition, intending to keep herself a virgin unless God revealed otherwise to her. Therefore, committing her virginity to the divine disposition, she consented to carnal coupling, not seeking it, but obeying the divine inspiration in either case.[60]

The popularity that this account achieved among subsequent theologians, in spite of its conspicuously contorted logic, and despite their rejection of Gratian's inclusion of sexual relations in the definition of marriage, testifies to their investment in avoiding making Mary a model for marital chastity.[61]

Whereas most laypeople did not read the Latin works of Gratian and other theologians, Gratian's logic was more widely available because it was echoed in vernacular forms, such as the late fourteenth-century manual *Le Ménagier de Paris,* written by a husband to instruct his young wife. In this book, the Annunciation is converted into a model of wifely obedience. "By God," says the husband,

> it is not always the season to say to one's ruler: "I will do naught, it is not reasonable"; greater good cometh by obeying, wherefore I take my ensample from the words of the Blessed Virgin Mary, when the Angel Gabriel brought her tidings that Our Lord should be conceived in her. She did not answer: "It is not reasonable, I am a maid and virgin, I will not suffer it, I shall be defamed"; but obediently she answered: *Fiat mihi secundum verbum tuum,* as who should say: Be it unto me according to thy word.[62]

The pairing of *maid* and *virgin* in the wording of the hypothetical answer suggests that one might expect Mary to object to the Incarnation on the grounds that it would violate her virginity. In this passage, Mary is not presented as a model for chaste marriage that would challenge the hierarchical separation of virginity and marriage, but as a model for wifely obedience to the marriage debt.

In the N-Town play, Mary's response to the idea of marrying Joseph recalls the terms of this passage from *Le Ménagier de Paris* but uses them to opposite effect, intervening to reshape the Virgin into a more controversial figure who models marital chastity and highlights inconsistencies in Church teachings that privilege virginity but require lay marriage. While the opening conflict with the bishop would have provided ample opportunity for Mary's submissiveness to be emphasized, as in the passage from the *Ménagier de Paris,* nothing of that nature is included. Instead, as we have seen, Mary initially refuses to marry, insisting that she maintain her virginity. She does not speak again until she voices her consent during the wedding ceremony, and, a few lines later, makes a vow of chastity, one of the few moments when the marriage ceremony in the play differs from the standard liturgical script. She vows:

> In chastyté to ledyn my lyff
> I xal hym nevyr forsake,
> But evyr with hym abyde.
> And, jentyll spowse, as ȝe an seyd,
> Lete me levyn as a clene mayd.
>
> (324–28)

The play calls attention both to her independence of mind and to her vow of chastity; it is Joseph's submission to God's authority that receives emphasis, and he seems neither interested in nor capable of exacting the marital debt.[63] On the contrary, Joseph himself insists on the prior condition "þat in bedde we xul nevyr mete," explaining with an almost submissive apology, "For, iwys, mayden suete, / An old man may not rage" (295–97). The play not only emphasizes the chastity of the marriage of Mary and Joseph, but by including the standard contemporary marriage liturgy of the time, it also portrays the marriage as paradigmatic, not exceptional, and as fully possible in fifteenth-century England.[64] A "clene mayd" need not restrict herself to the temple but can live in the world as a married woman, making "clene" married life a model for lay piety. In this way, the play suggests that a chaste marriage can be a model for ordinary people and that marriage can protect "chastyté."

The N-Town play shows that the chaste spiritual aspects of the holy couple's union are part of all marriages by including the ring exchange from the liturgy that specifically invokes the sacramental substance of marriage. The bishop instructs, "Joseph, with þis ryng now wedde þi wyff, / And be here hand now þu here take" (318–19), and Joseph responds, "Sere,

with þis rynge I wedde here ryff, / And take now here for my make" (320–21).
This brief exchange would have reminded the audience of the familiar
longer liturgical version, described and glossed in the Sarum Missal:

> Then shall the bridegroom place the ring upon the thumb of the bride,
> saying, *In the name of the Father*; then upon the second finger, saying, *and
> of the Son*; then upon the third finger, saying, *and of the Holy Ghost*; then
> upon the fourth finger, saying, *Amen,* and there let him leave it, accord-
> ing to *Decretum xxx q.v.c. Feminae* ad finem, because in that finger there
> is a certain vein which runs from thence as far as the heart; and inward
> affection, which ought to be fresh between them, is signified by the true
> ring of the silver.[65]

As this passage explains, the ring ceremony signals the "inward affection"
and the compatibility of that affection with the spirituality and grace of the
Trinity. Following the logic of this passage, Mary's dedication to God in
the temple, which is referred to in the beginning of the play, can be understood not as a dedication to celibacy but as an expression of the sacramental
aspect of all Christian marriages. Thus her initial problem of choosing between a spiritual life in the temple or earthly married life, which was posed
by her as a choice between earthly and heavenly bridegrooms, is resolved by
an incorporation of her aspirations for a "clene" life dedicated to God within
the rubric of marriage. By reminding the audience that the spirituality of
marriage is already promoted in the established marriage liturgy, the play
shows its audience that marriage can be part of a clean and holy life not just
for Mary and Joseph but for all married people. Thus, the N-Town play un-
settles the association of piety with celibacy, and marriage with sexuality,
which underpinned the outlawing of clerical marriage in the early twelfth
century, legislation that sought to maintain the clear hierarchy of clergy
over laity.

In the context of the N-Town play's promotion of marital spirituality, it is
striking to note that marriage was considered explicitly relevant to controversy over clerical authority by both Lollards and their orthodox opponents
in contemporary East Anglia. One of the many ways Lollards attacked the
validity of the hierarchy of clerical over lay religious authority was by criticizing clerical celibacy and promoting the virtues of marriage.[66] In *De Officio
Regis* and *De Veritate Sacrae Scripturae* Wyclif objects to the double standard

whereby priests instructed laypeople that marriage was honorable for them, while considering it "horrible" and "scandalous" for themselves.[67] Furthermore, in *Of Prelates* he criticizes priests for denigrating an institution whose virtue is upheld by Scripture (they "forsaken as venym matrimonye, þat is leffel bi holy writt").[68] The tract *Of Weddid Men and Wifis* points out that the Gospels do not forbid clerical marriage: "God ordeynede prestis in þe olde lawe to haue wyves, and nevere forbede it in the new lawe, neiþer bi Crist ne bi his apostlis, but raþere aprovede it."[69] Although Wyclif never went so far as to advocate clerical marriage or a reversal of the hierarchy of virginity over marriage, several of his followers did both, and the court records suggest that marriage was of particular interest to the East Anglian Lollards tried by Bishop Alnwich in Norwich from 1428 to 1431.[70] For example, William Bate of Sethyng, a tailor, allegedly claimed that the "chastite of prestes seculer ne regular ne of nunnes is not commendable, but all prestis and all nunnes may lefully be wedded and maried and use the comon lyf of wedlok, and that lyf ys more meritorie than is to lyve continent and chast."[71] By questioning the validity of clerical celibacy, the Lollards challenged the established understanding of marriage as a quintessentially lay practice. Their claim that marriage was superior to celibacy threatened to reverse a long-standing hierarchy that was understood, since the outlawing of clerical marriage in the twelfth century, to have larger implications for the relationship between lay and clerical authority.

Marriage, and the Virgin's marriage in particular, was seen by both sides as relevant to the larger issue of defining the extent of clerical prerogative. A fifteenth-century Lollard sermon on the Nativity, for example, treats the holy couple's marriage at length, making the story of the Virgin and Joseph's marriage into an argument for the virtues and the spiritual nature of marriage which reflects the logic of Augustine's defense of the Virgin's marriage. Deriving its impetus from the Gospel text in which "it seiþ þat Joseph cam to Bethleem wiþ Marie, his weddide wyif þat was so wiþ chyilde," the sermon explains that "men may haue autorite aʒenst hem þat seiyn þat fleschli couplynge of man and womman makeþ matrymonie, for a blessider matrimonie or wedlok þer neuere þan was þis, vnder whiche was born þat blesside chyld þat was boþe God and man."[72] Not only does the sermon use the precedent of Mary and Joseph's marriage to argue that sex between the partners cannot constitute marriage, it also quotes a portion of Augustine's explanation of how the holy couple fulfills all three goods of marriage, in spite of their chastity. Then the sermon concludes, "in þis text also a man may see and lerne what worschepe God haþ do to þe hooly order of matrimonie, syþþe he wolde not be born but vnder þis hooly ordere."[73] Thus, the Lollard sermon uses the theological history of the holy couple, enlisting orthodox teaching to argue for the spirituality of marriage.

At the same time, famous Lollard opponent and guardian of orthodoxy Roger Dymmok used Mary's sexual status to defend clerical celibacy. In his famous rebuttal to the Lollards, *The Book Against the Twelve Errors and Heresies of the Lollards,* Dymmok argues that the law of continence originated with the Virgin, and was exemplified by Christ and the Apostles, indicating that keeping such vows was both possible and enjoined by God:

> The law of continence took its origins from the blessed Virgin, mother of God, among the worshippers of God, and Christ and His apostles have exemplified, for men of the clergy, the purity of perpetual continence.[74]

According to Dymmok, vows of virginity were forbidden by the Jews, so the Virgin's vow of chastity was made only on the condition that it was pleasing to God:

> [F]or that reason, before she had been engaged to be married, the glorious Virgin made a vow of chastity, conditionally to be sure, if it were pleasing to God, but after the marriage was celebrated between her and Joseph, from divine inspiration, and with her husband in agreement, she explicitly professed her chastity with him.[75]

Unlike the Lollard sermon, Dymmok has made the marriage of the Virgin into a defense of the virtues of celibacy, rather than an argument for the sanctity of marriage. Although generally omitted from conventional narratives of the conflict between Lollardy and orthodoxy, these examples suggest that those most enmeshed in Lollard controversy recognized the importance of the example of the Virgin's marriage to their debates over the relative merits of marriage and celibacy, and they imply that the subject of Mary's marriage may have invoked this controversy for the fifteenth-century East Anglian audience of the N-Town plays.

Mary and Joseph's marriage was particularly relevant to the religious politics of fifteenth-century East Anglia, but historically its exegesis also had controversial implications. Ever since Pope Alexander III validated the definition of a marriage as an exchange of consent, there was conflict around the question of the necessity for clerical participation in weddings. Alexander and many other local and general councils declared emphatically that marriage should take place following the publication of the banns, in front of a church with the blessing of the parish priest. But according to Alexander's own rules, marriages were valid even if they had none of these characteristics, and court records suggest that these kinds of marriages in actuality were very common.[76] The ambiguity of these laws posed a serious problem: how could the Church insist that people be married in front of a church by a priest with proper witnesses and liturgy if the validity of a marriage would be upheld in an ecclesiastical court even if not performed this way? A large number and wide variety of local laws were enacted to address the problem by penalizing the participants, but the proliferation and variability of these local laws were in themselves symptomatic of the lack of control on the part of Church authorities.[77] This ambiguity was also evident in theological treatises, such as the early thirteenth-century *Summa Confessorum* of Master Thomas which says in the second chapter that "it is clear that a man and a woman can contract marriage by themselves, without a priest and without all others, in any place, so long as they agree in a permanent way of life," while insisting in the third chapter on the reading of the banns and on the liturgical ceremony.[78]

In addition, orthodox sermons and vernacular manuals for popular instruction contemporary with the N-Town plays systematically conflated what was considered legal and sacramental (consent between parties) with what was fully sanctioned by Church authorities (in church with a priest according to the standard liturgy). Robert of Brunne's manual *Handlying Synne* asserted:

> . . . do þo men ful ylle,
> Þat wedden any aзens here wylle;
> Here wyl behoueþ to-gedyr consente,
> Are þe prest do þe sacrament.[79]

Although Brunne emphasizes the role of choice and free will, he places both within the context of the priest's role in the liturgy. Similarly, Mirk's sermon for married people begins by stating that his purpose is to "schew

ʒow what þis sacrament is," but the couple's love for each other, the substance of the marriage sacrament, is placed only within the context of the
priest's role: "þe prest blessuth a ring, þat betokeneth God, þat hath neyther begynnyng ne endyng, and duth hit on hur fyngur þat haþ a veyne to
hure herte, tokenyng þat he schal loue God oure all thyng, and þanne hure
husbond."[80] These writings obscured the fact that weddings performed
by laypeople in secular locales were both sacramental and valid according
to the Church courts, even though they were not sanctioned by Church
authorities.

This conflation of valid and sacramental marriage with what was fully
sanctioned made possible the tendency of the Lollards in the Norwich
heresy trials to deny the sign of the marriage sacrament just as they denied
the form of the other sacraments and the need for priestly control. One
defendant allegedly claimed that "oonly consent of love betuxe man and
woman is sufficient for the sacrament of perfit matrimoyn withoute contract
of word or solennizacion in churche, for such solennizacion is but vayne-
glorie induced be covetise of prestes to gete mony of the puple."[81] This statement links the denial of the form of the sacrament to the broader Lollard critique of clerical authority and corruption and to their belief that laypeople
and priests were equally effective in the administration of the sacraments.
The form of the court depositions invited such an interpretation by consistently placing the denial of the need for words of consent immediately after
the denial of transubstantiation in the lists of the alleged heretical beliefs.
Although not noted by modern medievalists, technically speaking, however,
these claims were not heretical. The repeated insistence of the accused in the
depositions that "only consent of love in Jhu' Crist betuxe [*sic*] man and
woman of Cristene beleve ys sufficiant for the sacrament of matrimony" is
virtually identical to both legal and sacramental definitions.[82] In the formulation of Thomas Aquinas, the words by which the consent of matrimony
are expressed are the form of the sacraments and the external acts of the contracting parties are the matter.[83] This definition of the "sign" of the marriage
sacrament is consistent with Augustine's definition of the sacraments, often
quoted by medieval theologians: "a sacrament is the sign of a sacred thing"
or "a sacrament is the visible form of invisible grace."[84] What is unusual
about the sacrament of marriage is that the words spoken are those of the
couple, and it is their mutual faith and affection that gives their words the
status of the Word.

This parallelism uncovers the crucial fact that in the orthodox definition of the sacrament of marriage, the participation of the clergy was not
essential as it was to the other sacraments (exceptions were the rare baptism and penance *in extremis*). Hugh of Saint Victor, like several other theologians, anticipated this problem of clerical control inherent in defining
marriage as consent. In *On the Sacraments,* he imagines a counterargument:

> But you say: If after the first consent to the conjugal pact there is mar-
> riage straightway, what then does that authority mean which says that a
> legitimate marriage is made only . . . according to the law [which requires
> that she] . . . be blessed by the priest with prayers and oblations . . . [?]

In defending the definition of marriage as the exchange of vows, Hugh invokes a comparison between marriage and baptism *in extremis:*

> . . . where one's own will and legitimate vow assist, even without all
> these other things there can be legitimate marriage. For if marriage can-
> not be where these things are not, neither can baptism be where the con-
> secration of the font has not preceded the catechizing and exorcization
> of baptizing, and where the unction of oil and chrism do not follow.[85]

Since the sign of the sacrament of marriage was the exchange of words of
present consent, then it was the words of the couple, not those of the priest,
that had sacramental force. While to Hugh and to contemporary fifteenth-
century ears the term would have seemed a heretical oxymoron, marriage
was in a sense a "lay sacrament."

While the Norwich depositions indicate that the Lollards, and perhaps
other laypeople, may not have been aware of the ways in which, even in the
orthodox definition, the wedding did not require clerical participation, the
N-Town marriage play draws attention to it. In the play the marriage of
Mary and Joseph is performed in a manner that is both legal (consent between the parties) and officially sanctioned (at church with a priest according to the standard liturgy), but the notion that laypeople can function as
priests in the marriage ceremony is invoked by the framing of the holy
couple's marriage ceremony. The parental couple gives their blessing immediately after the priest, an addition not scripted by the official liturgy
for the ceremony. After the exchange of consent, vows, and the ring, and the

Alma Chorus, Mary asks, "To haue ȝoure blyssyng, fadyr, I falle ȝow before" (341), which the bishop grants: "He blysse ȝow þat hath non hendynge / *In nomine Patris, et Filii, et Spiritus Sancti*" (342–43). This portion follows the standard marriage liturgy, but afterward Mary deviates from the liturgical script by also asking for a blessing from her parents: "Fadyr and modyr . . . I pray ȝow here in þis plas / Of ȝoure blessynge, for charyté . . . On knes to ȝow I falle. / I pray ȝow, fadyr and modyr dere, / To blysse ȝoure owyn dere dowtere" (370, 374–75, 378–82), a request that her parents, Joachim and Anne, each grant in turn. The central role given to Mary's parents in the play reframes the marriage liturgy in a familial context.

In the dialogue and through the staging of the wedding vows and the liturgy, the N-Town play uses marriage to promote lay spirituality, suggesting that there was a formal similarity between theatrical representation and the performance of the marriage sacrament. The distinction between the dramatization of a play and the enactment of the marriage liturgy would have been especially volatile since theater in the Middle Ages was defined neither by a clearly differentiated space nor by a distinct set of professionals.[86] In performance, the role of the bishop, like the roles of the holy couple and their parents, would have been played by a member not of the clergy but of the laity, possibly a member of a religious guild. Thus, the very fact of performance would have suggested the idea that weddings might be performed by laypeople, and that ordinary people were capable of imitating or enacting the married roles of Mary and Joseph. Moreover, the N-Town play was most likely an open-air place-and-scaffold production performed in a secular locale, reminding the audience that weddings need not take place within the sacred space of a church. The inclusion of the vows from the standard liturgy not only pointed to the ways in which the wedding was a lay sacrament, it also suggested that the sacrament of marriage was itself a performance. Watching the wedding take place between two actors as part of a play would have encouraged the play's lay audience to think of weddings themselves as theatrical; just as the congregation within the church would have functioned as witnesses to the weddings performed there, so in the dramatic production, the audience of the play served as witnesses to the wedding.

Since the exchange of the words of mutual consent constituted a wedding, according to both legal and sacramental definitions, and since the lay participants' words of consent had sacramental force, the staging of the vows in a play raises questions about the distinction between the per-

formance of a play and the ritualized performance of the marriage sacrament. An implicit comparison is drawn between the act of speaking the
marriage vows, which constitutes the sign of the sacrament of marriage,
and the act of speaking, which is part of theater. When Joseph says, "I take
þe, Mary, to wyff" (310) and "with þis rynge I wedde here ryff" (320), his
words are performative in the sense that J. L. Austin made famous when
he defined it as the kind of speech in which "the issuing of the utterance
is the performing of the action," and indeed the wedding was one of Austin's defining examples in *How to Do Things with Words*.[87] As the N-Town
play demonstrates, although the bishop is present in the play, it is the
words of the couple themselves, the exchange of vows, that accomplishes
the marriage within the narrative of the play. Austin famously warns us
that performative utterances are "in a peculiar way hollow or void if said
by an actor on the stage," and we would hardly expect that a medieval audience would have understood the two people playing Mary and Joseph to
be considered married at the play's end.[88] Yet the staging of the wedding
in the N-Town marriage play nonetheless reminds us that medieval weddings are fundamentally lay performances, a fact perhaps made somewhat
more palpable by the fact that theater in the Middle Ages—unlike in Austin's time—was defined by neither a stage nor professional actors. As Pierre
Bourdieu reminds us in his sociological revision of Austin, words are only
performative in the appropriate institutional context. The "specific ef-
ficacy" of performative utterances, Bourdieu contends, "stems from the
fact that they seem to possess in themselves the source of a power which
in reality resides in the institutional conditions of their production and
reception."[89] The exchange of words of present consent in the medieval
wedding are performative because the institution of the Church and the
ecclesiastical courts upheld a definition of the wedding as an exchange
of vows. Despite the fact that the two people playing Mary and Joseph
would not have been considered married at the end of the N-Town play,
nonetheless the staging of the wedding in and of itself would have reminded the medieval audience that marriages needed neither clerical participation nor a church setting to be considered valid. Thus, by staging the
wedding, the N-Town marriage play shows how the sacrament of marriage enacts a more lay and communal standard of sacramentality. In doing
so, the marriage play not only teaches a lesson in marriage theology, as
I have been arguing, but contributes dramatically to a reformist theory
of marriage.

"The Trial of Mary and Joseph": Theater for Lay Piety

The performative nature of the marriage sacrament and its potential to advocate dramatically for lay piety is also explored in the trial play, in which a visibly pregnant Mary is brought to ecclesiastical court on accusations of adultery, and Joseph is accused of breaking his vow of chastity. Two disreputable characters named Reysesclaundyr ("Raise-Slander") and Bakbytere ("Back-Biter") accuse Mary openly, claiming to have seen her swollen belly, and they speculate about how she might have become pregnant. In doing so this pair disparages marriage and reduces it to mere sex, an approach to marriage that is linked to a literal mode of representation and interpretation that is rejected in the play. Explicitly posed against the detractors, the play stages a truth test that proves Mary's virtue and upholds the possibility of chaste marriage. Through the staging of the trial and the truth test in which Mary is exonerated, the play makes marriage a means of exploring its own dramatic representational practices. The status of marriage as a sacrament that could be performed by laypeople allows it to become a model for a sacramental theater that performs lay piety.

The apocryphal trial of the holy couple for adultery appears in other late medieval East Anglian stories of the Virgin such as the late medieval *Life of Saint Anne* and John Lydgate's *Life of Our Lady,* but only the N-Town play sets the scene in a contemporary court.[90] Although one of Mary's accusers is "Bakbytere," a figure familiar from sermons and confessional manuals, this scene does not invoke the penitential context, but instead resembles the dramatic manner in which proceedings would have been conducted in commissary court, where people were accused in open voice, an abbreviated oral procedure.[91] By invoking a range of legal procedures recognizable to a fifteenth-century audience, such as the accusation by public rumor, defamation, compurgation, the oath, and the ordeal, the play reminds its viewers of the central role that marriage played in contemporary courts.

The play opens with Den the Summoner addressing the audience directly, and summoning them to court, "I warne 30w here all abowte / Þat I somown 30w, all þe rowte!" (5–6), and asserting, "The courte xal be þis day!" (33). He lists a cross section of the urban community, from "Thom Tynkere" to "Miles þe myllere" and "Bette þe bakere," a range of people who might have been called to serve as witnesses in sexual cases tried in the lower ecclesiastical courts of medieval England. By identifying the people by trade, the summons further recalls the urban audience who would have witnessed the drama in late medieval towns. This passage has the effect not only of underlining the continuity between the contemporary urban courtroom and the fiction of the play itself, it also shows the central role that marriage played in the regulation of behavior in the urban community.

The detractors' accusations against Mary invoke the genre of antimatrimonial discourse both in their assumption that her alleged infidelity was inevitable and in their view that marriage is defined by sex. Speculating gleefully that "of hire tayle ofte-tyme be lyght" (96), and observing that her present girth is comparable to theirs ("here wombe doth swelle / And is as gret as þinne or myne! [80–81]), they blame marriage for Joseph's woes: "That olde cokolde was evyl begylyd / To þat fresche wench whan he was wedde" (98–99). In this way, the detractors echo the concerns of Joseph in the marriage play when he resisted marriage to Mary for fear of becoming cuckolded by his young wife. Their denigration of Mary's marriage is based in an understanding of marriage as merely sexual, rather than consisting of companionship or love, the essence of the marriage sacrament. Mary's crime, as they see it, is thus not the betrayal of Joseph's love or devotion, but the fact of her pregnancy, which they mistakenly take as a sign of her adultery.

The detractors' preoccupation with sex and their insistence on adultery is linked to the genre of fabliau in the play. The detractors accuse Mary of lying by comparing her story to that of a well-known misogynist lai, "The Snow Drop," about a woman who gets pregnant while her merchant husband is away, and swears she has been impregnated by swallowing a snowflake.[92] One detractor unknowingly turns this story into a parody of the Incarnation when he mockingly compares Mary's claim that she is innocent of breaking her vow of chastity to this fabliau:

In feyth, I suppose þat þis woman slepte
Withowtyn all coverte whyll þat it dede snowe;
And a flake þerof into hyre mowthe crepte,
And þerof þe chylde in hyre wombe doth growe.

(306–9)

This passage demonstrates a literal frame of mind and points to the absurdity of the idea that a woman could become pregnant without having had sex. The description of the wife's actions in "The Snow Drop" is unambiguously incriminating and clearly ascribes her pregnancy to her adulterous acts with a young lover:

And Love, which can't be hid from sight,
got both of them in such a stir
that soon he came to lie with her.
Their labors, though, were not in vain:
the wife got pregnant by her swain
and had his son; thus matters ran.[93]

The detractors believe that they have found a similarly clear-cut lie, a fabliau tale in which the old man, Joseph, is betrayed by his young lusty wife, Mary, and by a younger man. One speculates that: "Sum fresch ȝonge galaunt she lovyth wel more / Þat his leggys to here hath leyd!" (87–88), while the other gloats:

Now muste he faderyn anothyr mannys chylde,
And with his swynke he xal be fedde.
A ȝonge man may do more chere in bedde
To a ȝonge wench þan may an olde.
Þat is þe cawse such lawe is ledde,
Þat many a man is kokewolde.

(100–105)

In this passage, the detractor employs a logic focused on sex, arguing that the superiority of young men in bed makes the cuckolding of older husbands inevitable; no bonds of affection are considered. The detractors' focus on the sexual aspect of marriage is paired with an approach to representation that features the literal over the symbolic. Thus the detractors' version of events makes the story of the Incarnation into a standard *senex amans* fabliau plot.

The N-Town play, however, neatly inverts both the expectations of its characters and the conventions of the fabliau. When Mary refuses to represent the loquacious and lustful wife, and to tell her detractors the fabliau tale they desire, they accuse her of lying and insist that her body speaks for itself: "Þu art with chylde we se in syght; / To us þi wombe þe doth accuse!" (302–4). Here they invoke another stereotypical element of fabliaux: the association of a woman's speech with her body, and specifically with her sexuality. Generally this is a means of condemning her speech as lies and her body as overly carnal; the body is both the impetus for dissembling and, paradoxically, the source of literal truth that belies the claims of its owner.[94] The detractors' assertions are undermined, however, by the fact that the truth of Mary's words is clear to the play's audience from the beginning when she is identified as the Virgin Mary. The play overturns fabliau convention, moreover, by ascribing the values of carnal excess and bodily truth to the detractors themselves instead of Mary. For example, they harp on Mary's appearance, calling her "fresch and fayr . . . to syght" and "a ʒonge damesel of bewté bryght, / And of schap so comely also" (91, 94–95). Their repeated references to her physical appearance suggest that they are indulging their own libidinous fantasies. When one detractor speculates that "such a mursel, as semyth me, / Wolde cause a ʒonge man to haue delyght" (92–94), he clearly imagines himself cast in the role of her young lover. Their misreading of the significance of Mary's body serves to associate their own lustful fictions with their wrongheaded tale of her adultery. Blind to her true nature, they take a literal and sexualized approach to both representation and marriage.

The detractors' literal model of representation and interpretation not only invokes the paradigms of fabliau, it also engages the language of contemporary controversy about idolatry in fifteenth-century East Anglia. When the detractors focus excessively on Mary's appearance, they treat her as an object and enact the concerns of iconoclasts about the use of images by making Mary a means of indulging their lustful imaginings, rather than a way to achieve spiritual understanding.[95] Wyclif opposed what he saw as the excessive use of pageantry and images in the Church; he worried that images would not rouse the mind in spiritual intentions, as orthodox defenders claimed, but rather generate sensual desire instead: "so-called Christians, like animals or beasts, having forsaken the faith of spiritual believers today exceedingly indulge the senses: the sight in costly spectacles of church ornaments . . . and sensuous objects are provided by which all the senses are moved in irreligious ways."[96] As Sarah Stanbury has shown, this concern that images generate desire was often gendered so that "the power of images [was] coterminous with a certain sexualized or feminized agency" and, in sensational tales of Lollard abuses of images, a "specific equation is made between the hatred of idols and the fear of female saints."[97] In the N-Town play, Reysesclaundyr's and Bakbytere's lascivious focus on Mary's appearance invokes this gendered rhetoric of the feminized seduction of images. Their response to Mary also parodies the concern of Lollard iconoclasts and of nonheretical critics of images that worshippers failed to distinguish image from saint.[98] As one Lollard polemicist against images exclaims in horror:

> For summe lewid folc wenen þat þe ymagis doun verreyly þe myraclis of hemsilf, and þat þis ymage of þe crucifix be Crist hymsilf, or þe seynt þat þe ymage is þere sett for lickenesse. And þerefore þei seyn "þe swete rode of Bromholme," "þe swete rode of Grace," "þe swete rode at þe norþe dore," "oure dere Lauedy of Walsyngham" but nouȝt "oure Lauedy of heuene," ny "oure lord Iesu Crist of heuene" . . . And herby þe rude puple tristus vtterly in þes deade ymagis, and louen God and hese comandementis þe lesse . . .[99]

The detractors in the N-Town play enact the sin of the "lewid folc" described in this passage who mistake painted statues for the Virgin herself, believing that the truth of Mary's nature resides only in the tangible object of her body. They read her body mimetically, believing that the truth resides only in her appearance, whereas her body is both a tangible truth and a sign of a higher one.

In contrast to the literal-minded discourse of Reysesclaundyr and Bakbytere, the N-Town play includes a truth test that simultaneously exonerates Mary and Joseph, reveals the lies of their accusers, and functions as an alternative form of religious representation. When the bishop explains how the test will reveal the guilt or innocence of the person who takes it, he advertises the test as the opposite of, and an antidote to, the fabliau representational model of the detractors:

> Þat what man drynk of þis potacyon
> And goth serteyn in processyon
> Here in þis place þis awtere abowth,
> If he be gylty, sum maculacion
> Pleyn in his face xal shewe it owth.
> Iff þu be gylty, telle us, lete se.
>
> (237–42)

In this test, inner nature will be manifested as outward appearance; it will be possible to determine who is lying and who is telling the truth because the person's face will become the clear sign of guilt or innocence. This procedure will reground signs, so there is no longer a gap between the signifier and the signified, and it will no longer be possible to misread Mary's pregnant body as a sign of her guilt.

Unlike the detractors, whose accusations are based on a misreading of Mary's body and of her marriage to Joseph, the truth test enacts a sacramental model of representation, specifically inviting a comparison to the Mass. Mary refers to her body as a "tabernacle," invoking the frequent association of the Virgin's pregnant body with the Eucharist in late medieval painting.[100] As she circumnavigates the altar, Mary reasserts her initial claim that "I nevyr knew of mannys maculacion" (334), and the bishop is forced to confirm the truth of her words. Her words are shown to point beyond Mary herself to divine presence through the Incarnation:

> O, gracyous God, as þu hast chose me
> For to be þi modyr, of me to be born,
> Saue þi tabernacle, þat clene is kepte for þe,
> Which now am put at repref and skorn.
> Gabryel me tolde with wordys he[re]beforn
> Þat ʒe of ʒoure goodnes wold become my chylde.
>
> (338–43)

Instead of the tangible sign and consequence of her lust, her body becomes the visual sign of the divine child she carries within. Her denial of adultery is revealed not to be further evidence of her lust, a confirmation of the inherent connection between her speech and her carnality, as her accusers had thought, but instead her performance of the truth test demonstrates that she is both the reflection and embodiment of the divine. By invoking the Incarnation, the play enlists theological justification for embodied representation, one often cited by defenders of images, who believed that Christ's visible appearance on earth gave divine authority to images.[101] Thus, Mary's test becomes both a defense against the charge of adultery and a defense of the ability of theatrical religious representation to abide against idolatrous misreading and convey spiritual conviction. By identifying the truth test as providing a visible sign of invisible grace, the N-Town play identifies itself with what Sarah Beckwith has termed "sacramental theater." As Beckwith has argued, "Theater is not so much inimical to the sacramental disclosure of God as the perfectly consonant form for the religion of incarnation. Precisely because sacraments are best understood as actions and not things, it is in the theater of dramatic action that they are best understood."[102] Although Beckwith and others have focused on the similarities and tensions between the drama and the ritual of the Eucharist, this play invites us to consider the relationship between dramatic perform- ance and the sacrament of marriage.[103] Unlike the Eucharist in which the wafer is a material sign of the sacrament, the truth test is linguistic and thus resembles the marriage sacrament, in which the act of speaking consent constitutes the sign of the sacrament.

The truth test both invokes a sacramental model of representation and, in a deviation from contemporary court practices, recalls the anachronistic legal practice of the ordeal, a procedure in which God literally participates in identifying a person's assertions as true or false. Officially outlawed in 1215 by the Fourth Lateran Council, an ordeal was a mode of trial in which a suspect was subjected to a dangerous physical test and the result regarded as the immediate judgment of God.[104] The most common versions in En- gland involved being lowered into cold water or having one's hands burned with a red-hot iron; the survival or healing of the accused was seen as a sign of innocence. While Mary and Joseph are not subject to physical dan- ger, their test is similarly understood to enlist the direct intervention of God. Although the truth test in the N-Town play resembles the ordeal be- cause it is supposed to be the physical manifestation of God's will, it does not require any physical test of innocence, like hands that heal from a hot iron. In contrast to the traditional form of the ordeal, then, the play's truth test is not so much a spectacle as a test of language that will confirm who is speaking truthfully. In fact, while the bishop describes the test as one in which the faces will show guilt, when Mary and Joseph circumnavigate the altar it is precisely the *absence* of visible sign that demonstrates their inno- cence. Joseph says,

> This drynk I take with meke entent.
> As I am gyltles, to God I pray:
> Lord, as þu art omnypotente,
> On me þu shewe þe trowth þis day.
>
> (250–53)

The linguistic emphasis of the N-Town version is clear when compared with the versions of this episode in Lydgate's *Life of Our Lady* and in the Apocryphal Bible, a source for the play. In the latter, for example, Joseph does not speak at all; not his language but his appearance is emphasized: "Cum ergo bibisset securus Joseph at girasset altare, nullum signum peccati apparuit in eo."[105] In the N-Town play, like an ordeal, God's participation makes Joseph's language a sign of grace.

When the detractors are forced by the bishop to undergo the same test, it is not surprising that they are distinguished from the holy couple primarily by language. Whereas Mary and Joseph stick to the same story, the detractors change theirs. After drinking the potion, the first detractor exclaims:

> Out, out! Alas, what heylith my soulle?
> A, myn heed with fyre methynkyht is brent!
> Mercy, good Mary, I do me repent
> Of my cursyd and fals langage!
> > (364–67)

The first portion of his speech recalls the pain associated with the traditional ordeal by hot iron, but the only spectacle that ensues is possibly the actor's use of gesture or facial expression; the change in his story identifies his crime as linguistic.[106] In fact, the detractor's performance of the truth test produces a similar change in the bishop, who says,

> We all on knes fall here on grownd,
> Þu, Goddys handemayd, prayng for grace.
> All cursyd language and schame onsownd,
> Good Mary, forʒeve us here in þis place.
> > (370–73)

The play depicts the miracle of the truth test primarily as a transformation of language, explicitly eschewing the elaborate spectacle that a staged ordeal might produce.

Even the Incarnation is expressed as a linguistic performance rather than a dramatic spectacle. During her perambulation, Mary says,

> God, as I nevyr knew of mannys maculacion,
> But evyr haue lyued in trew virginité,
> Send me þis day þi holy consolacyon
> Þat all þis fayr people my clennes may se.
> > (334–37)

Although Mary invokes the language of spectacle, the truth of her words is confirmed by the absence of visible sign. As the bishop exclaims,

> Þis woman with chylde is fayr and clene,
> Withowtyn fowle spotte or maculacion!
>
> .   .   .   .
>
> It shewyth opynly by here purgacyon
> Sche is clene mayde, bothe modyr and wyff!
>   (348–49, 352–53)

Unlike those of her detractors, Mary's words do not change after she has drunk the potion. Thus, while Mary is associated with the body by the detractors, it is her language rather than her body that proves the divine meaning even of her body itself. By contrast, in *The Life of Our Lady,* Lydgate describes the audience's rapturous gaze as Mary processes around the altar:

> And all the people, be gan to gasen faste
> If any signe, did in hir apere
> Outhir in colour, in contenaunce or chere
> But all for nought, playnely as I tolde
> The more on hir, they loken and byholde
> The more she was, to her sight fayre
> And lyche as phebus, in Ioly grene maye
> Whan he hathe chasede, the derke mysty eyre
> Shyneth more bright, the clere somers daye
> Whan þikke vapours, be dreven clene awaye.[107]

In this passage Lydgate's narrative voice dwells lovingly on the sight of Mary's face. In the N-Town play, however, this obsession with Mary's body has been associated with the detractors who mistakenly equate the truth of Mary's body with her mere physicality, while her body is also the sign of the higher truth of the Incarnation. Whereas the detractors have taken her body as the literal sign of her sinful carnality, in fact her body is both sign and embodiment of God and, consequently, a model for a higher form of representation in the play.[108]

This final scene not only confirms theater's ability to stage spirituality, it also echoes the terms of the orthodox defense of images, implicitly defending its own theater against accusations of idolatry. In her allusion to the Incarnation, Mary recalls one of the reasons for images in conventional orthodox explanation, one version of which is provided by the figure of Pauper in the early fifteenth-century *Dives and Pauper*.[109] He explains that images have "been ordynyd to steryn manys mende to thynkyn of Cristys incarnacioun and of his passioun and of holye seyntys lyuys."[110] The dramatic and emotional response of Mary's accusers, after first witnessing her drink the truth potion and then drinking it themselves, asserts the power of the performance of the truth test, and of theater, to convert and elevate through the emotions, illustrating the second of Pauper's justifications of images: "Also þey been ordeynyd to steryn mannys affeccioun and his herte to deuocioun, for often man is more steryd be syghte þan be heryng or redynngge."[111] Instead of reducing the spiritual to the carnal, as the detractors had attempted, the play has raised the carnal detractors to a greater awareness of God and shown how divinely sanctioned theatrical performance can be a means to spiritual understanding.

"The Trial of Mary and Joseph" redefines the meaning of the marriage sacrament by tying the theatricality of marriage not just to the performative exchange of vows in the wedding but to married life more generally. In this formulation, not only the vows are given the status of sacramental signs, but other words and actions are also accorded sacramental force because they are the signs of the love between the couple that is the essence of the sacrament of marriage. By de-emphasizing the specificity of the sign of the marriage sacrament, N-Town rejects the heritage of twelfth-century theologians wishing to codify the seven sacraments and of canon lawyers seeking to identify an exact moment to mark the beginning of marriage. Instead, the N-Town play is true to an earlier theology, exemplified by Augustine's definition of marriage as the "affections of the mind," which focused not on the event of the wedding but on marriage as a way of life.[112] By reconstructing a broader understanding of the marriage sacrament as the wedded state, and by moving away from the limited definition of the sacrament that focused on the words of consent, the play makes a broader argument for the sanctity of married life. While true to earlier orthodox definitions of the sacrament, the play's redefinition of the marriage sacrament as the wedded state has unorthodox implications, because it validates lay piety and encroaches on the prerogatives of the clergy.

In conclusion, by suggesting that the promotion of theater is consistent with the use of marriage to promote a reformist agenda, I join a number of critics who have argued that reformed religion was not inherently antitheatrical. Although the "Tretise of Miraclis Pleyinge" was once taken to exemplify Lollard antitheatricality, Clifford Davidson has called the Lollard identification of the text into question, citing the text's orthodox view of the priesthood and the sacraments, and he cautions against assuming that either the followers of Wycliff or the members of the popular Lollard movement were "widely obsessed by any unique hatred of playing and the stage."[113] Ritchie Kendall has argued that Lollards developed their own theatrical modes of presentation. Competing with the drama for the same lay audience, Kendall claims, the Lollards developed a "displaced drama" in the agonistic accounts of heresy trials, such as the *Examination of William Thorp,* and in satiric dialogues, such as *Jack Upland.*[114] Without identifying the drama as Lollard per se, I join critics such as Robert Weimann, Sarah Beckwith, and Ruth Nisse, who have demonstrated that the drama and Wycliffite writings share reformist concerns.[115]

In teaching the theological history of the skirmishes around clerical control of weddings, the N-Town plays show that orthodox and heterodox positions overlap in their understandings of the wedding as a lay performance and marriage as a sacramental practice that does not depend on consummation. This overlap suggests that the subject of Mary and Joseph's marriage would have been of particular interest not only to heterodox extremists but also to the wealthy lay patrons of the numerous East Anglian wool churches and the many members of religious guilds and fraternities who exerted a gentler pressure on clerical monopoly. With their interest in the sacramental value of theater and their use of orthodox theology to promote marriage, the N-Town Mary plays should not be read as Lollard polemic but instead understood in the context of the broad spectrum of growing East Anglian lay piety. Furthermore, these N-Town plays show that marriage was a site of ideological contestation in the late Middle Ages, marking complex fissures and tensions in the fabric of East Anglian religious life. Like Chaucer's *Franklin's Tale* and Gower's *Traitié,* the N-Town plays suggest that the promotion of sacramental marriage was appealing to civic and bourgeois constituencies, supporting its association with the values of the lay middle strata.

CHAPTER FOUR

The Marriage of Love and Sex

Margery Kempe and Bourgeois Lay Identity

It is striking that one of the most widely read depictions of medieval marriage was written by a bourgeois woman. According to both *The Book of Margery Kempe* and surviving records, Margery Kempe was a member of the urban mercantile elite. Records from the town of Lynn verify that her father, John Brunham, was mayor of Lynn five times and was one of the town's two members of Parliament.[1] According to her book, Margery was herself a businesswoman, although evidently not a good one, for her attempts first at brewing and later at milling both failed. A variety of critics have noted the ways in which *The Book of Margery Kempe* seeks to reconcile the vocabulary and values of bourgeois mercantilism with spirituality. Sheila Delany has argued that the "cash nexus pervades [Margery's] consciousness" and that her narrative is shaped by "spiritual economics."[2] Similarly, David Aers has discussed the "market's permeation of religious consciousness" in the *Book*.[3] Sarah Beckwith has analyzed the interaction between bourgeois and clerical values in the text, arguing that it is "as much

as a bourgeois cry against clerical values, as it is a clerical cry against bourgeois ones."[4] More recently, Kathleen Ashley has argued, "Margery's autobiography symbolically enacts a solution to the cultural dilemma of how
to achieve spiritual validation while remaining an active member of mercantile society."[5] In this chapter, I argue that the sacramental marriage
model is central to Margery's attempt to reconcile her spiritual ambitions
with her bourgeois values. Margery's difficulties in doing so are due in part
to the ambivalent role granted to marital sex in two conflicting theological
paradigms. The sacramental model validated marriage as a virtuous practice but did not require marital sex, whereas the doctrine of the marital
debt required marital sex without treating it as virtuous. Margery draws on
the traditions of hagiography and mystical marriage imaginatively to reconcile these two traditions, seeking to create a union of sexually active bourgeois companionate marriage and spirituality which not only validates her
own position as bourgeois woman and aspiring saint but also helps to forge
an ideology of marriage that we now recognize as central to modern bourgeois identity.

The tension between the picture of her earthly marriage in *The Book* as
mutual on the one hand and sexually oppressive on the other is the result
of the incompatibility of bourgeois marriage practices with existing marriage models. Margery depicts her marriage to John primarily as a companionate relationship that is affectionate and mutual, reflecting the portrait
social historians have identified as characteristic of late medieval bourgeois marriage practices. But this bourgeois picture of mutuality in marriage is at odds with the picture of marital relations in the genre of hagiography to which Margery's text aspires, a genre that tends to emphasize the
sexual oppression of husbands, reflecting the poor reputation of marital
sexuality in theological writings and popular teaching.

Although her depiction of her marriage to John reflects the split between
love and sex, in her mystical marriage Margery creates a new bourgeois
model of marriage out of the pieces of received tradition which seeks to
reconcile marital sex with marital spirituality. Mystical marriage was conventionally reserved for virgins, but Margery participates in it as a married
woman, following the example of Continental holy women such as Saint
Bridget. She uses the sensuality of this tradition to make her relationship
to Christ an image of a new earthly model of marriage that unites love and
sex, making sex a spiritualized expression of love. Moreover, Margery's ide-

alized vision constructs marriage as the means through which she can express her private thoughts and feelings in *The Book*, making it the window onto an internal subjectivity or selfhood that is conveyed to an audience through her text. This notion of a public privacy, or rather the privacy that enables or forms a public sphere, has been central to historical notions of bourgeois identity, although typically located at a later period. In making this argument, I am suggesting that *The Book of Margery Kempe* not only revises existing models to create an idea of marriage more consistent with existing bourgeois values, but it also uses marriage to create a bourgeois ideology. Furthermore, in promoting the compatibility of earthly marriage with both sainthood and mystical marriage, Margery validates marriage as a moral practice, echoing the praise accorded it in contemporary conduct books widely read by bourgeois readers.

As we will see at the end of the chapter, this attempt to reconcile bourgeois marriage values and practices with Margery's spiritual goals proves threatening to a series of clerical authorities who see her marital behavior as engaging with contemporary religious politics. Despite her ability to pass tests of orthodoxy, Margery's marital conduct repeatedly earns her the epithet "Lollard." This suggests that her bourgeois marital behavior and emergent marital ideology, while not strictly unorthodox, are seen by many to be relevant to contemporary religious controversy about the relationship between lay and clerical authority, engaging the terms of the discussion in the previous chapter on the N-Town marriage plays. Like the other texts in this study, from Chaucer's *Franklin's Tale* to the N-Town plays, *The Book of Margery Kempe* appears to adapt marriage in unusual ways, but Margery's marital ideology is less the work of an eccentric individual than it is part of a larger body of writings, authored by and directed to the members of the emergent lay middle strata of society who appropriated clerical culture for their own ends.

Bourgeois Married Sainthood: Conflicting Values

Several critics have called attention to the ways in which *The Book of Margery Kempe* is not a factual account of Margery's life but a rhetorical construction that draws upon familiar genres and tropes to sanctify Margery. Lynn Staley, for example, has argued that the use of a scribe both provides a "fictional" witness to Margery's holiness and singularity, and allows Kempe the freedom of a social critic by invoking the conventions of sacred biography.[6] Beckwith has discussed Margery's version of *imitatio Christi,* a practice central to saints' lives, and Gail McMurray Gibson has described Kempe's *Book* as a "calculated hagiographical text" that replaces martyrdom by the sword with "martyrdom by slander."[7] Most recently, Katherine J. Lewis has argued that *The Book* was an attempt to create a specifically English cult.[8] Indeed, Kempe begins her *Book* much as Osbern Bokenham introduces his legend of Saint Mary Magdalene, presenting it as "a comfortabyl for synful wrecchys, wher-in þei may haue gret solas and comfort to hem and vndyrstondyn þe hy & vnspecabyl mercy of ower souereyn Sauyowr Cryst Ihesu" (1).[9] Not only Margery's narrative of her spiritual course but also her account of her earthly marriage should be understood as a rhetorical performance, a deliberate invocation of the hagiographical model, especially in its emphasis on her rejection of marital sex. When discussing sex, Margery depicts John as like the oppressive lustful husbands and authority figures who are characteristic in saints' lives, but in respect to other aspects of marriage her description is more companionate and as a result more consistent with typical bourgeois marriage practices of the period. Thus, the *Book*'s depiction of sexual oppression in marriage invokes hagiographical models of chaste marriage at odds with its bourgeois portrait of relative autonomy and equality in marriage.

Married saints began to appear with new frequency in the thirteenth and fourteenth centuries, a period of restricted canonization. Married saints were among the most popular, but few were sexually active saints whom Margery Kempe could emulate in her efforts to sanctify her own life as a married bourgeois mother of fourteen children. These married saints tended to have chaste marriages, like Saint Cecelia, or to achieve their greatest holiness after their husbands had died, when they became widows. As widows, they ascended to the middle rung of the three grades of chastity, which ranked widowhood above marriage, although below virginity. On the other hand, as many critics have noted, an increasing number of Continental holy women were wives and mothers, providing a key role model for Kempe in what Susan Dickerman has termed "their extension of the sphere of female religious activity into the midst of secular life" and in their adaptation of a range of affective pious practices, such as expressive crying and *imitatio Mariae.*[10] Margery specifically mentions Saint Bridget and

Marie d'Oignies, two married holy women, in her text. Unlike Margery, however, these two holy women achieved mystical marriage to God only as widows. Although Christ selects Bridget to be his spouse early in life in her vita, He indicates that their mystical marriage will take place only after her earthly husband has died: "I haue chosen þe and taken þe to mi spouse . . . þou assigned thi will into mi handes at þe time of diinge of þi husband."[11] Similarly, Marie d'Oignies's vita refers to the day of her death as her "wedding day," suggesting that her mystical marriage to God took place not on earth but in heaven after her death.[12] In this way, although Bridget and Marie provided Margery with a model for married lay sanctity, neither had a spiritual marriage to God that could be achieved during her earthly marriage; their model did not provide the opportunity for integrating these two kinds of marriage to the extent that Margery does in her book.

Although Margery clearly competes with the married holy women Marie d'Oignies and Saint Bridget in the *Book*, it is the virgin martyrs Saint Katherine and Saint Margaret, and others who dramatically eschew marriage, whose company she most often seeks in her visions.[13] Sarah Salih and Katherine J. Lewis have shown that in her *Book* Margery Kempe engages the tropes of the virgin martyr hagiographies in her confrontations with male secular and religious authorities, and in her resistance to marital sex.[14] Margery's obsession with these virgin martyrs is consistent with the ongoing popularity of virgin martyr legends in the fifteenth century, even among married laywomen.[15] In Osbern Bokenham's fifteenth-century East Anglian *Legendary,* for example, nine of the thirteen tales included concern virgins.[16] In these narratives the virgin saint characteristically suffers horrible torture to avoid marriage. Bokenham's legend of Saint Margaret, for example, describes how the tyrant Olibrius instructs his henchmen to torture Saint Margaret "Wyth glowynge ferbrondys faste you hye, / This wycchys sydys to brenne & sere / As longe as ye ony flesh fynde there!"[17] As Marc Glasser has wittily observed, "The typical virgin martyr legend is an ironic inversion of Paul's famous comment on marriage: it is better to burn than to marry."[18] Marriage in these tales is systematically associated with lust and idol worship, and virginity with Christian piety, as the legend of Saint Margaret illustrates. In this tale, Saint Margaret is pursued by the powerful tyrant whose offer of marriage is motivated by lust and comes with an attempt to seduce her to worship his gods. As in the passage cited above, Glasser has argued that the torture suffered by these saints often resembles sexual assault, symbolically linking torture with both marriage and sex.[19] The virgin martyr narratives are crucial to understanding Kempe's portrait of her sexual oppression in her earthly marriage to John.

Margery's narrative perhaps most directly follows the chaste marriage vitas when she reports that she repeatedly "cownseld hir husbond to levyn chast" (12). Chaste marriage vitas were themselves characteristically adaptations of the virgin martyr narratives in which the wife's avoidance of sex within marriage was almost as dramatic as the virgins' avoidance of marriage, suggesting that it was better to suffer horribly than to have marital sex. It is in the context of these saints' lives that Kempe's dramatic description of her horror of marital sex should be understood. Like the heroines of chaste marriage vitas, Margery depicts marital sex as a form of torture, claiming that "þe dette of matrimony was so abhominabyl to hir þat sche had leuar, hir thowt, etyn or drynkyn þe wose, þe mukke in þe chanel, þan to consentyn to any fleschly comownyng saf only for obedyens" (11–12). Margery's rejection of marital sex and her invocation of obedience, a trait she does not typically display elsewhere in the *Book,* are both familiar hagiographical tropes.

Despite her colorful rejection of marital sex, in this same passage Margery acknowledges that marital sex had been pleasurable to her in the past, in contrast to the typical married saint. For example, in Bokenham's account, before marriage Saint Elizabeth makes a vow "shewyng þat no lust of flessh founde / In no maner wyse in hyr myght be" that if her husband died before her, she would not remarry, insisting instead "perpetuel continence þat she shulde obserue."[20] Margery, on the other hand, concedes that her marriage has been lustful, admitting that sex had not always been repulsive to her, as her later regrets illustrate. She repeatedly rejects the earlier pleasure she had in marital sex as when she tells John that they "had dysplesyd God be her inordynat lofe & þe gret delectacyon þat þei haddyn eyþyr of hem in vsing of oþer" (12). In this passage, the earthly lust is not ascribed to a desiring husband, as in the legend of Saint Cecelia, or to a heathen king, as in the legend of Saint Margaret, but to John and even to Margery herself. Margery places her discussion of the pleasure of marital sex into the framework of a conversion narrative, contrasting her past desires for John with her current state, in which "sche had no lust to comown wyth hir husbond" (14). It is only after her conversion that the narrative ascribes marital desire exclusively to Margery's husband and associates it systematically with her oppression. For example, Margery describes John's response to her suggestion that they abstain from marital sex in the following way: "Hir husbond seyd it wer good to don so, but he mygth not ȝett, he xuld whan God wold. And so he vsyd her as he had do be-for, he wold not spar. And euyr sche preyd to God þat sche mygth levyn chast" (12). In this passage, even John acknowledges the virtue of marital chastity, but unable to control his desire he imposes his lust forcefully on his wife, Margery, fulfilling the role of the sexually oppressive husband characteristic of chaste marriage vitas.

This acknowledgment of Margery's earlier desire for her husband suggests that we should understand Margery's rejection of marital sex as part of a rhetorical performance rather than an authentic account of her feelings toward sex with her husband. By contrast, several critics have taken Margery's narrative of her sufferings of marital sexuality as a straightforward account of her experience, arguing that her text reflects the kind of oppression medieval wives — even bourgeois wives — suffered in a world where they had limited legal rights and were taught to be subordinate to their husbands by clerics and other writers. David Aers, for example, claimed that Margery "was forced to endure years of compulsory sexuality . . . against which Margery expresses the deepest repugnance and pain," and Sheila Delany argued that "like any medieval woman, Margery is born the property of her father; on her marriage this right is transferred to her husband . . . Having no right of property over her own body, Margery must endure legal rape when persuasion fails."[21] These readings are consistent with scholarship by social historians who have treated the *Book* as evidence of medieval marriage practices.[22]

These readings of Margery's experience of sex as a site of marital oppression have centered on the scene in which John once again rejects her request for a vow of mutual chastity. On a hot midsummer evening when Margery and her husband, John, are returning from York, he proposes,

Margery, grawnt me my desyr, & I schal grawnt ȝow ȝowr desyr. My fyrst desyr is þat we xal lyn stylle to-gedyr in o bed as we han do be-for; þe secunde þat ȝe schal pay my dettys er ȝe go to Iherusalem; & þe thrydde þat ȝe schal etyn & drynkyn wyth me on þe Fryday as ȝe wer wont to don. (24)

When Margery initially rejects his offer, on the grounds that she cannot break her Friday fast, he threatens to rape her: "'Wel,' he seyd, 'þan schal I medyl ȝow a-geyn'" (24).

Although it is true that medieval women were legally subject to marital rape, and although the autonomy of medieval women was unarguably curtailed by marriage, we should also consider the ways in which this dramatic portrayal of John as oppressive and driven by lust is consistent with the portrait of husbands and male authorities in saints' lives. John's violent threat is a modified version of the torture inflicted by male authorities on the bodies of the virgin saints who resist marriage, which, as we have seen, often figures rape and is motivated by lust. Indeed, as Sarah Salih has shown, the vocabulary of virgin saints' lives is invoked in the passage immediately preceding John's proposal when he asks,

> "Margery, yf her come a man wyth a swerd & wold smyte of myn hed les þan I schulde comown kendly wyth ʒow as I haue do be-for, seyth me trewth of ʒowr consciens—for ʒe sey ʒe wyl not lye—whþyr wold ʒe suffyr myn hed to be smet of er ellys suffyr me to medele wyth ʒow a-ʒen as I dede sum-tyme?" . . . And þan sche seyd wyth gret sorwe, "For-soþe I had leuar se ʒow be slayn þan we schuld turne a-ʒen to owyr vnclennesse." (23)

With its repetition of the word *suffyr* this passage equates decapitation with marital sex, depicting these experiences as such comparably horrible fates that choosing between them would be difficult. In an ironic inversion of the typical virgin martyr narrative, instead of agreeing to have her head cut off rather than suffer again the defilement of marital sex, Margery hypothetically offers to sacrifice John's life as an index of her commitment to chastity and "clennesse."[23]

Indeed, John's question about whether Margery would rather have his head cut off or sleep with him suggests a specific awareness of the hagiographical genre and, as Aers has observed, is similar to dialogue from the legend of Saint Cecelia.[24] In Bokenham's version of the story, Cecelia warns her husband in their bedchamber on their wedding night:

> An aungel of god a louere haue I,
> Wych my body kepyth wyth greth jelusy.
> Where-fore, yf he neuere so lytyl may proue
> That þou me touche wyth vnclene loue
> Wy[t]h wyl me to defoulen flesshly,

Anoon wyth þe he wyl ben angry
And ful cruelly on þe veniaunce take.[25]

Like the passage quoted above from *The Book of Margery Kempe,* here marital sex is also depicted as "vnclene." Indeed, in an earlier passage Margery
recounts praying to God that she might live chaste and be protected from
her husband's lust. Like Cecelia, she is protected from her husband's advances by a threat of divine violence, but the threat of bodily harm comes
not from Margery or from an angel but directly from the mouth of Christ.
In a previous chapter, Margery reports that when she prayed to God that
she might remain chaste, "Cryst seyd to hir mende, 'Þow must fastyn þe
Fryday boþen fro mete & drynke, and þow schalt haue þi desyr er Whit-
sonday, for I schal sodeynly sle þin husbonde'" (21). This threat of violence against John is not carried out, but Margery reports that God gives
her His immediate protection from her husband's advances: "aftyr hyr husbond wold haue had knowlach of hir as he was wone be-for, & whan he
gan neygh hir, sche seyd 'Ihesus, help me' & he had no power to towche
hir at þat tyme in þat wyse, ne neuyr aftyr wyth no fleschly knowyng" (21).
Like a virgin martyr assailed by a lusting heathen, Margery prays to God
to protect her aspirations to chastity. Furthermore, the description of John
as having "no power" invokes the language of the miracles that protect
chaste and virgin saints from their assailants. In fact, the impact of John's
threat to "meddle" with Margery in their exchange in York is tempered by
John's admission that he had not "medelyd wyth hir" for eight weeks prior
because he was afraid, since Margery had earlier warned him that he would
be slain suddenly (23).

Unlike Saint Cecelia, and most saints in their vitas, however, Margery
does not rely on miracles or divine intervention but uses her earthly pow-
ers to escape marital sex without suffering dramatic physical torture. In
contrast to aristocratic saints such as Saint Margaret and Saint Elizabeth,
who are represented in their vitas as subject to the patriarchal authority of
fathers and secular rulers, in this scene Margery Kempe uses her status as
a bourgeois businesswoman to negotiate her way out of the marital debt.
Specifically, in exchange for John freeing her from her obligations to have
marital sex, she offers to relieve him of his financial debts. She responds to
his petition as follows: "Sere, yf it lyke 3ow, 3e schal grawnt me my desyr,
& 3e schal haue 3owr desyr. Grawntyth me þat 3e schal not komyn in my

bed, & I grawnt ȝow to qwyte ȝowr dettys er I go to Ierusalem" (25). Here Margery defuses the threat of rape by offering money in exchange for liberation from the marital debt. Thus, Margery's portrait of herself as the victim of a hierarchical marriage is tempered by her ability to act as her own agent in what is literally a financial settling of sexual obligation.

Instead of seeing this scene as emblematic of the victimization of Margery and other women in medieval marriage, I join Lynn Staley and Deborah S. Ellis in arguing that Margery has the upper hand in the financial bargaining with her husband and it is in fact John more than Margery who risks becoming an object of exchange.[26] Although critics have often assumed that Margery has this bargaining power because of the money she inherited from her father, according to the system of *couverture* all land and chattels owned by the wife, including any property she inherited during her marriage, was subject to her husband's control. A married woman's inability to hold chattels or property independently of her husband prevented her, under common law, from contracting debts, buying or selling land independently, or making a testament.[27] Margery probably operated as a *femme sole,* a legal status that allowed wives to operate businesses with financial independence from their husbands.[28] She says that she ran first a brewery and later a horse-mill, but by her own account, by the time of her negotiation with John both of these enterprises had failed and thus could not have provided much financial bargaining power. Aside from the possibilities offered by operating as a *femme sole,* a wife like Margery Kempe could not literally have been financially independent of her husband, but nonetheless, there are several legal situations in which a husband like John would have needed his wife's permission to sell the property. This would have been the case, for example, if they held the property together in *jointure,* an alternative to dower, in which the husband agreed to hold his land in joint tenancy with his wife.[29] More indirectly, a wife's claim to dower and dowry after her husband's death could effectively discourage prospective buyers.[30] Although *The Book of Margery Kempe* does not supply the details to verify that any of these options provide the particular explanation for Margery's depiction of her financial independence in marriage, even this brief account of medieval property law suggests a variety of ways in which Margery may have been able to use money as a source of bargaining power.[31]

Margery's relative power in her marriage is characteristic of bourgeois companionate marriage, despite the narrative's invocation of the trope of marital sexual oppression crucial to the genre of hagiography that her text emulates. Many saints' lives depict their heroines as subject to their father's will in marriage, reflecting a practice used only by the very top layers of aristocratic society. Indeed medieval saints, including the ones Margery mentions in her text, are often from the upper ranks of the aristocracy, where the families played a determining role in arranging marriages, since the transmission of patrimony was a primary concern. By contrast, social historians have shown that bourgeois women like Margery Kempe often had considerable freedom to choose a husband and to arrange the marriage contract.[32] This freedom to choose a husband on the part of bourgeois women is in evidence in the advice poem "The Good Wife Taught Her Daughter," in which the mother advises her daughter to consult only her friends about any marriage proposal she receives; she does not say that they or her family should determine her decision.[33] Indeed, Margery Kempe fits the pattern of late marriage in late medieval English urban society which historians have tied to the freedom to choose a spouse and to companionate marriage; while the legal marriage age for girls was twelve, Margery Kempe recounts that she was married at twenty years or older.[34]

With the notable exception of Margery's description of her sexual oppression in marriage, the *Book* generally describes her marriage as affectionate and mutual, rather than hierarchical. In the first chapter, for example, Kempe describes recovering from her madness, and requesting from her husband the keys to the buttery, but "Hyr maydens & hir kepars cownseld hym he xulde delyuyr hir no keys, for þei seyd sche wold but ȝeue awey swech good as þer was . . . Neuyr-þe-lesse, hir husbond, euyr hauyng tendyrnes & compassyon of hir, comawndyd þei xulde delyuyr to hyr þe keyys" (8). In this passage, "tendyrnes & compassyon" are clear indicators of affection, and John's willingness to give her the keys suggests that he trusts his wife, rather than striving to rule over her.[35] This trust on John's part in this early scene is echoed in a later one, when Margery is challenged by the "worschepful doctowr" in York (122), and she reports that John has given her his permission to travel around the country on pilgrimage. This freedom to travel is later clearly linked to gender and other kinds of insubordination, when the archbishop of York expresses anxiety on behalf of the duke of Bedford that Margery "cownseledyst my Lady Greystokke to forsakyn hir husbonde" (133). In this context Margery's freedom to travel alone seems unusual for a married woman. John does not begrudge her independence but instead feels compassion for her travails. When Margery comes to Lambeth palace in London and is reviled by a woman who "seyd ful cursydly to hir in þis maner, 'I wold that þu wer in Smythfeld, & I wold beryn a fagot to bren þe wyth; it is pety þat þow leuyst,'" Kempe reports that "hir husbond suffred wyth great peyn & was ful sory to heryn hys wyfe so rebukyd" (36). Here and in other scenes John is given the part of the compassionate companion who supports his wife through her difficulties in her attempts to practice her own independent form of piety. This is in contrast to John's depiction as an oppressive authority figure who seeks to sully her piety and purity by exacting the marital debt.

Given Margery's description of companionate marriage in the *Book,* why then does Kempe construct this narrative of oppression under the marriage debt? Why is Margery's oppression in marriage constructed as exclusively sexual? When John responds to Margery by saying that her refusal of the marital debt makes her "no good wyfe" (23), like the husband or parents who try to enforce the debt in other chaste marriage narratives, he represents the well-articulated doctrine that insisted that sex was part of marriage. And yet, as we have seen, conceding to the marital debt was not part of being a good saint. This is because while the sacramental model suggested that marriage could be holy, it did not validate marital sex. The scene in York in which Margery negotiates with John dramatizes the tension between the two models of marriage by showing that there was a discrepancy between the criteria for being a good saint and a good wife. This scene can thus be understood as a dramatization of the conflict between two theological understandings of marriage: the sacramental understanding that validated marital sanctity apart from marital sexuality, and the doctrine of the marital debt which required marital sex.

We have seen that the sacramental model followed Augustine's definition of marriage as the "affections of the mind," an intangible state that does not depend on carnal knowledge, dignifying marriage as a spiritual practice. Thus, although the sacramental model of marriage did much to improve the reputation of marriage by defining it as a spiritual practice whose substance was love, it did little to improve the poor reputation of marital sex. The doctrine of the marital debt, on the other hand, seemed to contradict the sacramental definition by requiring marital sex—even non-

procreative sex—specifying that each party had the right to ask for sex
and in turn the obligation to comply with the other spouse's requests.[36]
Theological understandings of the marital debt were based on the following well-known text of 1 Corinthians:

> Let the husband pay the debt to his wife, and the wife also in a like man-
> . ner to the husband. The wife does not have power over her own body,
> but the husband; likewise, the husband does not have power over his
> own body, but the wife . . . You must not refuse each other, except per-
> haps by consent for a time that you give yourself to prayer . . . *But I say
> this by way of concession, not by command.*[37]

Saint Paul's text suggests that marital sex is a remedy for those who cannot
contain themselves rather than a positive good. Medieval theologians differentiated among three levels of sinfulness in regards to marital sex—
rendering the debt, which was sinless; exacting the debt because of incon-
tinence, which was venially sinful; and uniting for the satisfaction of lust,
which was mortally sinful—but in no case was the act accorded positive
spiritual value. Even rendering the debt, while sinless, was not considered
inherently virtuous. Thus, the theology of the marital debt did not suggest
that marital sex had any particular relationship to the love, the sacramental essence of marriage.[38] Furthermore, the problems of regulating marital
sex received greater emphasis in penitential and sermon traditions than
did the spirituality of marriage.[39]

The separation between the theology of the marital debt and the sacramental definition explains the absence of any developed account of the relationship between love and sex in medieval marriage. In fifteenth-century
England, sex did not have the same associations with love, selfhood, and
personal identity as it does today. As Pierre Payer observes:

> The concept of sex or sexuality as an integral dimension of human
> persons, as an object of concern, discourse, truth and knowledge, did
> not emerge until well after the Middle Ages. Medieval theologians and
> canon lawyers did not talk about sex as such because they had no lan-
> guage with which to do so. The words "sex," "sexual" and "sexuality,"
> and their counterparts in other European languages, are of relatively re-
> cent vintage and have no counterparts in medieval Latin.[40]

This claim is further confirmed by a brief survey of some of the terms used in *The Book of Margery Kempe* to describe marital sex: "fleschly comownyng" (12), "to-gedyr in o bed as we han do be-for" (24), and "I medyl 3ow a-geyn" (24). None of these expressions suggest any connection between the affection of the sacramental tradition and the compulsory sex required by the doctrine of the marital debt. This theological context explains why Margery separates her description of her affectionate relationship with her husband from her depiction of the oppression of marital sex; it also explains why the hagiographies of married saints tend to exclude marital sex from their accounts.

Even within canon law, there was a tension between these two models of marriage: one that required marital sex without according it virtue, and the other that gave marriage spiritual virtue but did not make sexual relations essential. As we have seen in the previous chapter, after much theological debate about the role of sex in marriage which generated many complex multipartite definitions, consent alone became the definition of marriage. However, the tension between the sacramental model of marriage and the marital debt persisted in a number of ancillary laws surrounding the dissolution of marriage. For example, in spite of the fact that marriage did not require consummation to be valid, inability to consummate a marriage was considered grounds for divorce and impotence was considered an impediment to marriage.[41] In addition, although a couple was considered married at the moment they exchanged vows of present consent, canon law allowed the marriage to be dissolved within two months if the marriage remained unconsummated and the couple made a mutual decision to enter a monastery.[42] Thus, while consent alone was required to make a marriage, marital sex was required to make it indissoluble.

In this way, the marital conflict over sex between Margery and John is both a financial transaction and a negotiation of the criteria for being a good saint and being a good wife. This negotiation attempts to reconcile the doctrines of the marital debt and the sacramental view of marriage, recalling the juggling act of theologians. Unlike N-Town's "Joachim and Anna" or "The Marriage of Mary and Joseph," *The Book of Margery Kempe* does not draw on the sacramental model of marriage to sanctify her affectionate relationship to John, perhaps because this model does little to validate sexually active marriage. The depiction of earthly marriage in the book shows the ongoing difficulties of reconciling the expe-

rience of ordinary bourgeois marriage with the received theological ideologies of marriage.

A Bourgeois Mystical Marriage: Combining Love and Sensuality

Kempe deliberately remakes her marriage to Christ in the image of earthly
marriage, using it as a place imaginatively to construct a bourgeois ideology. Central to this construction is the manipulation of the traditions of
sacramental marriage and mystical marriage to imagine a theology of marriage that unites love and sex. By fashioning a model of marriage in which
sex becomes an expression of love, Kempe creates a new ideology of marriage in her depiction of her spiritual marriage to Christ which reconciles
the ideals of the companionate marriage she has had with her earthly husband, John, with sexuality in marriage. In her visions, Margery extends the
sacramental model of marriage to include married sexuality, drawing on
the model of mystical marriage that takes sensuality to be an expression of
spiritual love. As is consistent with a book that draws self-consciously on
saints' lives and other traditions of devotional writing, Margery's text deliberately manipulates this established tradition to serve her own purposes.
In this way, like the N-Town marriage plays, The Book of Margery Kempe
strategically deploys orthodox theology and the established genres of devotional writings.

Some critics have been scandalized by the conflation of images of earthly
lovemaking with mystical marriage, and have suggested that this illustrates
Margery's failure as a mystic. For example, Wolfgang Riehle claims, "She
draws a much too forceful analogy between her mystical love and her earlier married sexuality . . . In Margery there is frequently a crude realism
which intrudes in a very embarrassing manner."[43] Other critics ascribe this
conflation of earthly and mystical marriage to her personal history. For example, Anthony Goodman has suggested that it is Margery's troubled relationship with her father and her dissatisfaction with her earthly marriage
that causes her to substitute God for her husband.[44] As others have argued,
however, if Margery Kempe's mysticism is notable for its unabashed sexuality, in this regard it follows the tradition of bridal mysticism embraced by
such figures as Mechthild of Magdeburg, Marie d'Oignies, and other beguines.[45] Although the earthliness of Margery's mystical visions has clear

Continental precedents, I agree with Riehle's and Goodman's suggestion that Kempe goes further than these holy women in making her mystical marriage a specific response to her earthly marriage.

Even compared to the mystical marriages of Continental holy women such as Bridget, Margery's marriage to God is described in the especially quotidian terms of her bourgeois earthly marriage. As Susan Dickerman argues, "To a much greater degree than any other pious woman, Margery was inclined to interpret her spiritual experience in social terms."[46] Kempe's Christ tells her that he accompanies her on her daily activities "whan þu syttest at þi mete, I sytte wyth þe; whan þow gost to þi bed, I go wyth þe; &, whan þu gost owt of towne, I go wyth þe" (31), and on one occasion finds her a babysitter when he asks her to take on a spiritual task (48).[47] But Kempe's description of her relationship to God is perhaps most earthly in its use of sensual and even explicitly sexual terms. Although mystical marriage imagery is often sensual, Margery Kempe's version makes her relationship to Christ into an image of ordinary sex, particularly located in her bourgeois household. A classic example can be found in the instructions of Kempe's Christ: "[I]t is conuenyent þe wyf to be homly wyth hir husbond . . . Þerfore most I nedys be homly wyth þe & lyn in þi bed wyth þe" (90). This is a specifically earthly image of marital sexuality imagined in the domestic space of the bed. Later in the same passage, Christ seems to describe marital sex when he counsels her that "whan þu art in þi bed, take me to þe as for þi weddyd husbond, as they derworthy derlyng" (90). Next, Margery's Christ describes a spiritual version of ordinary gestures of affectionate lovemaking: "wil þat þu loue me, dowtyr, as a good wife owyth to loue hir husbonde. & perfor þu mayst boldy take me in þe armys of þi sowle & kyssen my mowth, myn hed, & my fete as swetly as thow wylt" (90). This is notable not only for its similarity to earthly marriage but also for its attempt to combine love and sex, usually separated in accounts of earthly marriage. Unlike images of devotion based on a courtly model in which neither marriage nor consummation is ever reached, Margery is able to achieve both in her vision, integrating love and sex in a way not found in her descriptions of her marital interactions with John. What we have here is not simply a misunderstanding of the tradition of mystical marriage, or a mere reflection of the Continental tradition of bridal mysticism, but a deliberate use of mystical marriage to construct a model of marriage that combines love and sex.

This conflation of the sensual and the spiritual in marriage imagery was part of Saint Bernard's teaching on the Song of Songs and central to the development of the traditional imagery of mystical marriage. In one of his sermons, Bernard explained why bodily experience is integral to spiritual understanding: "Because we are carnal and born of the concupiscence of the flesh, it is necessary that our desire, our love, originate in the flesh."[48] Bernard described an ascent from the flesh to the spirit, a progression that was not to be reversed; he was careful to distinguish this physical experience of spirituality from the stimulus of the earthly world.[49] Bernard's exegesis of the marital imagery, however, often appears to collapse metaphoric and literal, and thus to unsettle the clarity of the hierarchy of the spiritual over the material world. In one of his sermons, for example, he says,

> [W]hen the mind is enraptured by the unutterable sweetness of the Word, so that it withdraws, or rather is transported, and escapes from itself to enjoy the Word . . . A mother is happy in her child; a bride is even happier in a bridegroom's embrace. The children are dear, they are pledges of his love, but his kisses give her greater pleasure.[50]

Here Bernard characteristically uses erotic and ecstatic fleshly language to describe a spiritual union that denies the flesh. This passage depends on the metaphor of the soul as a bride of Christ and yet omits any overt indication that the imagery is metaphoric.

In the previous chapter, we saw a similar conflation in *Holy Maidenhood,* in which marriage to Christ is described not as analogous to earthly marriage but as a preferable version of the same relationship.[51] Similarly, Alan de Lille instructs virgins: "If you want to marry an earthly husband for riches, consider that earthly riches are deceptive and transitory, for they pass away either in the present life or at least in death. Therefore marry him whose treasures are incomparable, whose riches are immutable, where thief does not steal nor moth corrupt."[52] These are two examples of the many late medieval texts in which the mystical marriage Bernard meant to apply allegorically to male virgins was adapted in a provocatively literal sense to apply to women.[53] The integrity of the boundary between the celibate contemplative life that marked clergy and the active married life of the laity depended on the clarity of this vulnerable distinction between literal and metaphoric marriage.

The integrity of this boundary was more stable for Saint Bernard, who wrote in Latin exclusively to those of the contemplative life, than for later vernacular devotional writers. In his first sermon on the Song of Songs, Bernard identifies his audience clearly as the monastic spiritual elite:

> The instructions that I address to you, my brothers, will differ from those I should deliver to the people in the world, at least the manner will be different. The preacher who desires to follow St. Paul's method of teaching will give them milk to drink rather than solid food, and will serve a more nourishing diet to those who are spiritually enlightened . . . "We have a wisdom to offer those who have reached maturity," in whose company, I feel assured, you are to be found . . . Be ready then to feed on bread rather than milk.[54]

In his view, these sermons on the Song of Songs and the quest for true spiritual life were the exclusive prerogative of his monastic audience; he distinguishes his audience broadly from the "people in the world," whom he evidently regards with some distaste.[55] Bernard's appropriation of this secular vocabulary of marriage exclusively for monastic use relied on the clarity and stability of boundaries between clergy and laity, celibacy and marriage, lately and definitively established by a series of laws and legislation passed against clerical marriage, culminating in Lateran II in 1139. In this cultural environment there was little anxiety that people seriously devoted to the contemplative life could possibly be married in any literal sense.

These boundaries were not as stable in fifteenth-century East Anglia where a growth of vernacular devotional literature was part of a development of lay piety. The works of Bernard's later followers are especially careful to draw attention to Bernard's distinction between the physical experience of spirituality and the stimulus of the earthly world. For example, in the fifteenth-century Middle English translation of *The Fire of Love*, Richard Rolle of Hampole's *De Incendio Amoris* describes love for God in the following way:

> [W]hen I felt fyrst my hert wax warme, and treuly, not ymagynyngly, bot als it were with sensibyll fyre, byrned. I was forsoth meruayld as þe byrnyng in my saule byrst vp . . . oft-tymes haue I gropyd my breste, sekandly whedyr þis birnynge wer of any bodely cause vtwardly. *Bot*

when I knew þat onely it was kyndyld of gostely caus inwardly, and þat þis
brynnynge was noȝt of fleschly lufe ne concupiscens, in þis I consaued it was þe
gyft of my maker. (My italics)[56]

Rolle includes an extra sentence to distinguish heavenly sensation from
sexual lust, attempting to draw a clear line between heavenly and earthly
love. But the fact that Rolle felt he needed this extra sentence suggests that
he was aware of the fragility of such a division in a model of devotion that
made bodily experience so crucial to spiritual understanding.[57]

It is just this boundary that Rolle so anxiously polices which Margery
transgresses in her revision of the tradition of mystical marriage. Directly
after the account of her marriage to God, Margery alludes directly to Rolle's
The Fire of Love. In this passage she too describes the way her love burns
for God:

> Also owr Lord ȝaf hir an-oþer tokne, þe whech enduryd a-bowtyn xvj
> ȝer & it encresyd euyr mor & mor, & þat was a flawme of fyer wondir
> hoot & delectabyl & ryth comfortabyl, nowt wastyng but euyr incres-
> yng, of lowe, for, thow þe wedyr wer neuyr so colde, sche felt þe hete
> brennyng in hir brest & at hir hert, as verily as a man schuld felyn þe
> material fyer ȝyf he put hys hand or hys fynger þerin. (88)

In Margery's version, Rolle's careful distinction between the heavenly derived experience of spiritual ecstasy and earthly sensation is notably absent.
Margery makes mystical marriage into a resource for exploring the continuity between love and sensuality, which were completely separated in the
theology of earthly marriage.

Kempe deliberately emphasizes the continuities between spiritual and
earthly marriage revealing the shared theological traditions behind both.
Although many other mystics employ a literalized and sexualized imagery
of mystical marriage, compared with the vitas of other mystics Kempe's account of her marriage to God more closely resembles earthly marriage and,
throughout her book, the marital imagery is more fully developed. By comparison, even the famous account of Catherine of Siena's mystical marriage
to Christ in Raymond of Capua's vita, in which He places a ring on her hand,
does not so closely resemble the marriage liturgy, nor is the image of Catherine as a bride of Christ such a dominant image in the rest of her vita.[58] At the

center of the narrative, when Kempe describes a vision in which she is married to God, she draws heavily on the standard marriage liturgy:

> [Þ]e Fadyr toke hir be þe hand in hir sowle be-for þe Sone & þe Holy Gost & þe Modyr of Ihesu and alle þe xij apostelys & Seynt Kateryn & Seynt Margarete & many oþer seyntys & holy virgynes wyth gret multitude of awngelys, seying to hir sowle, "I take þe, Margery, for my weddyd wyfe, for fayrar, for fowelar, for richar, for powerar so þat þu be buxom & bonyr to do what I byd þe do." (87)

Margery's staging of the wedding invokes the ceremony of the dedication for nuns that built on the tradition of the Song of Songs and echoed the earthly marriage ceremony. Margery's version differs significantly from these, however, because, needless to say, God does not speak as part of the dedication ceremony for nuns. His speaking role in this passage is instead that of a husband in the earthly marriage ceremony. Margery's selection of the liturgy to describe her mystical marriage both reminds her readers of how much spiritual and earthly marriage ceremonies share and also demonstrates the ways in which the theology of the sacramentality of marriage and mystical marriage overlap and inform each other.

It is not incidental that Kempe chooses to emphasize the exchange of vows, since, as we have seen, this exchange was the sign of the sacrament. These vows were themselves the sign and substance of the love between the couple, which was in turn the sign and substance of God's love or grace. In this way, the married couple's love was technically of the same substance as God's love. The theory behind these connections would have been understood by laypeople like Margery Kempe because they were often explained in teachings on the marriage ceremony in lay sermons and handbooks for parish clergy and implied in the liturgy itself. For example, the "Sermon de Nupcijs" in *Mirk's Festial* explains, "Þerefore þe prest blessuth a ring þat betokeneth God, þat hath neyther begynnyng ne endyng and duth hit on hur fyngur þat haþ a veyne to hure herte, tokenyng þat he schal loue God oure all thyng, and þanne hure husbond."[59] Thus, the inclusion of the exchange of consent suggests that mystical and earthly marriage shared a common substance of God's love. As Hugh of St. Victor explains, "Matrimony was a sacrament of a kind of spiritual society . . . through love between God and the soul, and in this society the soul was the bride and God was the bridegroom."⁶⁰ In this way, Margery's mystical marriage reveals a continuity between earthly and spiritual marriage theology which seeks to overcome the aggressively maintained separation established by the Church between the two kinds of marriage.

Marriage as Bourgeois Ideology

We have seen that Margery Kempe reconceived mystical marriage to include not only marriage but also marital sexuality, overcoming the medieval inability to link love and sex together into a viable model of marriage. In doing so, Kempe articulates two ideas that we now recognize as characteristic of bourgeois values: the moral valuation of marriage, and the idea that sex is an expression of love. The relationship between *The Book of Margery Kempe* and bourgeois identity is also evident in the parallel between Margery's promotion of mystical marriage and the promotion of marriage in conduct manuals, which were increasingly popular in the late Middle Ages among the middle classes, especially members of the urban patriciate, like Margery Kempe.⁶¹ Margery's mystical marriage to Christ shares much with contemporary conduct manuals, including an emphasis on private and individual interaction that is paradoxically tied to public status.

Although Margery Kempe recognizes that mystical marriage was usually reserved for virgins, she constructs her spiritual experience as a mystical marriage despite being married, reflecting a bourgeois valuation of marriage. Margery is aware that she is exceptional, as she demonstrates when she speaks to Christ about their marriage: "Lord Ihesu, þis maner of leuyng longyth to thy holy maydens." He answers:

3a, dowtyr, trow þow rygth wel þat I lofe wyfes also, and specyal þo wyfys whech woldyn levyn chast . . . for, þow þe state of maydenhode be mor parfyte & mor holy þan þe state of wedewhode, & þe state of wedewhode mor parfyte þan þe state [of] wedlake, зet dowtyr I lofe þe as wel as any mayden in þe world. (48–49)

Although Kempe's Christ acknowledges the traditional role of marriage as the bottom rung in the hierarchy of the three grades of chastity, He also suggests that, at least in some cases, married women were as capable as virgins of achieving sanctity.

The words of Kempe's Christ find an echo in the late fourteenth-century text *Le Ménagier de Paris*, a "treatise on moral and domestic economy," written by a wealthy businessman to instruct his young wife. The author says of "the name of virginity" that "concerning the which name the holy writings of my lord saint Augustine and my lord saint Gregory and many others say and bear witness that all worthy women who have been, are and shall be, of whatsoever estate they be or have been, may be named and called virgins."[62] The author proceeds to use the parable of Saint Matthew about the pearl of great price to describe virginity not as physiological but as a more abstract quality of worthiness:

> By the treasure found in a field and by the precious stone we may understand every good and worthy woman; for in whatsoever estate she be, maid, wife or widow, she may be compared unto the treasure and the precious stone; for she is so good, so pure, so stainless that she is pleasing unto God Who loveth her as a holy virgin, whatsoever be her estate, maid, wife or widow. And certes, a man in whatever estate he be, noble or not, can have no better treasure than a worthy and wise woman.[63]

A correlation is established here between the three grades of chastity used to categorize women—maid, wife, widow—and the three estates that apply to class—noble, cleric, laborer. Just as virginity is no longer given pride of place, so too nobility is unsettled from the top of the pyramid. Like the lesson of Chaucer's *Wife of Bath's Tale,* nobility of character is emphasized over nobility of blood; it is the woman's inner nature—"so good, so pure"— rather than her social or marital status that makes her a "treasure." In a move we can see as characteristic of middle strata values, the hierarchy of status is replaced by a hierarchy of virtue. This passage echoes the broader message of many courtesy books: that virtue comes from behavior rather than estate, a message that may explain the appeal of courtesy books for the urban elite. For example, a passage from "Urbanitatis" states: "In halle, in chambur, ore where þou gon, / Nutur & good maners makeþ man."[64]

Contemporary behavioral manuals like these, popular among the urban elite, were being produced in increasing volume in the late Middle Ages. They sought to regulate behavior previously the subject matter of sermons,

confessional handbooks, and saints' lives, combining moral teaching with
a new interest in manners. The "Lytylle Childrenes Lytil Boke," for example, borrows the authority of clerics when it begins its long discourse
on table manners:

> Lytylle childrene, here ye may lere
> Moche curtesy þat is wrytyne here;
> For clerkis that the vij arteȝ cunne,
> Seyn þat curtesy from hevyn come
> Whan Gabryelle oure lady grette,
> And Eliȝabeth with Mary mette.[65]

Here Gabriel and Elizabeth become advocates not for piety but for polite-
ness, and the biblical exegesis familiar from sermons is enlisted in the service of a middle strata agenda. A similar rivalry with clerical culture for
moral authority can be found in the beginning of Caxton's *The Book of
the Knight of the Tower,* in the book's parable of its own origin, where the
Knight enlists the help of clerics in garnering exempla for his book. Marriage is also the context for moral instruction in this book, since the Knight
is inspired to write it for his young daughters in a courtly vision in which
he remembers his love for his dead wife.

Ownership of conduct manuals was just one of the many ways the
fifteenth-century middle strata showed an increased interest in the regulation of behavior—sexual and otherwise—which had in earlier centuries
been the province of the Church. For example, as Marjorie K. McIntosh
has argued, fifteenth-century local courts, peopled largely by the middling
classes, encroached on the jurisdiction of the ecclesiastical courts and
the higher secular courts by defining misconduct not in moral terms but
as a disruption of community harmony.[66] Both religious and trade guilds,
dominated by the wealthy and influential members of urban society, grew
in size and number throughout this period and sought to control the
conduct of their members. For example, the guild of the Virgin Mary at
Kingston-on-Hull expelled convicted members who were felons or anyone
found to be "a blackguard, lover of law-suits, libeler, bully, night-walker,
destroyer of goods, liar, harlot, excommunicate, or guilty of any other crime
injurious to the good name of the guild and the brethren thereof."[67] Many
guilds punished antisocial behavior themselves, requiring offenders to

submit to arbitration by other guild members. Both Margery and her father belonged to the prestigious Trinity Guild of Lynn. Given this context
in which bourgeois individuals and institutions began to appropriate religious authority for their own social purposes, it is not surprising that
Margery adapts her mystical marriage to God to her bourgeois vocabulary
and experience.

Not only the similarity of Margery's Christ to the voice of contemporary conduct manuals but also her insistence upon her experience as private helps us to understand its bourgeois nature. Indeed, as Lee Patterson
has argued in his discussion of the construction of bourgeois identity in
Chaucer's *Canterbury Tales,* "The focus on the realm of private value defined by its apartness from the public world of event" is something "we have
come to recognize as a central characteristic of bourgeois liberalism."[68] The
association of privacy with Margery's relationship to Christ is first introduced when Kempe describes how, thinking she might die in childbirth,
she summoned her confessor to reveal a secret: "[S]che sent for hyr gostly
fadyr, for sche had a thyng in conscyens whech sche had neuyr schewyd
be-forn þat tyme in alle hyr lyfe" (6–7). When her confessor is too hasty
in his criticism, she is unable to complete her confession and this undis-
closed secret precipitates madness. The aborted exchange with her confessor is replaced by a private exchange with Christ, who appears—not
coincidentally—at her bedside, a space lately identified with her marriage,
"in lyknesse of a man, most semly, most bewtyuows, & most amyable þat
euyr myght be seen wyth mannys eye" (8). Her mystical marriage is meto-
nymically linked to her inner and personal life, and the content of her secret
is never revealed in the whole of her book, in spite of her evident penchant
for self-display. Later, when God offers to marry Margery, He phrases it as
an offer to show her His innermost secrets: "Dowtyr, I wil han þe weddyd
to my Godhede, for I schal schewyn þe my preuyteys & my cownselys" (86).
Here and elsewhere in the narrative, Margery's relationship to Christ is
identified as a sharing of the private, a kind of lay piety that circumvents
the need for priestly intervention.

The imagery of marriage is associated not only with privacy but also with
Margery's developing sense of her individualized selfhood. In a description
that predicts the later scene of mystical marriage, Christ reassures Margery
that he will grant her mystical marriage despite her lack of virginity. He
tells her she will have

a syngulcr louc in Hcuyn, a synguler reward, & a synguler worshep. &, for-as-mech as þu art a mayden in þi sowle, I xal take þe be þe hand in Hevyn & my Modyr be þe oþer hand, & so xalt þu dawnsyn in Hevyn wyth oþer holy maydnes & virgynes, for I may clepyn þe dere a-bowte & myn owyn derworthy derlyng. I xal sey to þe, myn owyn blyssed spowse. (52–53)

The repetition of the word *synguler* indicates that her mystical marriage makes her unique and is not an option available to all. This passage suggests that Margery's singularity and her mystical marriage stem from the purity of her inner self. Virginity and the ability to participate in mystical marriage with God are thus represented not as a physiological state but as a representation of inner virtue, reflecting what Clarissa W. Atkinson has identified as a larger shift in the later Middle Ages from a physical to a moral or spiritual definition of virginity.[69] In this way, Kempe follows the traditional understanding of mystical marriage as a representation of the state of mind ready to receive God, but transforms it into a description of individualized selfhood.

The effect of using mystical marriage as a vocabulary for developing Margery's individuality is intensified by the rare use of the first person narration to describe mystical marriage. Other accounts of mystical marriage, such as the famous vision of mystical marriage experienced by Catherine of Siena, tend to be in the vita, written in third person by the saint's biographer, rather than in the revelations, where the first person is used.[70] As Margery explains in the preface, however, her book is not written as a chronological sequence of events but is structured by her own consciousness: "Thys boke is not wretyn in ordyr, euery thyng aftyr as it were don, but lych as þe mater cam to þe creatur in mend . . ." (5). The book, and evidently her memory, begins with marriage, as the first phrase of the book demonstrates: "Whan þis creatur was xx 3er of age or sumdele mor, sche was maryed to a worschepful burgeys . . ." (6). From here, the narrative moves quickly to the arrival of Christ at her bedside, setting the scene for her later development of mystical marriage. Thus, as Nancy Partner has observed, the narrative voice and structure of *The Book* place marriage at the center of her sense of self.[71]

Although Margery describes her relationship to Christ as private and intimate, and her marriage as linked to the secrets of her inner life,

nonetheless, this construction is also public and social. Kempe's description of her exchange with Christ in which he requests that she wear white
clothes shows the penchant for translating the private and personal into a
public display that is ultimately linked to her social aspirations. When
Margery complains that she is suffering reproof for wearing white clothes,
as he has instructed her to do, Christ compares her situation to one in which
a man chooses to dress his wife to display his wealth: "dowtyr, þe mor
schame, despite, & reprefe þat þu sufferyst for my lofe, þe bettyr I lofe þe,
for I far liche a man þat louyth wel hys wyfe, þe mor enuye þat men han to
hir þe bettyr he wyl arayn hir in despite of hir enmys. & ryth so, dowtyr, xal
I faryn wyth þe" (81).[72] In a characteristically bourgeois move, Margery's virtue, not ostensibly derived from her social or sexual status, is translated
back into a claim to higher social standing, and her religious aspirations
are directly linked to social goals. Here, Margery plays on the common
medieval understanding that dress should fit vocation, which is reflected
in the carefully chosen habits of the different religious orders and in the
sumptuary laws.[73]

Indeed, the fixation of Kempe's Christ on her clothing and food in this
and other passages resembles the obsession with these topics in conduct
manuals consumed by a late medieval bourgeois audience who were concerned with their social standing. For example, in *The Knight of La Tour-
Landry,* the knight devotes a whole section of his book to fasting, and his instructions echo those of Christ in the *Book*: "Affter, my faire doughtres, ye
aught to fast, as long as ye be to wedde, iij dayes a woke, forto holde lowe
youre flesshe, to kepe you chaste and clene, in Goddes seruice. And yef ye
may not fast somoche, fast the Friday in the worshipe of Cristes passion that
he suffered for us." The knight, like Kempe's Christ, also takes an interest
in clothing: "And therfor, faire doughtres, here is a faire ensaumple how
folke aught beter to arraie hem on holydayes in worshipe and for the loue of
God that sendithe alle, and for the loue of hys blessed moder and saintes,
thanne for to plese the sight of worldely peple."[74] Like Margery's Christ in
the passage quoted above, here the knight also claims that the divine audience is more important than the earthly audience for his daughters' clothing, but nonetheless he reminds his readers that clothing and manners, however privately directed, inevitably have public implications. Margery's and
the knight's interest in clothing and appearances should not be belittled as
superficial. As Susan Crane has recently argued of chivalric court culture,

clothing and other aspects of public appearance were not thought "to falsify personal identity but, on the contrary, to establish and maintain it," noting that "a striking congruence, though hardly an equivalence, links this medieval understanding to the postmodern perception that the ongoing gestures of self-presentation amount to the very constitution of the self, not just its secondary modeling."[75] In their interest in clothing and food as constructing the self, conduct books can be seen to reflect this construction, one that was adapted by bourgeois readers such as Margery Kempe, as they adapted other elements of aristocratic culture to their own ends.

Although a private revelation, as early as the first page *The Book of Margery Kempe* claims to be written for the public consumption of readers so that they may be inspired to strengthen their faith. This paradoxical tendency toward the display of the private can also be found in the many moments in her text that are poised between autobiography and theater, such as her account of her marriage to God. Returning to a passage discussed earlier in the chapter, we can see that even the vision of her wedding that takes place in her soul is constructed as a dramatic performance, complete with the heavenly witnesses of

> þe Sone & þe Holy Gost & þe Modyr of Ihesu and alle þe xij apostelys & Seynt Kateryn & Seynt Margarete & many oþer seyntys & holy virgynes wyth gret multitude of awngelys . . . (87)

Although the reader is reminded with the phrases "in hir sowle" and "to hir sowle" that the scene is a vision staged only in the private space of her mind, this inner space is nonetheless populated by a vast audience, possibly one large enough to fill up even the largest church in East Anglia. Not only does Margery allude to a "gret multitude" of angels and "many" saints, but the list format of her description also serves to emphasize the size of her audience. This wedding scene and Margery's depiction of her mystical marriage to God more generally are characterized by a "privateness oriented to an audience," and by a "[s]ubjectivity, [that] as the innermost core of the private, was always already oriented to an audience," which Jürgen Habermas has suggested became characteristic of the bourgeois family in the public sphere.[76] Thus, Margery's construction of mystical marriage can be seen to resemble and perhaps anticipate the later construction of ordinary bourgeois marriage.

The Politics of Marital Sanctity

Margery's elaboration of married bourgeois spirituality, understood by her as a private revelation but manifested publicly by her white clothes and solitary travels, is seen by others in her *Book* to have distinct public and political implications. Lynn Staley notes how her clothes function in the text to dramatize the "hostility aroused by Margery's non-conformity."[77] Staley and others have remarked on the passages in which Margery repeatedly earns the epithet of "Lollard" from townspeople and Church authorities throughout her journeys.[78] Observing that her belief in the sacraments frees her from these accusations of heresy and demonstrates that Margery is not fundamentally a Lollard, these critics have commented on the ways in which Margery triggers concerns about Lollardy, including her refusal to swear, her penchant for preaching as a laywoman, which hints at the superfluity of the clergy, and her familiarity with the vernacular Bible; but few have commented on the centrality of Margery's marital status to the issue of her heresy in the *Book*. An exception is Ruth Nisse, who has shown that the *Book* reflects the ways Lollardy was broadly associated with sexual as well as social disruption in the contemporary cultural imagination.[79] More specifically, I will argue here that by seeming to blur the division between marriage and virginity, Margery's white clothes engender charges of heresy, demonstrating the way marital status functioned in the contemporary debate about the extent of clerical authority.

The link between heresy and marital status is evident in the first question the archbishop poses to her when examining her as a heretic. He asks not about her beliefs in the sacraments or the priesthood, but rather about her sexual status: "'Why gost þu in white? Art þu a mayden?' Sche, knelyng on hir knes be-for hym, seyd, 'Nay, ser, I am no mayden; I am a wife.' He comawndyd hys mene to fettyn a peyr of feterys & seyd sche xulde ben feteryd, for sche was a fals heretyke" (124). The archbishop clearly understands Margery's white clothes to be a sign of her maidenhood.[80] Earlier in the text, when Christ tells Margery to wear white clothes, she initially objects: "yf I go arayd on oþer maner þan oþer chast women don, I drede þat þe pepyl wyl slaw[n]dyr me" (32). This passage suggests that clothes were a familiar marker of sexual and religious status and that there was a widely recognized distinction between the clothing worn by virgins and by chaste married women. In this passage, it is the archbishop's discovery of Margery's transgression of the categories of virgin and wife that generates a specific accusation of heresy.

The archbishop's response to Margery's donning of white clothes shows that he saw her appropriation of the privileges of a virgin by a married woman as a specific political statement about the relative merits of marriage and virginity which implicitly challenged clerical prerogative. As we have seen in the previous chapter, the dismantling of the hierarchy of virginity over marriage was part of the larger Lollard project of eroding the privilege of the clergy. This connection is also made in *The Book of Margery Kempe* since the first specific command the archbishop directs at her after questioning her prerogative to wear white clothes is as follows: "Þow schalt sweryn þat þu [ne] xalt techyn ne chalengyn þe pepil in my diocyse" (125–26). Margery's appropriation of the garb of celibacy is thus linked by the archbishop to a larger appropriation of the role of cleric, and specifically of the role of a preacher. When later asked to explain why she wears white clothes, Margery responds that she does so because the Lord has told her to do so in a revelation (116), and indeed the book had earlier included the Lord's instructions to Margery: "I sey to þe I wyl þat þu were clothys of whyte & non oþer colowr, for þu xal ben arayd aftyr my wyl" (32). Thus, Margery's white clothes become an emblem of her unseating of the division between marriage and celibacy, as well as a sign of her direct relationship to God which does not depend on the mediation of clerical authority.[81]

When the archbishop instructs her not to teach, Margery recognizes that he is commenting both on her appropriation of clerical authority as a layperson, and on her inversion of the gender hierarchy. She responds by insisting that the Gospel provides a precedent for women speaking of God, and then "a gret clerke browt forth a boke & leyd Seynt Powyl for hys party a-geyns hir þat no woman xulde prechyn" (126). For orthodox authorities, there was a direct association between the hierarchy of men over women (understood to be the basis of marriage) and the hierarchy of clerics over laypeople. These hierarchies were seen not only as analogous but also as mutually dependent. This interdependence is clear in the following excerpt from an antiheretical tract written to refute the ideas of Walter Brut. Brut was tried for his heretical beliefs, including his arguments that women could preach:

> Women are not permitted to teach men publicly in church . . . The hierarchy of the Church was ordained and arranged on the pattern of the

hierarchy of Heaven . . . So ought it to be in the hierarchy of the Church that the greater ones, that is, bishops and archbishops, ought by the light and grace of their teaching to purify through intermediaries, that is priests and preachers, to enlighten and help the lesser lay people, namely women, and not vice versa.[82]

Perhaps because of this connection between masculine and clerical authority, the figure of the Lollard woman preacher loomed large in the contemporary imagination, although as Shannon McSheffrey has shown, they were less common in practice.[83]

In addition to invoking specifically the specter of a woman preacher, Margery's clothes appear to signal both the absence of a husband's authority over his wife and also a broader disruption of male authority. After Margery is examined on her principles of belief in another scene, the mayor says to her, "I wil wetyn why þow gost in white clothys, for I trowe þow art comyn hedyr to han a-way owr wyuys fro us & ledyn hem wyth þe" (116). In this way, Margery's white clothes are taken as a threat not just to clerical authority but also to the authority of men over their wives in marriage, on which the mayor understands the social order to depend. As Lynn Staley has noted, the "mayor, the local representative of authority and degree, sees Margery's white clothing as a sign she intends to upset those hegemonies upon which late medieval society was supposedly based and lead away 'our wives.'"[84] In the chapterhouse in York, Margery is asked whether she has her husband's permission to go on pilgrimage by herself: "'Hast þu an husbond?' Sche seyd '3a.' 'Hast þu any lettyr of recorde?'" (122). Orthodox authorities asserted, in addition to limiting her ability to teach, that a woman's movements should be restricted. Another passage from the tract written to refute the ideas of Walter Brut asserts: "She is not able to have the authority of teaching because her sex does not permit her to be free to go out, 'because you will be under the power of the man and he will rule over you': Genesis 3:16."[85] This explains why this question about Margery's marital status and whether or not she has permission from her husband to travel alone on pilgrimage preface a subsequent inquiry by the clerical authorities into her position on the articles of the faith. In this way, the companionate nature of Margery's bourgeois marriage, which allows her relative autonomy, is seen to conflict with ecclesiastical norms.

Although Margery's behavior raises concerns about heresy and repeatedly earns her the epithet "Lollard," when interrogated about her beliefs she answers appropriately, confirming her belief in the sacraments, transubstantiation, the priesthood, and the value of celibacy.[86] When a "gret clerke" tests her by asking how the words *"crescite & multiplicamini"* are to be understood, she gives a conventionally appropriate answer: "Ser, þes wordys ben not vndirstondyn only of begetyng of chyldren bodily, but also be purchasyng of vertu, whech is frute gostly, as be heryng of þe wordys of God, be good exampyl ȝeuyng, be mekenes & paciens, charite & chastite, & swech oþer" (121). As Ruth Nisse has observed, this passage was seen by Dymmok and others to "signal Lollard arguments against vows of continence."[87] Margery openly acknowledges the value of the "gostly" fruit of chastity, suggesting that not everyone should marry and thus rejecting the Lollard argument that priests should marry. Although Margery confirms her belief in the orthodox tenets specifically chosen to identify Lollards, her behavior invokes the broad association of Lollardy in the contemporary imagination with sexual and social transgression, and with political challenges to both Church and state.

Both the mayor and the archbishop, representing respectively secular and religious authority, have trouble responding precisely because she cannot be easily located in what they construct as a binary between heresy and orthodoxy. As John H. Arnold has recently argued in reference to Margery's trials, critical attempts to locate Margery definitively as either orthodox or dissentist are misplaced, since "orthodoxy and heresy were not clearly defined and were certainly not self-evident to learned commentators."[88] Like the N-Town Mary plays discussed in the previous chapter, the *Book of Margery Kempe* draws on the orthodox theology of marriage but calls attention to the aspects of this theology most useful to the promotion of bourgeois lay piety. Thus, despite Margery's own repeated insistence on her "singularity," her promotion of marital sanctity ties her to a broader emergent group: the lay middle strata of late medieval England.

In this, *The Book of Margery Kempe* takes up a place within a range of late medieval texts, authored by and directed to the members of the middle strata, from Gower's *Traitié* to Chaucer's *Franklin's Tale* to the N-Town plays, all of which use marriage to formulate an ideology for members of the emergent middle strata, and to justify their new position within late medieval English society. Although *The Book of Margery Kempe* may arguably constitute the most transgressive attempt to reorder medieval social hierarchy in this group of texts, my readings demonstrate their shared concern with

exploiting the contradictions of existing marital writings and marriage theology to privilege the values of the middle strata, encroaching on the prerogatives of both aristocracy and clergy. As we have seen, the promulgation
of the notion that marriage was especially moral and spiritual, despite its
roots in orthodox theology, was seen as overtly political in the late Middle
Ages when the hierarchy of clergy over laity was under siege by both Lollard extremists and by more moderate constituencies of reformists.

This cultural history is worth remembering, especially at a time when
marriage has again become a source of religious and political controversy.
Recent controversies over gay marriage have led to heated political conflict in American courts and legislatures, with conservative voices attacking
judges and gay and lesbian political organizations for their "activism," for
transforming the "holy" and "private" institution of marriage into a political tool in their effort to reorganize status in American life. The insistence
of critics, especially conservative Protestant religious voices, on defining
marriage as between a man and a woman and as a privileged site of virtuous
behavior, even as the "cornerstone of civilization," as some have argued,
ignores not only the historically troubled relationship between marital
sexuality and Christian spirituality, but also the ways in which marriage
has previously been used as an ideological instrument to promote social
and religious change. Just as writers such as Geoffrey Chaucer, John Gower,
and Margery Kempe found marriage to be a particularly useful institution
with which to reformulate the status quo and to justify a reordering of medieval social hierarchy, so too gays and lesbians in contemporary America
(and elsewhere) are attempting to use marriage to establish and legitimize
their own place in society. At least since the late Middle Ages, marriage has
been "political" and a tool of "activists," and those who look to the past to
find legitimacy for their claims of marriage as part of "traditional family
values" will have difficulty finding a stable starting point. Although this
book is a study of late medieval English literature, I hope that it has offered
insights not only into the intersections between literature, theology, and social change in late fourteenth- and fifteenth-century England, but has also
shown that marriage has historically been a political institution, an ideological locus for the working out of profound religious and social tensions
and ideals.

NOTES

Introduction

1. This phrase comes from a passage in *De Consensu Evangelistarum* in which Augustine discusses the marriage of Mary and Joseph. See *Saint Augustin: Sermon on the Mount, Harmony of the Gospels, Homilies on the Gospels,* trans. William Findlay, 1st ser., vol. 6, *A Select Library of the Nicene and Post-Nicene Fathers of the Christian Church,* ed. Philip Schaff (Grand Rapids: Eerdmans, 1954), 102–3. A fuller citation of this passage can be found in my N-Town chapter.

2. A number of tensions within medieval marriage are aptly traced by Conor McCarthy in *Marriage in Medieval England: Law, Literature and Practice* (Rochester, NY, and Woodbridge, Suffolk: Boydell Press, 2004). Some of the other tensions McCarthy notes are: (1) the contrast between marriage as individual consent and as family alliance, and (2) between the courts' emphasis on verbal formulae and the notion of intentionality inherent in marital consent.

3. *Robert of Brunne's "Handlying Synne,"* ed. Frederick J. Furnivall, part 1, EETS, o.s. 119 (London: Oxford University Press, 1901), 58. There are many examples of this same paradox. One is in a sermon by Honorius of Autun which instructs, "Let husbands love their wives with tender affection; let them keep faith with them in all things . . . In the same way, women should love their husbands deeply, fear them and keep faith with a pure heart." See D. L. d'Avray and M. Tausche, "Marriage Sermons in *Ad Status* Collections of the Central Middle Ages," *Archives d'histoire doctrinale et littéraire du moyen âge* 47 (1980): 78. A fictional version can be found among other commonplaces of marital teaching in Chaucer's *Parson's Tale* (ll. 925–35). See *The Riverside Chaucer,* ed. Larry D. Benson (Boston: Houghton Mifflin, 1987), 321.

4. Mary Poovey, *Uneven Developments: The Ideological Work of Gender in Mid-Victorian England* (Chicago: University of Chicago Press, 1988), 3–4.

5. On the outlawing of clerical marriage, see James A. Brundage, *Law, Sex and Christian Society in Medieval Europe* (Chicago: University of Chicago Press, 1987), esp. 214–22, and Jo Ann McNamara, "Chaste Marriage and Clerical Celibacy," in

Sexual Practices and the Medieval Church, ed. Vern L. Bullough and James Brundage (Buffalo: Prometheus Books, 1982), 22–33.

6. The fuller quotation from 1 Corinthians 7:8–9 (DV) is: "I say to the unmarried and to the widows: It is good for them to continue, even as I. But if they do not contain themselves, let them marry. For it is better to marry than to be burnt."

7. On the marital debt, see Pierre J. Payer, *The Bridling of Desire: Views of Sex in the Later Middle Ages* (Toronto: University of Toronto Press, 1993), 89–97; Brundage, *Law, Sex and Christian Society in Medieval Europe,* esp. 241–42, 358–60, 505–7; Thomas N. Tentler, *Sin and Confession on the Eve of the Reformation* (Princeton: Princeton University Press, 1977), 170–74; and Elizabeth M. Makowski, "The Conjugal Debt and Medieval Canon Law," *Journal of Medieval History* 3 (1977): 99–114.

8. *Saint Augustin: Anti-Pelagian Writings,* trans. Peter Holmes and Robert Ernest Wallis, 1st ser., vol. 5, *A Select Library of the Nicene and Post-Nicene Fathers of the Christian Church,* ed. Philip Schaff (Grand Rapids: Eerdmans, 1956), 268.

9. On the development of the marriage sacrament, see G. Le Bras, "La doctrine du mariage chez les théologiens et les canonistes depuis l'an mille," *Dictionnaire de Théologie Catholique,* ed. A. Vacant et al., vol. 9, II, cols. 2123–2317; Seamus P. Heaney, *The Development of the Sacramentality of Marriage from Anselm of Laon to Thomas Aquinas* (Washington, DC: Catholic University of America Press, 1963); and Edward Schillebeeckx, *Marriage: Human Reality and Saving Mystery,* trans. N. D. Smith (New York: Sheed and Ward, 1965). On marital affection, see John T. Noonan, Jr., "Marital Affection in the Canonists," *Studia Gratiana* 12 (1967): 479–509; and Michael Sheehan, "Maritalis Affecto Revisited," in *The Olde Daunce: Love, Friendship, Sex and Marriage in the Medieval World,* ed. Robert R. Edwards and Stephen Spector (Albany: State University of New York Press, 1991), 32–56.

10. Hugh of Saint Victor, *On the Sacraments of the Christian Faith,* trans. Roy J. Deferrari (Cambridge: Medieval Academy of America, 1951), 326.

11. Dyan Elliott, *Spiritual Marriage: Sexual Abstinence in Medieval Wedlock* (Princeton: Princeton University Press, 1993), 141 and 132–94; McNamara, "Chaste Marriage and Clerical Celibacy"; and Margaret McGlynn and Richard J. Moll, "Chaste Marriage in the Middle Ages: 'It Were to Hire a Greet Merite,'" in *Handbook of Medieval Sexuality,* ed. Vern Bullough and James A. Brundage (New York: Garland, 1996), 103–22.

12. On the increase in chaste marriage vitas, see Marc Glasser, "Marriage in Medieval Hagiography," *Studies in Medieval and Renaissance History,* n.s. 4 (1981): 3–34.

13. Elliott, *Spiritual Marriage,* 12.

14. On consent, see Charles Donahue, Jr., "The Canon Law on the Formation of Marriage and Social Practice in the Later Middle Ages," *Journal of Family History* 8 (1983): 144–58, and "The Policy of Alexander the Third's Consent Theory of Mar-

riage," in *Proceedings of the Fourth International Conference of Medieval Canon Law, Toronto, 21–25 August 1972*, ed. Stephen Kuttner, Monumenta Iuris Canonici, ser. C, subsidia, vol. 5 (Vatican City: Biblioteca Apostolica Vaticana, 1976); Michael M. Sheehan, *Marriage, Family and Law in Medieval Europe: Collected Studies*, ed. James K. Farge (Toronto: University of Toronto Press, 1996); Constance M. Rousseau and Joel T. Rosenthal, eds., *Women, Marriage, and Family in Medieval Christendom: Essays in Memory of Michael M. Sheehan* (Kalamazoo: Medieval Institute Publications, 1998); and John Noonan, "Power to Choose," *Viator* 4 (1973): 419–34.

15. R. H. Helmholz, *Marriage Litigation in Medieval England* (London: Cambridge University Press, 1974), esp. 25–47; Martin Ingram, "Spousal Litigation in the English Ecclesiastical Courts c.1350–c.1640," in *Marriage and Society: Studies in the Social History of Marriage*, ed. R. B. Outhwaite (London: Europa, 1982), 35–57; Michael Sheehan, "The Formation and Stability of Marriage in Fourteenth-Century England: Evidence of an Ely Register," *Mediaeval Studies* 33 (1971): 228–63 (reprinted in *Marriage, Family and Law in Medieval Europe: Collected Studies*, ed. James K. Farge [Toronto: University of Toronto Press, 1996]); and Frederik Pedersen, *Marriage Disputes in Medieval England* (London: Hambledon Press, 2000).

16. On linguisitic performativity, see J. L. Austin, *How to Do Things with Words* (Cambridge: Harvard University Press, 1962). For a more substantial discussion of the relationship between Austinian linguistic performativity and sacramentalism, see my N-Town chapter.

17. Norman P. Tanner, ed., *Heresy Trials in the Diocese of Norwich 1428–31*, Camden 4th ser., vol. 20 (London: Royal Historical Society, 1977), 166. Also see 17, 61, and 160.

18. Ibid., 160.

19. On the family in religious practice, see R. N. Swanson, *Religion and Devotion in Europe c.1215–c.1515* (New York: Cambridge University Press, 1995), esp. 122–26. On the family and East Anglian religious culture, see Gail McMurray Gibson, *The Theater of Devotion: East Anglian Drama and Society in the Late Middle Ages* (Chicago: University of Chicago Press, 1989), 19–46.

20. Gibson, *Theater of Devotion*, 80. For examples of married lay couples and families in the religious art of the late Middle Ages, see Eamon Duffy, *The Stripping of the Altars: Traditional Religion in England 1400–1580* (New Haven: Yale University Press, 1992), esp. figs. 124–26. Baptismal fonts were often decorated with scenes depicting marriage and the other sacraments. See Ann Eljenholm Nicols, *Seeable Signs: The Iconography of the Seven Sacraments 1350–1544* (Rochester: Boydell Press, 1994).

21. Glasser, "Marriage in Medieval Hagiography."

22. See Gail McMurray Gibson, "Saint Anne and the Religion of Childbed: Some East Anglian Texts and Talismans," in *Interpreting Cultural Symbols: Saint Anne in Late Medieval Society*, ed. Kathleen Ashley and Pamela Sheingorn (Athens: University of Georgia Press, 1990), 95–110; Kathleen Ashley, "Image and Ideology: Saint Anne

in Late Medieval Drama and Narrative," in *Interpreting Cultural Symbols,* ed. Ashley and Sheingorn, 111–30, and Introduction, in *Interpreting Cultural Symbols,* ed. Ashley and Sheingorn, 1–68.

23. Sylvia L. Thrupp, *The Merchant Class of Medieval London* (Chicago: University of Chicago Press, 1948), 161–63; and Gibson, *Theater of Devotion,* 67–106.

24. See Duffy, *Stripping of the Altars,* 123–26. Duffy also notes the custom of leaving intensely personal family items such as wedding rings and bed linen to be converted into vestments or ornaments for images and thus used on the altar or in the course of the liturgy, 334.

25. On books of hours, see Roger S. Wieck, *Time Sanctified: The Book of Hours in Medieval Art and Life* (New York: Braziller, 1988).

26. Thrupp, *Merchant Class,* 184.

27. For further discussion of this point, see my N-Town chapter. In "Did the Medieval Laity Know the Canon Law Rules on Marriage? Some Evidence from Fourteenth-Century York Cause Papers," *Mediaeval Studies* 56 (1994): 111–52 (revised in *Marriage Disputes in Medieval England,* 59–84), Frederik Pedersen has shown, based on an analysis of the fourteenth-century York Cause Papers, that laypeople understood, among other technicalities, that marriages were *legal* without a priest. Whereas laypeople may have understood that these marriages were *legal,* this does not mean that they understood them to be *sacramental,* as the evidence from the Norwich trials demonstrates.

28. Thrupp, *Merchant Class,* 299.

29. Paul Strohm, *Social Chaucer* (Cambridge: Harvard University Press, 1989), 1–23.

30. Thrupp, *Merchant Class,* 299.

31. Scholars have argued that the growing number of bourgeois readers and a corresponding increase in the availability of reading material contributed to the growth of conduct literature. Evidence from the manuscripts and ownership of printed editions suggest that even poems written for aristocrats were more widely read by people of the merchant class. In *The Matter of Courtesy: Medieval Courtesy Books and the Gawain-Poet* (Woodbridge, Suffolk: Brewer, 1985), Jonathan Nicholls notes, for example, that a manuscript of the conduct poem "Urbanitas" also contained a copy of a code for freemasons, concluding that manuscript evidence suggests that courtesy literature was more appealing to merchants than aristocrats. Alternatively, conduct manuals may have found a shared audience in gentry and urban elites, reflecting the increasing social mobility between these classes in the late Middle Ages. On this subject, see especially Mark Addison Amos, "'For Manners Make Man': Bourdieu, de Certeau, and the Common Appropriation of Noble Manners in the *Book of Courtesy,*" in *Medieval Conduct,* ed. Kathleen Ashley and Robert L. A. Clark (Minneapolis: University of Minnesota Press, 2001), 23–48. For

a discussion of conduct literature as an expression of bourgeois ethos, see Claire Sponsler, *Drama and Resistance: Bodies, Goods, and Theatricality in Late Medieval England* (Minneapolis: University of Minnesota Press, 1997), 54–55; Seth Lerer, *Chaucer and His Readers: Imagining the Reader in Late-Medieval England* (Princeton: Princeton University Press, 1993), 88–90; Barbara Hanawalt, "'The Childe of Bristowe' and the Making of Middle-Class Adolescence," in *Bodies and Disciplines: Intersections of Literature and History in Fifteenth-Century England,* ed. Barbara A. Hanawalt and David Wallace (Minneapolis: University of Minnesota Press, 1996); Felicity Riddy, "Mother Knows Best: Reading Social Change in a Courtesy Text," *Speculum* (1996): 66–86; Kathleen Ashley, "The Miroir des Bonnes Femmes: Not for Women Only?" in *Medieval Conduct,* ed. Ashley and Clark, 86–105; and Anna Dronzek, "Gendered Theories of Education in Fifteenth-Century Conduct Books," in *Medieval Conduct,* ed. Ashley and Clark, 135–59.

32. *English Guilds,* ed. Joshua Toulmin Smith, EETS, o.s. 40 (London: Trübner, 1870), 22–23.

33. *The Babees Book,* ed. F. J. Furnivall, EETS, o.s. 32 (London: Trübner, 1868), 187.

34. See Christopher Dyer, *Standards of Living in the Later Middle Ages: Social Change in England c. 1200-1520* (Cambridge: Cambridge University Press, 1989), 13–14; and *Statutes of the Realm* (London: Eyre and Strahan, 1810–28), 1:380.

35. *Rotuli Parliamentorum,* ed. John Strachey (London, 1767–77), 2:278. See discussion in Strohm, *Social Chaucer,* 5–7.

36. Dyer, *Standards of Living,* 27–48.

37. Nigel Saul, *Knights and Esquires: The Gloucestershire Gentry in the Fourteenth Century* (Oxford: Clarendon Press, 1981), 25, 241, and more broadly, 205–53. Also see M. M. Postan, *Essays on Medieval Agriculture and General Problems of the Medieval Economy* (New York: Cambridge University Press, 1973), 186–213.

38. Saul, *Knights and Esquires,* 25.

39. E. W. Ives, *The Common Lawyers of Pre-Reformation England* (New York: Cambridge University Press, 1983), 32.

40. R. L. Storey, "Gentleman-Bureaucrats," in *Profession, Vocation and Culture in Later Medieval England: Essays in Memory of A. R. Myers,* ed. Cecil H. Clough (Liverpool: University of Liverpool Press, 1982), 90–129; and Chris Given-Wilson, *The English Nobility in the Late Middle Ages: The Fourteenth-Century Political Community* (New York: Routledge and Kegan Paul, 1987), 17.

41. *Early English Meals and Manners,* ed. Frederick J. Furnivall, EETS, o.s. 32 (London: Oxford University Press, 1868), 271.

42. *The Babees Book,* ed. Furnivall, 119.

43. Thrupp, *Merchant Class,* esp. 155–287; Lee Patterson, *Chaucer and the Subject of History* (Madison: University of Wisconsin Press, 1991), 330–31; and Amos, "For Manners Make Man."

44. Although not focused on genre per se, Glenn Burger has recently made a similar argument in *Chaucer's Queer Nation* (Minneapolis: University of Minnesota Press, 2003), arguing that what lies behind the focus on the middle strata in the *Canterbury Tales* "is the construction of 'bourgeois' lay models of identity as copies of clerical (especially monastic) and aristocratic 'originals.' . . . [One of] the most notable locations for such copying in the *Canterbury Tales* [is] . . . the idea of companionate marriage" (xxi).

45. Michel de Certeau, *The Practice of Everyday Life,* trans. Steven Rendall (Berkeley: University of California Press, 1984), xiii, 32, and 166.

46. Fredric Jameson, *The Political Unconscious: Narrative as a Socially Symbolic Act* (Ithaca: Cornell University Press, 1981), 105.

47. See Strohm, *Social Chaucer,* 47–83. Although scholars have long tried to place Chaucer as either aristocratic or bourgeois, Strohm argues that "Chaucer's social grouping was not simply an uneasy amalgam of aristocratic and merchantile elements, but was itself a distinct segment of society" (10).

48. Saul, *Knights and Esquires,* 25, 241, and more broadly, 205–53. Also see Postan, *Essays on Medieval Agriculture,* 186–213.

49. C. S. Lewis, *The Allegory of Love: A Study in Medieval Tradition* (New York: Oxford University Press, 1936), 13–14; and Georges Duby, *Medieval Marriage: Two Models from Twelfth-Century France,* trans. Elborg Forster (Baltimore: Johns Hopkins University Press, 1978).

50. Henry Ansgar Kelly, *Love and Marriage in the Age of Chaucer* (Ithaca: Cornell University Press, 1975).

51. Neil Cartlidge, *Medieval Marriage: Literary Approaches, 1100-1300* (Cambridge: D. S. Brewer, 1997); and Kathryn Jacobs, *Marriage Contracts from Chaucer to the Renaissance Stage* (Gainesville: University Press of Florida, 2001).

52. For a classic discussion of the medieval concept of *sponsus regni* which underlies much of this discussion, see E. H. Kantorowicz, *The King's Two Bodies: A Study in Medieval Political Theology* (Princeton: Princeton University Press, 1957), 221–26.

53. David Wallace, *Chaucerian Polity: Absolutist Lineages and Associational Forms in England and Italy* (Stanford: Stanford University Press, 1997), 295.

54. Louise Olga Fradenburg, *City, Marriage, Tournament: Arts of Rule in Late Medieval Scotland* (Madison: University of Wisconsin Press, 1991), xiv.

55. She argues that the depiction of marriage in French works on the household can be linked to Charles V's use of sacramental marriage theology to allow him "both a priestly function and a husband's authority and power," whereas English texts reflect Richard II's more embattled kingship, constructing "power as a bond of duty." See Lynn Staley, *Languages of Power in the Age of Richard II* (University Park: Pennsylvania State University Press, 2005), 85, 267, and 271.

56. Although in essence a bond between individuals, as M. Teresa Tavormina has argued of medieval marriage in *Kindly Similitude: Marriage and Family in Piers*

Plowman (Cambridge: D. S. Brewer, 1995), "it was a private bond with significant public ramifications," a claim she explains as follows: "The multiple interests that marriage brought into play contributed largely to these public aspects of marriage; family, neighbors, friends, associates, patrons and lords might all have some stake in a marriage, in various emotional, legal, social and political ways" (45). Like Tavormina, I draw on legal and social history and a combination of sermons, theology, and liturgy, as well as other literary texts to supply the contexts for my readings.

57. Sarah Beckwith, *Signifying God: Social Relation and Symbolic Act in the York Corpus Christi Plays* (Chicago: University of Chicago Press, 2001); and Miri Rubin, *Corpus Christi: The Eucharist in Medieval Culture* (New York: Cambridge University Press, 1991).

58. Beckwith shows, for example, how the organization of the York Corpus Christi play was "one of the political mechanisms of labor regulation in the city"; *Signifying God,* xvi and 23–55.

59. Burger, *Chaucer's Queer Nation,* 45.

60. George Lyman Kittredge, "Chaucer's Discussion of Marriage," *Modern Philology* 9 (1911–12): 435–67; reprinted in *Chaucer and His Poetry* (Cambridge: Harvard University Press, 1915).

61. In his discussion of the *Merchant's Tale,* Patterson argues that marriage was an instance of the realm of the private and of "socially undetermined subjectivity" which he links to bourgeois ideology. See Patterson, *Chaucer and the Subject of History,* 322–66. A more overt link between marriage and the middle strata ("gentils," composed of, in my terms, the upper ranks of the middle strata) is made by Burger in *Chaucer's Queer Nation.*

62. None of the other tales of the "marriage group" are as centrally concerned with sacramental marriage. Whereas the *Wife of Bath's Prologue* and *Tale* both end with an image of marital mutuality, most of her text is consumed by issues of marital sovereignty and the promotion of marital sexuality which are antithetical to the sacramental model. Although January's image of marriage as a "paradys" in the *Merchant's Tale* might arguably be tied to an idealized version of sacramental marriage, the tale's ascription of this vision to the repulsive and self-deceiving January makes it impossible to take seriously. Finally, the *Clerk's Tale*—the fourth member of Kittredge's group—presents a politicized image of marriage as governance that the *Franklin's Tale,* with its emphasis on marital mutuality, is often seen deliberately to counter.

63. Elizabeth Porter, "Gower's Ethical Microcosm and Political Macrocosm," in *Gower's* Confessio Amantis*: Responses and Reassessments,* ed. A. J. Minnis (Cambridge: D. S. Brewer, 1983), 135–62; and Staley, *Languages of Power,* esp. 339–55.

64. For the term *public poetry,* see Anne Middleton, "The Idea of Public Poetry in the Reign of Richard II," *Speculum* 53 (1978): 94–114.

Chapter One.   *Married Friendship*

1. See, for example, R. M. Lumiansky, *Of Sondry Folk: The Dramatic Principle in the Canterbury Tales* (Austin: University of Texas Press, 1955), 180–93. For an early influential example of this position, see George L. Kittredge, *Chaucer and His Poetry* (Cambridge: Harvard University Press, 1915), 204.

2. Henrik Specht, *Chaucer's Franklin in the* Canterbury Tales*: The Social and Literary Background of a Chaucerian Character* (Copenhagen: Akademik Forlag, 1981). For a similar argument, see Gordon Hall Gerould, "The Social Status of Chaucer's Franklin," *PMLA* 41 (1926): 262–79.

3. See Nigel Saul, "The Social Status of Chaucer's Franklin: A Reconsideration," *Medium Aevum* 52 (1983): 10–26; and Paul Strohm, *Social Chaucer* (Cambridge: Harvard University Press, 1989), 106–9.

4. Rodney Hilton, "Warriors and Peasants," *New Left Review* 83 (1974): 83–94; J. L. Bolton, *The Medieval English Economy, 1150-1500,* 2nd ed. (London: Dent, 1980), 246–86; papers collected in *The Transition from Feudalism to Capitalism,* ed. Rodney Hilton (London: New Left Books, 1976); and Lee Patterson, *Chaucer and the Subject of History* (Madison: University of Wisconsin Press, 1991), 324–27.

5. Kathryn Jacobs, "The Marriage Contract of the *Franklin's Tale*: The Remaking of Society," *The Chaucer Review* 20 (1985): 132–43.

6. Lynn Staley, *Languages of Power in the Age of Richard II* (University Park: Pennsylvania State University Press, 2005), 1–73, Lee Patterson, "Court Politics and the Invention of Literature: The Case of Sir John Clanvowe," in *Culture and History 1350-1600: Essays on English Communities, Identities and Writing,* ed. David Aers (Detroit: Wayne State University Press, 1992), 7–41; Paul Strohm, "Politics and Poetics: Usk and Chaucer in the 1380s," in *Literary Practice and Social Change in Britain, 1380-1530,* ed. Lee Patterson (Berkeley: University of California Press, 1990), 83–112.

7. C. Stephen Jaeger, *Ennobling Love: In Search of a Lost Sensibility* (Philadelphia: University of Pennsylvania Press, 1999), and *The Origins of Courtliness: Civilizing Trends and the Formation of Courtly Ideals 939-1210* (Philadelphia: University of Pennsylvania Press, 1985).

8. Jaeger, *Ennobling Love,* 6, 5, ix.

9. Richard Firth Green uses this same term, *ennobling love,* in *Poets and Princepleasers: Literature in the English Court in the Late Middle Ages* (Toronto: University of Toronto Press, 1980), 124. On the relevance of this paradigm to later medieval texts, see especially Larry D. Benson, "Courtly Love and Chivalry in the Later Middle Ages," in *Fifteenth-Century Studies: Recent Essays,* ed. Robert F. Yeager (Hamden, CT: Archon Books, 1984), 241. In his classic account, Maurice Keen deems ennobling love a crucial element of the "methodology of chivalry." See *Chivalry* (New Haven: Yale University Press, 1984), 102–24.

10. Quoted and translated in Benson, "Courtly Love and Chivalry in the Later Middle Ages," 241. For the French, see Mareschal Bouicicault, *Livre des faits du Mareschal de Bouicicault,* in *Collection complète des mémoirs relatifs à l'histoire de France,* ed. Claude B. Petitot (Paris: Foucault, 1825), 6:393.

11. Geoffrey Chaucer, *The Riverside Chaucer,* ed. Larry D. Benson (Boston: Houghton Mifflin, 1987), 178. All other references will be to this edition and will be cited in the text.

12. Stephen Knight, "The Social Function of Middle English Romances," in *Medieval Literature: Criticism, Ideology and History,* ed. David Aers (New York: St. Martin's Press, 1986), 99–122. Examples of this romance paradigm cited by Knight include Chrétien de Troyes' twelfth-century *Le Chevalier au Lion* and Malory's fifteenth-century "Tale of Gareth."

13. Margaret Adlum Gist, *Love and War in the Middle English Romances* (Philadelphia: University of Pennsylvania Press, 1947), esp. 31–35. Gist's examples include *King Horn* and the late fourteenth-century or early fifteenth-century *Sultan of Babylon.*

14. Even later at the end of the tale when Pluto causes Arcite's death at the request of Saturn and Theseus substitutes Palamon for his dead friend, Emily is still given no voice in the narrative. Instead, she is instructed by Theseus, "That ye shul of youre grace upon hym rewe, / And taken hym for housbonde and for lord" (3080–81), despite the fact that her opposition to marriage is clear earlier when she prays to Diana to help her remain chaste (2294–2330).

15. David Aers, *Chaucer, Langland and the Creative Imagination* (Boston: Routledge & Kegan Paul, 1980), 161.

16. "Sir Launfal," in *The Middle English Breton Lays,* ed. Anne Laskaya and Eve Salisbury (Kalamazoo: Medieval Institute Publications, 2001), 220. Since the Franklin identifies his own tale as a Breton lai, I have drawn most of my examples of romance from the eight surviving Middle English examples of this subgenre, several of which are from the Auchinleck manuscript thought to be known to Chaucer. Most scholars now agree that Chaucer drew on a general familiarity with the genre of the Breton lai rather than on any specific lost lai. In *Sir Thopas,* Chaucer apparently parodied popular tail-rhyme romances, such as *Sir Launfal,* illustrating his familiarity with the genre. The fact that Thomas Chestre's version of *Sir Launfal* drew on earlier Middle English versions of the tale suggests a continuous telling of this tale from the time of Marie de France to Chaucer. See Laskaya and Salisbury, 201. For a summary of the relevant scholarship on the *Franklin's Tale,* and the Breton lai, see Robert R. Edwards, "The Franklin's Tale," in *Sources and Analogues of* The Canterbury Tales, ed. Robert M. Correale and Mary Hamel (Cambridge: D. S. Brewer, 2002), 1:212–13.

17. Andreas Capellanus, *The Art of Courtly Love,* trans. John Jay Parry (New York: Columbia University Press, 1990), 185. An alternate translation is: "Love does

not usually survive being noised abroad." *Andreas Capellanus on Love,* ed. P. G. Walsh (London: Duckworth, 1982), 283.

18. Geoffroi de Charney, *The Book of Chivalry,* trans. Elspeth Kennedy, in *The Book of Chivalry of Geoffroi de Charny: Text, Context and Translation,* ed. and trans. Richard E. Kaeuper and Elspeth Kennedy (Philadelphia: University of Pennsylvania Press, 1996), 119.

19. On medieval scientific treatises addressing lovesickness, see Mary Frances Wack, *Lovesickness in the Middle Ages: The* Viaticum *and Its Commentaries* (Philadelphia: University of Pennsylvania Press, 1990).

20. Marie de France, "Equitan," in *The Lais of Marie de France,* trans. Robert Hanning and Joan Ferrante (Durham: Labyrinth Press, 1978), 61. "Equitan" is listed as an example of the type of lai Chaucer drew on in the *Franklin's Tale* in Germaine Dempster and J. S. P. Tatlock, "The Franklin's Tale," in *Sources and Analogues of Chaucer's Canterbury Tales,* ed. W. F. Bryan and Germaine Dempster (New York: Humanities Press, 1958), 387–90.

21. *The Sarum Missal in English,* trans. Frederick E. Warren, part 2 (London: De La More Press, 1911), 146.

22. On the importance of dilation to *ars praedicandi,* see James J. Murphy, *Rhetoric in the Middle Ages: A History of Rhetorical Theory from Saint Augustine to the Renaissance* (Berkeley: University of California Press, 1974), 269–355.

23. D. L. d'Avray and M. Tausche, "Marriage Sermons in *Ad Status* Collections of the Central Middle Ages," *Archives d'histoire doctrinale et littéraire du moyen âge,* 47 (1981), 106: "Ubi autem dicitur in Gen. quod tulit dominus unam de costis Adam, et ex illa formavit mulierem, datur intelligi quod voluit dominus uxorem esse sociam mariti sui, non dominam, unde de capite non formavit eam, non ancillam, unde non est formata de pedibus viri, unde non debet conculcari nec contempni a viro, sed eam diligere tanquam se ipsum, cum sint una caro" (their translation).

24. D'Avray and Tausche, "Marriage Sermons." For other examples, see this article and B. Hauréau, *Notices et extraits de quelques manuscrits latin de la Bibliothèque Nationale* (Paris: Librairie Klincksieck, 1890), 189–202.

25. *The Riverside Chaucer,* 321. On the similarity of marriage sermons to each other and their important role in disseminating marriage teachings to the laity, see D. L. d'Avray, *Medieval Marriage Sermons: Mass Communication in a Culture Without Print* (New York: Oxford University Press, 2001), 1–30.

26. Susan Crane, *Gender and Romance in Chaucer's* Canterbury Tales (Princeton: Princeton University Press, 1994), 93. For a similar analysis of this passage, see Angela Jane Weisl, *Conquering the Reign of Femeny: Gender and Genre in Chaucer's Romance* (Cambridge: D. S. Brewer, 1995), 108.

27. Guillaume de Lorris and Jean de Meun, *The Romance of the Rose,* trans. Charles Dahlberg (Hanover, NH: University Press of New England, 1983), 170.

Amor ne peut durer ne vivre,

s'el n'est en queur franc et delivre.

Por ce revoit l'en ensement,

de touz cues qui prumierement

par amors amer s'entreseulent,

quant puis espouser s'entreveulent,

enviz peut entr'eus avenir

qua ja s'i puisse amors tenir;

car cil, quant par amors amoit,

serjant a cele se clamoit

qui sa mestresse soloit estre:

or se claime seigneur et mestre

seur li, que sa dame ot clamee

quant ele iert par amors amee.

Guillaume de Lorris and Jean de Meun, *Le Roman de la Rose,* ed. Félix Lecoy (Paris: Editions Champion, 1966), 2:37. On the Franklin's homily as a restatement of Amis's advice in the *Roman de la Rose,* see Robert P. Miller, "The Epicurean Homily on Marriage by Chaucer's Franklin," *Mediaevalia* 6 (1980): 151–86.

28. Aers, *Chaucer, Langland and the Creative Imagination,* 160–69.

29. Kittredge, "Chaucer's Discussion of Marriage," *Modern Philology* 9 (1912): 435–67.

30. For representative examples of readings in this vein, see Miller, "The Epicurean Homily"; Russell A. Peck, "Sovereignty and the Two Worlds of the *Franklin's Tale,*" *Chaucer Review* 1 (1967): 262; and Gary D. Schmidt, "The Marriage Irony in the Tales of the Merchant and Franklin," in *Portraits of Marriage in Literature,* ed. Anne C. Hargrove and Maurine Magliocco (Macomb: Western Illinois University Press, 1984), 97–106.

31. Weisl, *Conquering the Reign of Femeny,* 107.

32. Judith Ferster, "Interpretation and Imitation in Chaucer's *Franklin's Tale,*" in *Medieval Literature,* ed. Aers, 148–68.

33. I borrow these terms from Seymour Chatman, *Story and Discourse: Narrative Structure in Fiction and Film* (Ithaca: Cornell University Press, 1978), esp. chap. 2.

34. For the literary mode of representing "reality" in a text as an index of cultural values, see Erich Auerbach, *Mimesis: The Representation of Reality in Western Literature,* trans. Willard R. Trask (Princeton: Princeton University Press, 1953), esp. 23.

35. Cited in Eric Kooper, "Loving the Unequal Equal: Medieval Theologians and Marital Affection," in *The Olde Daunce: Love, Friendship, Sex and Marriage in the Medieval World,* ed. Robert R. Edwards and Stephen Spector (Albany: State University of New York Press, 1991), 50. For a similar use of the vocabulary of friendship to describe

marriage, see the beginning of Augustine's influential treatise *De bono coniugali*: "Forasmuch as each man is part of the human race, and human nature is something social, and hath for a great and natural good, the power also of friendship . . . Therefore the first natural bond of human society is man and wife." *Saint Augustin: On the Holy Trinity, Doctrinal Treatises, Moral Treatises,* trans. Peter Holmes and Robert Ernest Wallis, 1st ser., vol. 3, *A Select Library of the Nicene and Post-Nicene Fathers of the Christian Church,* ed. Philip Schaff (Buffalo: Christian Literature Co., 1956), 399.

36. Thomas Aquinas, *Commentary on the* Nicomachean Ethics, trans. C. I. Litzinger (Chicago: Henry Regnery, 1964), 2:764.

37. Sermon 59 in *On the Song of Songs,* trans. Kilian Walsh and Irene M. Edmonds (Kalamazoo: Cistercian Publications, 1979), 3:121.

38. *Aelred of Rievaulx, Spiritual Friendship,* trans. Mary Eugenia Laker (Kalamazoo: Cistercian Publications, 1974), 63. On the phrase "loving the unequal equal," see Kooper, "Loving the Unequal Equal." On the relevance of this passage to the *Franklin's Tale,* see James I. Wimsatt, "Reason, Machaut, and the Franklin," in *The Olde Daunce,* ed. Edwards and Spector, 205. On the relationship between friendship and marriage in the *Franklin's Tale,* see Robert Lane, "The Franklin's Tale: Of Marriage and Meaning," in *Portraits of Marriage in Literature,* ed. Hargrove and Magliocco, 107–24.

39. Mutuality was also considered a more general characteristic of friendship, even apart from discussions of marriage as an instance of friendship. In his commentary on Aristotle's *Nicomachean Ethics,* for example, Aquinas asserts, "Friendship is a kind of equality precisely as it requires mutual love . . . in friendship the act of one is not sufficient but the acts of two mutually loving one another must occur" (*Commentary on the* Nicomachean Ethics, 727). Aquinas emphasizes mutuality in his commentary on *The Ethics*: "We say friendship is benevolence with corresponding requital inasmuch as the one loving is loved in return, for friendship has a kind of exchange of love after the manner of commutative justice" (*Commentary on the* Nicomachean Ethics, 709).

40. See for example, Cicero, *De Senectute, De Amicitia, De Divinatione,* trans. William Armstead Falconer (1923; rpt. Cambridge: Harvard University Press, 1996), 191.

41. Aquinas, *Commentary on the* Nicomachean Ethics, 703.

42. Ibid., 726.

43. Aelred of Rievaulx, *Spiritual Friendship,* 179.

44. In "Of Time and Tide in the *Franklin's Tale,*" *Philological Quarterly* 45 (1966): 688–711, Chauncey Wood explores the possibility that Aurelius did not use magic to remove the rocks but simply predicted the tide. On the tension between Dorigen's marriage vow and her promise to Aurelius, see Alan T. Gaylord, "The Promises in the *Franklin's Tale,*" *ELH* 31 (1964): 331–65.

45. Aelred of Rievaulx, *Spiritual Friendship,* 183.

46. *Romance of the Rose,* trans. Dahlberg, 103. "Ceste fet connoistre et savoir, / des qu'il ont perdu leur avoir, / de quele amor cil les amoient / qui leur amis devant

estoient; / car cels que bencürtez donc, / maleürtez si les estone / qu'il devienent tuit anemi." *Le Roman de la Rose,* ed. Lecoy, 1:150. For the influence of Aelred's writings on Jean de Meun, see Lionel J. Friedman, "Jean de Meun and Ethelred of Rievaulx," *L'Esprit Createur* 2 (1962): 135–41.

47. Cicero, *De Amicitia,* 131–32. For similiar passages, see Aelred of Rievaulx, *Spiritual Friendship,* 173, 179.

48. See, for example, Peter of Blois, "Tract de Amicitia Christiana": "In his verbis, sicut ait B. Ambrosius, dedit nobis formam amicitia, quam sequamur, ut secreta nostra revelemus invicem, et amicorum voluntatem alterutram faciamus" (PL 207:887).

49. Cicero, *De Amicitia,* 155.

50. Ibid., 157.

51. Jerome, "Adversus Jovinanum," in *St. Jerome: Letters and Select Works,* trans. W. H. Fremantle, 2nd ser., vol. 6, *A Select Library of the Nicene and Post-Nicene Fathers of the Christian Church,* ed. Philip Schaff and Henry Wace (New York: Christian Literature Co., 1893), 383. This passage from Jerome is especially relevant to the Franklin's tale, since a later passage of the same piece of writing is a plausible source for Dorigen's complaint. See Dempster and Tatlock, "The Franklin's Tale," in *Sources and Analogues of Chaucer's Canterbury Tales,* ed. Bryan and Dempster, 395; and Edwards, "The Franklin's Tale," in *Sources and Analogues of the Canterbury Tales,* ed. Correale and Hamel, 256–65.

52. D'Avray and Tausche, "Marriage Sermons," 78. For another classic example of this tension, see Hugh's *De Sacramentis*: "For since [woman] was given as a companion [*socia*], not a servant or a mistress, she was to be produced not from the highest or from the lowest part but from the middle . . . She was made from the middle, that she might be proved to have been made for equality of association. Yet in a certain way she was inferior to him, in that she was made from him, so that she might always look to him as to her beginning and cleaving to him indivisibly might not separate herself from that association which ought to have been established reciprocally." See *On the Sacraments of the Christian Faith,* trans. Roy J. Deferrari (Cambridge: Medieval Academy of America, 1951), 329.

53. In "Honour in Chaucer," *Essays and Studies* 26 (1973): 1–19, D. S. Brewer also links Dorigen's trouthe to private value, but, unlike me, he sees this as consistent with chivalric norms. In *A Crisis of Truth: Literature and Law in Ricardian England* (Philadelphia: University of Pennsylvania Press, 1999), 332, Richard Firth Green argues that in the Middle Ages, "promises constituted a kind of private law" so that Dorigen's conflicting obligations would have been seen to be her and her husband's individual concern.

54. On friendship and the monastic tradition, see Brian Patrick McGuire, *Friendship and Community: The Monastic Experience 350–1250* (Kalamazoo: Cistercian Publications, 1988); Jean Leclerq, *Monks and Love in Twelfth-Century France* (Oxford:

Clarendon Press, 1979); Reginald Hyatte, *The Arts of Friendship: The Idealization of Friendship in Medieval and Early Renaissance Literature* (New York: E. J. Brill, 1994), 43–86; and for a general introduction to the theory of Christian friendship, see Adele Fiske, "Paradisus Homo Amicus," *Speculum* 40 (1965): 436–59.

55. Gervase Mathew, "Ideals of Friendship," in *Patterns of Love and Courtesy*, ed. John Lawlor (Evanston: Northwestern University Press, 1966), 45–53. Mathew notes that this English romance was composed c. 1200 but maintained its popularity through the fifteenth century. The fact that *Amis and Amiloun* is found in the Auchinleck manuscript suggests that it may be particularly relevant to Chaucer. On male friendship in romance and in the courtly tradition, also see Hyatte, *The Arts of Friendship*, 87–135; and Lee Patterson, *Negotiating the Past: The Historical Understanding of Medieval Literature* (Madison: University of Wisconsin Press, 1987), 132–41.

56. Cicero, *De Amicitia*, 207.

57. See, for example, Jerome's letter to Rufinus, often cited in the friendship literature: "Let those who will, allow gold to dazzle them and be bourne along in splendor, their very baggage glittering with gold and silver. Love is not to be purchased, and affection has no price. The Friendship which can cease has never been real." See *St. Jerome: Letters and Select Works*, ed. Fremantle, 6.

58. Jaeger, *Ennobling Love*, 13.

59. See Eve Kosofsky Sedgwick's groundbreaking book *Between Men: English Literature and Male Homosocial Desire* (New York: Columbia University Press, 1985), esp. 1–20. On the relevance of the term *homosocial* to the construction of "ennobling love" see Jaeger, *Ennobling Love*, 15. Although most critics agree that medieval male friendships, including monastic friendships, had an erotic dimension, they disagree on the utility and accuracy of applying the term *homosexual* to these medieval writings. For a landmark argument in favor of using the term, see John Boswell, *Christianity, Social Tolerance and Homosexuality* (Chicago: University of Chicago Press, 1980). For one example of an opposing viewpoint, see McGuire, *Friendship and Community*. Although monastic authorities made regulations to preclude sexual relations between monks, and specific sex acts such as sodomy were highly punishable by Church law, nonetheless friendship was used to describe intense bonds of friendship between men that often seemed to include an erotic or sexual dimension. On the politics of and the penalties for what we would now call homosexual acts, see Michael Goodich, *The Unmentionable Vice: Homosexuality in the Later Medieval Period* (New York: Dorset Press, 1979).

60. On the overlapping of *amicitia* and *amor*, see Boswell, *Christianity, Social Tolerance and Homosexuality*, 46–47; McGuire, *Friendship and Community*, xv; Peter Drake, *Medieval Latin and the Rise of the European Love-Lyric* (Oxford: Clarendon Press, 1965), 1:232; and Patterson, *Negotiating the Past*, 132–37.

61. See Guillaume de Lorris and Jean de Meun, *La Roman de la Rose*, trans. Dahlberg. For the *Miroir de Mariage*, see Eustache Deschamps, *Oeuvres complètes de*

Eustache Deschamps, ed. Auguste H. E. Queux de Saint-Hilaire and Gaston Raynaud (Paris: Firmin Didot, 1878–1903; rpt. New York: Johnson Reprint Corp., 1966), vol. 9. For "Against Marrying," see *Gawain on Marriage: The Textual Tradition of the De Coniuge Non Ducenda with Critical Edition and Translation,* ed. A. G. Rigg (Toronto: Pontifical Institute of Mediaeval Studies, 1986).

62. *Andreas Capellanus on Love,* ed. Walsh, 289. On rivalry in courtship as a threat to male friendship, see Cicero's *De Amicitia,* 144–45.

63. Compare Giovanni Boccaccio, *Il Filocolo,* trans. Donald Cheney (New York: Garland, 1985), 254 ff. Identified as a source by Dempster and Tatlock in *Sources and Analogues of Chaucer's* Canterbury Tales, 377–83, and by Robert R. Edwards in *Sources and Analogues of the* Canterbury Tales, ed. Correale and Hamel, 1:221–38.

64. Thomas Aquinas, *Commentary on Aristotle's* Nicomachean Ethics, trans. C. I. Litzinger (Chicago: Regnery, 1964: repr., Notre Dame, IN: Dumb Ox Books, 1993), 757. On politics and friendship, see Michael Pakaluk, "Political Friendship," in *The Changing Face of Friendship,* ed. Leroy S. Rouner (Notre Dame, IN: University of Notre Dame Press, 1994), 197–213; John M. Cooper, "Political Animals and Civic Friendship," in *Friendship: A Philosophical Reader,* ed. Neera Kapur Badhwar (Ithaca: Cornell University Press, 1993), 303–26. On Aristotle's theory of friendship, see Paul Schollmeier, *Other Selves: Aristotle on Personal and Political Friendship* (Albany: State University of New York Press, 1994), esp. 75–96; and Suzanne Stern-Gillet, *Aristotle's Philosophy of Friendship* (Albany: State University of New York Press, 1995), esp. 147–77.

65. *Nicomachean Ethics,* 757–58. Aquinas comments on this passage that there is no justice under tyranny because "the tyrant does not strive for the common good, but for his own" (*Commentary,* 760).

66. John of Salisbury, *Policraticus,* ed. Cary J. Nederman (New York: Cambridge University Press, 1990), 25.

67. Aristotle's *Nicomachean Ethics* and his *Politics* and other classical writings influenced Florentine thinkers in their formulation of political theory on civic values. See Quentin Skinner, *The Foundations of Modern Political Thought,* vol. 1 (Cambridge: Cambridge University Press, 1978), 27; J. G. A. Pocock, *The Machiavellian Moment: Florentine Political Thought and the Atlantic Republican Tradition* (Princeton: Princeton University Press, 1975); and Richard C. Trexler, *Public Life in Renaissance Florence* (New York: Academic Press, 1980), 18. For the influence of Florentine political thought on Chaucer's *Canterbury Tales,* see David Wallace, *Chaucerian Polity: Absolutist Lineages and Associational Forms in England and Italy* (Stanford: Stanford University Press, 1997).

68. Quoted in Antony Black, *Guilds and Civil Society in European Political Thought from the Twelfth Century to the Present* (Ithaca: Cornell University Press, 1984), 78.

69. On the lack of precision in the medieval political vocabulary used to describe community, see Jeannine Quillet, "Community, Counsel and Representation," in *The Cambridge History of Medieval Political Thought c. 350–1450,* ed. J. H. Burns (New

York: Cambridge University Press, 1988), 520–72. "Common profit," for example, an extension of the classical concept of *res publica,* loosely came to mean the interests of the whole community, as opposed to those of an individual or a particular group. This term was used to justify a wide variety of political interests, all of which claimed to be operating in the interests of the people, from justifying the traditional three estates of society to justifying royal behavior to justifying the interests of a more inclusive government.

70. Saul, "Social Status," 17–19.

71. Gerald Harriss, "Political Society and the Growth of Government in Late Medieval England," *Past and Present* 138 (1993): 33; and Michael Bennett, "Careerism in Late Medieval England," in *People, Politics and Community in the Later Middle Ages* (New York: St. Martin's Press, 1987), 19–39.

72. Saul, "Social Status," 19.

73. Rodney H. Hilton, *The English Peasantry in the Later Middle Ages* (Oxford: Clarendon Press, 1975), 26.

74. See Saul, *Knights and Esquires,* 106–19; and A. L. Brown, *The Governance of Late Medieval England 1272–1461* (Stanford: Stanford University Press, 1989), 192–93.

75. Saul, *Knights and Esquires,* 119–28. Also see H. M. Cam, "The Theory and Practice of Representation in Medieval England," in *Historical Studies of the English Parliament,* vol. 1, ed. E. B. Fryde and Edward Miller (Cambridge: Cambridge University Press, 1970), 262–78.

76. Saul, "Social Status."

77. M. V. Clarke, *Medieval Representation and Consent* (New York: Russell and Russell, 1964), 325.

78. Cited in Brown, *The Governance of Late Medieval England,* 186. For a full discussion of parliamentary *plena potestas,* see J. G. Edwards, "*Plena Potestas* of English Parliamentary Representatives," in *Historical Studies of the English Parliament,* ed. Fryde and Miller, 136–49. *Plena potestas* not only allowed members of Parliament to bring to Parliament the grievance of the community, it also empowered them (to the king's advantage) to consent to taxation on behalf of their community.

79. J. R. Maddicott, "Parliament and the Constituencies," in *The English Parliament in the Middle Ages,* ed. R. G. Davies and J. H. Denton (Philadelphia: University of Pennsylvania Press, 1981), 61.

80. Clarke, *Medieval Representation and Consent,* 13.

81. G. L. Harriss, "The Formation of Parliament, 1272–1377," in *The English Parliament in the Middle Ages,* ed. H. G. Richardson and G. O. Sayles (Manchester: Manchester University Press, 1981), 72.

82. Wallace, *Chaucerian Polity,* 2.

83. Burger, *Chaucer's Queer Nation,* 37–77, esp. 51.

84. Wallace, *Chaucerian Polity,* 2.

85. Judith Ferster, *Fictions of Advice: The Literature and Politics of Counsel in Late Medieval England* (Philadelphia: University of Pennsylvania Press, 1996), 21. On the growth of government as a consolidation of royal power, see Harriss, "Political Society and the Growth of Government in Late Medieval England."

86. For an alternate reading that argues for the relevance of contemporary parliamentary events in understanding the *Franklin's Tale*, see Staley, *Languages of Power*, 62–73.

Chapter Two.   *Public Voice, Private Life*

1. There are, however, some studies of Gower and of the courtly tradition that give the *Traitié* brief mention. See Lynn Staley, *Languages of Power in the Age of Richard II* (University Park: Pennsylvania State University Press, 2005), 347–48; Edward Donald Kennedy, "Gower, Chaucer, and French Prose Arthurian Romance," *Mediaevalia* 16 (1993): 69–74; William Calin, "John Gower's Continuity in the Tradition of French *Fin Amor*," *Mediaevalia* 16 (1993): 91–111; J. A. W. Bennett, "Gower's 'Honeste Love,'" in *Patterns of Love and Courtesy: Essays in Memory of C. S. Lewis*, ed. John Lawlor (Evanston: Northwestern University Press, 1966), 113–14, Gervase Mathew, "Marriage and *Amour Courtois* in Late Fourteenth-Century England," in *Essays Presented to Charles Williams* (London: Oxford University Press, 1947), 134, and *The Court of Richard II* (London: John Murray, 1968), 78. Brief mention of the poem also occurs in formal studies, such as M. Dominica Legge, *Anglo-Norman Literature and Its Background* (Oxford: Clarendon Press, 1963), 358. The two most lengthy discussions of the *Traitié* are not more than seven pages each: John H. Fisher, *John Gower: Moral Philosopher and Friend of Chaucer* (New York: New York University Press, 1964), 83–88; and R. F. Yeager, *John Gower's Poetic: The Search for a New Arion* (Cambridge: D. S. Brewer, 1990), 85–92. Also see Yeager, "John Gower's French," in *A Companion to Gower*, ed. Siân Echard (Cambridge: D. S. Brewer, 2004), 148–50, and "John Gower's Audience: The Ballades," *Chaucer Review* 40 (2005): 81–105.

2. The *Traitié* follows the *Confessio* in MSS 36–38, 40–41, 43, 46; *Vox Clamantis* in MSS 50 and 51; and the *Cinkante Balades* in the Trentham MSS. For a discussion of the manuscripts of the *Traitié*, see G. C. Macaulay, *The Complete Works of John Gower*, vol. 1 (Oxford: Clarendon Press, 1899), lxxxiv–lxxxv; and Fisher, *John Gower*, 83 and 345 n. 35.

3. *Traitié pour Essampler les Amantz Marietz*, in *The Complete Works of John Gower*, ed. Macaulay, 1:379–92. All citations will be from this edition and will be cited in the text. Unless otherwise noted, the translations are my own.

4. James I. Wimsatt, *Chaucer and His French Contemporaries: Natural Music in the Fourteenth Century* (Toronto: University of Toronto Press, 1991), 30. For the influence of these courtly poets on Gower's oeuvre, see Yeager, *John Gower's Poetic*.

5. For an analysis of the academic effect of the Latin glosses of Gower's English poem, the *Confessio Amantis,* see Rita Copeland, *Rhetoric, Hermeneutics and Translation in the Middle Ages: Academic Traditions and Vernacular Texts* (New York: Cambridge University Press, 1991), 202–20. Richard Emmerson has subsequently demonstrated, however, that the Latin prose commentary of the *Confessio* was not always arranged in the margins of the manuscript page, as Copeland and others assumed. See "Reading Gower in a Manuscript Culture: Latin and English in Illustrated Manuscripts of the *Confessio Amantis,*" *SAC* 21 (1999): 143–86.

6. See John J. McNally, "The Penitential and Courtly Traditions in Gower's *Confessio Amantis,*" in *Studies in Medieval Culture,* ed. John R. Sommerfeldt (Kalamazoo: Western Michigan University Press, 1964), 74–94; G. R. Owst, *Literature and the Pulpit in Medieval England: A Neglected Chapter in the History of English Letters and of the English People* (Oxford: Blackwell, 1966). For an analysis of the role of exempla in the *Confessio,* see Larry Scanlon, *Narrative, Authority, and Power: The Medieval Exemplum and the Chaucerian Tradition* (New York: Cambridge University Press, 1994), 245–97.

7. George R. Coffman, "John Gower in His Most Significant Role," in *Elizabethan Studies and Other Essays in Honor of George F. Reynolds,* ed. George Fulmer Reynolds, University of Colorado Studies B, vol. 2, no. 4 (Boulder: University of Colorado Press, 1945), 52–61, and "John Gower, Mentor for Royalty: Richard II," *PMLA* 9 (1954): 953–64.

8. Elizabeth Porter, "Gower's Ethical Microcosm and Political Macrocosm," in *Gower's* Confessio Amantis*: Responses and Reassessments,* ed. A. J. Minnis (Cambridge: D. S. Brewer, 1983); Russell A. Peck, *Kingship and Common Profit in Gower's* Confessio Amantis (Carbondale: Southern Illinois University Press, 1978); Frank Grady, "The Lancastrian Gower and the Limits of Exemplarity," *Speculum* 70 (1995): 552–75, and "The Generation of 1399," in *The Letter of the Law: Legal Practice and Literary Production in Medieval England,* ed. Emily Steiner and Candace Barrington (Ithaca: Cornell University Press, 2002), 202–29; Judith Ferster, *Fictions of Advice: The Literature and Politics of Counsel in Late Medieval England* (Philadelphia: University of Pennsylvania Press, 1996), 108–36; Andrew Galloway, "The Politics of Pity in Gower's *Confessio Amantis,*" in *The Letter of the Law,* ed. Steiner and Barrington, 67–104, and "Gower in His Most Learned Role and the Peasants' Revolt of 1381," *Mediaevalia* 16 (1993): 329–47; Steven Justice, *Writing and Rebellion: England in 1381* (Berkeley: University of California Press, 1994), 208–22. Especially relevant to my subject here is Lynn Staley's brief reading in *Languages of Power,* 347–48, of the *Traitié* in the context of the Trentham manuscript, which was prepared for Henry VI and where the poem appeared with a range of other poetry concerned with princely address: "In Praise of Peace," "Rec celi Deus," *Cinkante Balades,* and "Henrici quarti." This is only one of ten manuscripts of the *Traitié,* however. In my

own reading, the *Traitié* refers to but does not participate in Gower's preoccupation with kingship.

9. Gower was married near the beginning of the year 1398. It is likely that Gower was born c. 1330, so he would have been almost seventy years old, certainly an advanced age for a first marriage! See Macaulay, vol. 1, lxxxiii; Fisher, *John Gower,* 58–59. For the translation of this passage, see Fisher, *John Gower,* 86.

10. Although there are no surviving records of the Inns of Court before 1422 that could confirm Gower's status as a lawyer, his poetry demonstrates an extensive knowledge of the language of law French, and technical knowledge of legal terms and particular contemporary cases. In the *Mirrour,* he describes himself wearing rayed sleeves, a costume associated with the legal profession. His legal knowledge is also implied by his involvement in a series of real estate transactions in the 1360s, and by the fact that Geoffrey Chaucer requested him as the executor of his will. See Fisher, *John Gower,* 37–69, 313–18, and "A Calendar of Documents Relating to the Life of John Gower the Poet," *JEGP* 52 (1959): 1–23. Although hampered by the fact that John Gower was a common name in the fourteenth century, on the basis of his tomb's coat of arms, Fisher has linked Gower to the family of Robert Gower of Kent, a retainer of David Strabolgi, earl of Athol from before 1329 to 1335. If Fisher's hypothesis is correct, Gower was from a minor gentle family that served a prominent noble house.

11. On Gower's life records and especially his tomb, see John Hines, Nathalie Cohen, and Simon Roffy, "Iohannes Gower, Armiger, Poeta: Records and Memorials of His Life and Death," in *A Companion to Gower,* ed. Echard, 23–41.

12. See N. Denholm-Young, *The Country Gentry in the Fourteenth Century* (Oxford: Clarendon Press, 1969), esp. 4–5; and Nigel Saul, *Knights and Esquires: The Gloucestershire Gentry in the Fourteenth Century* (Oxford: Oxford University Press, 1981), 17–29.

13. Bennett, "Gower's 'Honeste Love,'" 116.

14. Henry Ansgar Kelly, *Love and Marriage in the Age of Chaucer* (Ithaca: Cornell University Press, 1975), 20.

15. The *Traitié* is perhaps following up on the moment at the end of the *Confessio* when Amans is revealed to be John Gower himself and is thrown out of the court of love by Venus, a gesture that may suggest Gower's rejection of *fin amor.* See the end of this chapter for further discussion.

16. Unlike other knights, Gawain was not associated with a particular lady and so in later writings became a target for those wanting to criticize the attitudes toward love and the way of life that he represented. On this subject, and for a reading of the *Traitié*'s references to Gawain in the context of French prose romance, see Kennedy, "Gower, Chaucer, and French Prose Arthurian Romance," 55–90. The stanza on Lancelot and Tristan from the *Traitié* is as follows:

Comunes sont la cronique et l'istoire
De Lancelot et Tristrans ensement;
Enquore maint lour sotie en memoire,
Pour essampler les autres du present:
Cil q'est guarni et nulle garde prent,
Droitz est qu'il porte mesmes sa folie;
Car beal oisel par autre se chastie.

[The chronicle and the story
Of Lancelot and Tristram are similarly well known;
Always remember their folly
In order to warn others in the present time:
It is just that he who is warned and does not take heed
Should bear his lunacy in the same way,
Since a beautiful bird is rebuked by another.]

(XV.1.1–7)

17. For example, in *Erec and Enide,* married life saps Erec's commitment to chivalry and makes him indolent and unmanly: "He no longer cared for the tournament, only for dallying with his wife." See *Chrétien de Troyes: Arthurian Romances,* ed. William W. Kibler (New York: Penguin Books, 1991), 67. Another example can be found in *Yvain,* when Gawain urges a newly married hero to resist letting marriage make him weak. See *Arthurian Romances,* 326–27. For a discussion of these passages and the tendency for marriage to be seen as opposed to chivalric values and chivalric masculinity, or for, in his words, examples of the "conflict between marriage and personal endeavor" in the romance, see Neil Cartlidge, *Medieval Marriage: Literary Approaches, 1100–1300* (Cambridge: D. S. Brewer, 1997), 48–50.

18. Translated by Kennedy, "Gower, Chaucer, and French Prose Romance," 71.

19. Mathew, *The Court of Richard II,* 78.

20. "Mais ainsi come l'en doit vouloir garder l'onnour de sa dame en tant comme a lui touche et pour l'amour que l'on y a, l'en y doit garder son honnour mesmes pour l'onnour de sa (f. 100r) dame et l'amour que elle lui monstre. C'est a entendre que de vos manieres, de vos estas et de la valeur de vos corps vous devez en telle maniere ordener que la renommee de vous soit tele et si bonne, si grant et si honorable que l'en doie tenir de vous grans comptes et de vos grans biens a l'ostel et aux champs et especialment de faiz d'armes de pays et des faiz d'armes de guerres ou les grans honnours sont congneuz. Et ainsi seront vos dames et devront estre plus honnorees quant elles avront fait un bon chevalier ou un bon homme d'armes." Geoffroi de Charny, *The Book of Chivalry,* trans. Elspeth Kennedy, in *The Book of Chivalry of Geoffroi de Charny: Text, Context and Translation,* ed. and trans. Richard E.

Kaeuper and Elspeth Kennedy (Philadelphia: University of Pennsylvania Press, 1996), 118–21.

21.   *The Confessio Amantis,* book 1, ll. 2660–61, *The Complete Works of John Gower,* ed. Macaulay, 2:105, 108.

22.   In Machaut's *Fonteinne Amoureuse,* the fountain is engraved with pictures of the lovers of Troy, including Helen, Paris, and Achilles, who are also in the *Traitié.* See Guillaume de Machaut, The Fountain of Love (La Fonteinne Amoureuse) *and Two Other Love Vision Poems,* ed. and trans. R. Barton Palmer (New York: Garland, 1993), 61.

23.   On this subject, see Lee Patterson, *Chaucer and the Subject of History* (Madison: University of Wisconsin Press, 1991), 84–164.

24.   Achilles first uses this phrase about Patroclus, line 10337. See Benoît de Sainte-More, *Le Roman de Troie,* ed. Leopold Constans, 6 vols. (Paris: Firmin Didot, 1904–12). On this point, see Patterson, *The Subject of History,* 117.

25.   On the "wikked wives" catalogue, see Alcuin Blamires, *Woman Defamed and Woman Defended: An Anthology of Medieval Texts* (Oxford: Clarendon Press, 1992), esp. 10. Some popular and influential examples of this misogynist cataloguing impulse occur in Jerome's *Adversus Jovinianum* and in Walter Map's *De Nugis Curialium.* On "wikked wives," also see Katharina M. Wilson and Elizabeth M. Makowski, *Wykked Wyves and the Woes of Marriage: Misogamous Literature from Juvenal to Chaucer* (Albany: State University of New York Press, 1990). On the misogynist tradition more broadly, also see R. Howard Bloch, *Medieval Misogyny and the Invention of Western Romantic Love* (Chicago: University of Chicago Press, 1991); and Frances Lee Utley, *The Crooked Rib* (Columbus: Ohio State University Press, 1944).

26.   Lines 715–16, 725–6, 737–9. See Benson, ed., *The Riverside Chaucer,* 114–15.

27.   Scholars believe that the prototype for this book was taught at Oxford and at other universities. See Wilson and Makowski, *Wykked Wyves,* 158; and Robert A. Pratt, "Jankyn's Book of Wicked Wives: Medieval Antimatrimonial Propaganda in the Universities," *Annuale Mediaevale* 3 (1962): 5–27. Also see the reference to the schools in the quotation from *The Romance of the Rose* cited immediately below. The Wife specifies that this book has material from a number of sources, including "Ovides Art" (Ovid's *Ars Amatoria*), one of the sources for the *Traitié* and "Theofraste" ("The Book of Theophrastus"). "The Book of Theophrastus" no longer exists, but it is found in many misogynist compilations and is quoted as authoritative on marriage not only in Chaucer's *Wife of Bath's Tale* but also in such divergent works as John of Salisbury's *Policraticus,* Deschamps' *Miroir de Mariage,* and *Le Roman de la Rose.* The text was so representative of medieval misogyny that Christine de Pizan refuted it in her defense of women in *Le Livre de la Cité des Dames.* See Christine de Pizan, *The Book of the City of Ladies,* trans. Earl Jeffrey Richards (New York: Persea Books, 1982), 118.

28. On the links between the misogynist and misogamous tradition, see Wilson and Makowski, *Wykked Wyves*.

29. *The Romance of the Rose,* trans. Dahlberg, 157. The original reads:

> Ha! Se Theofratus creüsse,
> ja fame espousee n'eüsse.
> Il ne tient pas home por sage
> qui fame prent par mariage,
> soit bele ou lede, ou povre ou riche,
> car il dit, et por voir l'afiche,
> en son noble livre *Aureole,*
> qui bien fet a lire en escole,
> qu'il i a vie trop grevaine,
> pleine de travaill et de paine
> et de cotenz et de riotes,
> par les orguenz des fames sotes,
> et de dangiers et de reproches
> qu'el font et dient par leur boches,
> et de requestes et de plaintes
> qu'el treuvent par achesons maintes.

Guillaume de Lorris et Jean de Meun, *Le Roman de la Rose,* trans. Félix Lecoy (Paris: Editions Champion, 1966), 2:10–11.

30. For example, Jerome's *Adversus Jovinianum* includes a passage from Theophrastus arguing that it is impossible for anyone to attend to his books and his wife, and also cautions men against marriage by claiming that a celibate man could better devote himself to God. See *St. Jerome: Letters and Select Works,* 2nd ser., vol. 6, *A Select Library of the Nicene and Post-Nicene Fathers of the Church,* ed. Philip Schaff and Henry Wace (Grand Rapids: Eerdmans, 1954), 382–83 and 351. Marriage was seen as inadvisable for philosophers and clergy, and also for knights. This is illustrated by the advice of the friend Repetoire de Science to the protagonist in the *Miroir de Mariage,* by the courtly French ballad writer Deschamps.

31. Andreas Capellanus, *Andreas Capellanus on Love,* trans. P. G. Walsh (London: Duckworth, 1982), 157. "Dicimus enim et stabilito tenore firmamus amorem non posse suas inter duos iugales extendere vires." The possibility that this text is a parody only supports further my claim that the trope was a familiar one.

32. Eustache Deschamps, *Oeuvres complètes de Eustache Deschamps,* ed. Auguste H. E. Queux de Saint-Hilaire and Gaston Raynaud (Paris: Firmin Didot, 1878–1903; rpt. New York: Johnson Reprint Corp., 1966). I have adapted the translation by Sylvia Huot, "The *Miroir de Mariage*: Deschamps Responds to the *Roman de la Rose,*" in *Eustache Deschamps, French Courtier-Poet,* ed. Deborah M. Sinnreich-Levi (New York: AMS Press, 1998), 134.

33. Lines 9156–59, *Miroir de Mariage,* in *Oeuvres complètes,* vol. 9. Trans. by Huot, "Deschamps Responds," 138. Deschamps' ascription of this praise of marriage to the figure of "Folie" is especially interesting in view of Gower's own repeated use of that term in the *Traitié* to describe the actions of lovers who love outside of marriage. Although we cannot prove that Gower had a refutation of the *Miroir* in mind when he wrote the *Traitié,* it is nonetheless clear from his language and the terms of his argument, as well as from the ballad form, that he was deliberately responding to and refuting the courtly tradition.

34. In "Gower's Women in the *Confessio,*" *Mediaevalia* 16 (1993): 223–38, A. S. G. Edwards notes Gower's lack of interest in the women in the *Confessio.* For a more standard reading that argues for Gower's favorable approach to women, see Derek Pearsall, "Gower's Narrative Art," *PMLA* 81 (1966): 475–84; and Linda Barney Burke, "Women in John Gower's *Confessio Amantis,*" *Mediaevalia* 3 (1977): 238–59.

35. *The Romance of the Rose,* trans. Dahlberg, 166.

> Cist Herculés avoit, selonc
> L'auteur Solin, .vii. piez de lonc,
> n'onc ne pot a quantité graindre
> nus homz, si com il dit, attaindre.
> Cist Herculés ot mout d'encountres,
> il vainqui .xii. horribles montres;
> et quant ot vaincu le dozieme,
> onc ne pot chevir du trezieme,
> ce fu de Deïanira,
> s'aime, qui li descira
> sa char de venin toute esprise
> par la venimeuse chemise.
> Si ravoit il por Yolé
> Son queur ja d'amors affolé.
> Ainsinc fu par fame dontez
> Herculés, qui tant ot bontez.

Le Roman de la Rose, ed. Lecoy, 2:29–30. For a similar treatment of the tale, see Walter Map, *De Nugis Curialium, Courtiers' Trifles,* ed. and trans. M. R. James (Oxford: Clarendon Press, 1983), 304–7.

36. Ovid, *Metamorphoses,* trans. Rolfe Humphries (Bloomington: Indiana University Press, 1955), 213.

37. This shift of focus from Deianira to Hercules is all the more remarkable, given that one of Gower's Ovidian sources, *The Heroides,* tells the tale explicitly from the perspective of Deianira. Ovid's *Heroides* is written in the form of letters, and includes a letter from Deianira to Hercules and not vice versa. See Heroides IX, *Ovid: Heroides and Amores,* trans. Grant Showerman (Cambridge: Harvard University Press, 1914), 108–21.

38. The *Confessio Amantis,* book 2, ll. 2145–2326, *The Complete Works of John Gower,* ed. Macaulay, 2:188–93.

39. Jerome, *Adversus Jovinianum,* in *St. Jerome: Letters and Select Works,* trans. W. H. Fremantle, 2nd ser., vol. 6, *A Select Library of the Nicene and Post-Nicene Fathers of the Christian Church* (New York: Christian Literature Co., 1893), 385.

40. The *Confessio Amantis,* book 8, ll. 2621–39, *The Complete Works of John Gower,* ed. Macaulay, 3:457–58. See Kelly, *Love and Marriage in the Age of Chaucer,* 130.

41. Walter Map, *De Nugis Curialium,* 293–95. This passage comes from the section entitled "A Dissuasion of Valerius to Rufinus the Philosopher that he should not take a Wife," a short tract against marriage that was perhaps written earlier than the main text and was certainly circulated separately (see 288 n. 2). For similar arguments, see the discourse of the Friend in *The Romance of the Rose,* trans. Dahlberg, 159; and Jerome, *Adversus Jovinianum,* chaps. 47–48, in *St. Jerome: Letters and Select Works,* 383–85.

42. For example, Jerome describes Lucretia as one "who would not survive her violated chastity, but blotted out the stain upon her person with her own blood," and Chaucer's *Legend of Good Women* refers to her as a "noble wyf" who "was of love so trewe / Ne in hir wille she chaunged for no newe," and as one who "loved clennesse and eke trouthe." Jerome, *Adversus Jovinianum,* in *St. Jerome: Letters and Select Works,* 382. Chaucer's "Legend of Good Women," *The Riverside Chaucer,* ed. Larry D. Benson, 3rd ed. (Boston: Houghton Mifflin, 1987), 620.

43. The *Ancrene Wisse,* for example, instructs:

> Bathsheba, by uncovering herself in David's sight, caused him to sin with her, a holy king though he was, and God's prophet. . . . [T]his man, because of one look cast on a woman as she washed herself, let out his heart and forgot himself, so that he did three immeasurably serious and mortal sins: with Bathsheba, the lady he looked at, adultery; on his faithful Knight, Uriah, her lord, treachery and murder. . . . For this reason, it was commanded in God's law that a pit should always be covered, and if anyone uncovered a pit and a beast fell in, the one who had uncovered the pit had to pay for it. This is a most fearsome saying for a woman who shows herself to the eyes of men. She is symbolized by the one who uncovers the pit.

See *Anchorite Spirituality,* ed. and trans. Anne Savage and Nicholas Watson (New York: Paulist Press, 1991), 68–69. The phrase Bathsheba "caused him to sin" suggests that she is responsible for his actions, and this phrase is given as the cause of a whole chain of evil occurrences ending with the death of her husband. Her guilt is amplified by the immediate reference to David as a holy man and prophet. According to this passage, her fault is uncovering herself to his eyes, organs well known in the ecclesiastical discourses of sermons and confessors' handbooks as channels and even origins of lustful feelings.

44. See the *Miroir de Mariage,* 9:174–75; and *The Book of the Knight of the Tower,* trans. William Caxton, ed. M. Y. Offord, EETS, s.s. 2 (New York: Oxford University Press, 1971), 107.

45. The association of woman with body and spirit with man has become a critical commonplace. On this issue, see especially Bloch, *Medieval Misogyny,* 22–28; Caroline Walker Bynum, "And Woman His Humanity: Female Imagery in the Religious Writing of the Later Middle Ages," in *Fragmentation and Redemption: Essays on Gender and the Human Body in Medieval Religion* (New York: Zone Books, 1991), 151–80; and Rosemary Radford Ruether, "Misogynism and Virginal Feminism in the Fathers of the Church," in *Religion and Sexism: Images of Woman in the Jewish and Christian Traditions,* ed. Rosemary Radford Ruether (New York: Simon and Schuster, 1974), 150–83.

46. Quoted in D. L. d'Avray and M. Tausche, "Marriage Sermons in *Ad Status* Collections of the Central Middle Ages," *Archives d'histoire doctrinale et littéraire du moyen âge* 47 (1981): 79.

47. On the poem as a promotion of marriage reflecting contemporary commonplaces, see Fisher, *John Gower,* 84.

48. Translated by Fisher, *John Gower,* 84.

49. The *Confessio Amantis,* book 7, ll. 4233–37, *The Complete Works of John Gower,* ed. Macaulay, 3:353.

50. *Fasciculus Morum: A Fourteenth-Century Preacher's Handbook,* ed. and trans. Siegfried Wenzel (University Park: Pennsylvania State University Press, 1989), 649. "Luxuria est concubitus desiderium supra modum et contra racionem effluens." Similarly, in Chaucer's *Canterbury Tales,* the Parson's explication of conventional Church teaching lists several acceptable reasons for sex in matrimony: aside from engendering children and rendering the marital debt, sex in marriage can be useful "to eschewe leccherye and vileynye" (ii. 938–39). See "The Parson's Tale," *Riverside Chaucer,* 322. Also see Thomas N. Tentler, *Sin and Confession on the Eve of the Reformation* (Princeton: Princeton University Press, 1977), 168–70; and Pierre Payer, *The Bridling of Desire: Views of Sex in the Later Middle Ages* (Toronto: University of Toronto Press, 1993), 84–110.

51. "Quantus sit honor coniugii seu matrimonialis sacramenti patet ex hoc quod dominus ordinem coniugalem per se in paradiso instituit, cum alii ordines per homines et extra paradysum voluptatis postmodum fuerint instituti." Quoted in d'Avray and Tausche, "Marriage Sermons," 87. A similar passage can be found in the marriage sermon in John Mirk, *Mirk's Festial: A Collection of Homilies,* part 1, ed. Theodor Erbe, EETS, e.s. 96 (London: Oxford University Press, 1905), 290.

52. *Fasciculus Morum,* 677.

53. For more on this topic, see chap. 3 on the N-Town Plays.

54. Scanlon claims that scholars have spoken "perhaps too grandiosely, of a *De Casibus* tradition," but agrees that Boccaccio's text was widely circulated and influential. See *Narrative, Authority and Power,* 119–34. For a discussion of *De Casibus* and

its influence on Chaucer, see Henry Ansgar Kelly, *Chaucerian Tragedy* (Cambridge: D. S. Brewer, 1997), esp. 11–38. On Boccaccio and English tragedy, also see Henry Ansgar Kelly, *Ideas and Forms of Tragedy from Aristotle to the Middle Ages* (Cambridge: Cambridge University Press, 1993), 169–75; D. W. Robertson, Jr., "Chaucerian Tragedy," in *Chaucer Criticism,* ed. Richard J. Schoeck and Jerome Taylor, vol. 2 (Notre Dame, IN: University of Notre Dame Press, 1961), 86–121; and William Farnham, *The Medieval Heritage of Elizabethan Tragedy* (Berkeley: University of California Press, 1936).

55. Translation of text A (the first version of c. 1360) by Kelly, *Chaucerian Tragedy,* 26, based on *De Casibus Virorum Illustrium, a Facsimile of the c. 1520 Paris Edition,* ed. Lewis Brewer Hall (Gainesville: University Press of Florida, 1962). An alternative translation of text A is *Giovanni Boccaccio: The Fates of Illustrious Men,* trans. Louis Brewer Hall (New York: Frederick Ungar, 1965), 2.

56. Trans. Kelly, *Chaucerian Tragedy,* 26.

57. As Kelly has observed, not all of Boccaccio's tales seem to follow his intentions; some tell of undeserved misfortunes. See *Chaucerian Tragedy,* 11–38.

58. This separation is often made palpable in legendaries by the depiction of the saints' torturers as non-Christian officers of the secular law whose punishments conflict with divine justice, and by the elaborate descriptions of torture that the saint does not feel. For example, *The Golden Legend* describes the torture of Saint Agatha by a consular official, Quintianus, who tries to force her to sacrifice to his gods. After the first stage of her torment she is visited and healed by the Apostle Peter in Christ's name, showing the powerlessness of earthly punishment. When Quintianus threatens her with greater torture, she confronts him with his powerlessness over her: "Your words are silly and useless, they are wicked and pollute the air! You mindless wretch, how can you want me to adore stones and abandon the God of heaven who has healed me?'" Her words emphasize the gap between heavenly and earthly justice, and the fact that miracles connected to Agatha continue to take place after her death implies that she is rewarded in heaven for her suffering at the hands of the officials of secular law. See Jacobus de Voragine, *The Golden Legend,* trans. William Granger Ryan (Princeton: Princeton University Press, 1993), 156. For another version of the Agatha legend showing the same split between secular and sacred authority, see *The South English Legendary,* ed. Charlotte D'Evelyn and Anna J. Mill, vol. 1, EETS, o.s. 235 (London: Oxford University Press, 1956), 56. For a discussion of the split between the grisly tortures of the saints in the *South English Legendary* and the representation of these figures as experiencing no pain, see Karen Winstead, *Virgin Martyrs: Legends of Sainthood in Late Medieval England* (Ithaca: Cornell University Press, 1997), 73–74.

59. *Middle English Dictionary,* s.v. *contestable* or *constable.*

60. An adulterous wife forfeited her claim to the estate of her husband and any *inter vivem* gifts she had received from him prior to marriage. While he escaped

criminal penalties for homicide, a husband who killed his adulterous wife forfeited his claims to her dowry. Other penalties for adultery included fines, penitential processions, public whippings, and, in very rare cases, castration or the death penalty. Richard M. Wunderli, *London Church Courts and Society on the Eve of the Reformation* (Cambridge: Medieval Academy of America, 1981), 85–88.

61. James Brundage, *Law, Sex and Christian Society in Medieval Europe* (Chicago: University of Chicago Press, 1987), 249–50, 319–23; Sir Frederick Pollock and Frederic William Maitland, *The History of English Law Before the Time of Edward I,* 2nd ed. (Cambridge: Cambridge University Press, 1952), 2:490–91; Wunderli, *London Church Courts,* 91–92; and Barbara A. Hanawalt, *"Of Good and Ill Repute": Gender and Social Control in Medieval England* (Oxford: Oxford University Press, 1998), 127. On French literature and law of rape, see Kathryn Gravdal, *Ravishing Maidens: Writing Rape in Medieval French Literature and Law* (Philadelphia: University of Pennsylvania Press, 1991). On the importance of rape to Gower's *Confessio Amantis,* see Carolyn Dinshaw, "Rivalry, Rape and Manhood: Gower and Chaucer," in *Chaucer and Gower: Difference, Mutuality and Exchange,* ed. R. F. Yeager (Victoria: English Literary Studies, 1991), 130–52.

62. Porter, "Gower's Ethical Microcosm and Political Macrocosm," 135–36.

63. Diane Watt, *Amoral Gower: Language, Sex and Politics* (Minneapolis: University of Minnesota Press, 2003), 3. Similarly, Russell Peck has emphasized Gower's preoccupation with "the individual's responsibility within the larger social context" (xvix) in *Kingship and Common Profit in Gower's* Confessio Amantis, and Anne Middleton has argued of the *Confessio* that, despite its dedication to two successive kings, "the king is not the main imagined audience, but an occasion for gathering what is on the common mind." See Middleton, "The Idea of Public Poetry in the Reign of Richard II," *Speculum* 53 (1978): 107.

64. The *Confessio Amantis,* book 7, ll. 4248–51, *The Complete Works of John Gower,* ed. Macaulay, 3:353–54.

65. Quoted in Paul Strohm, *Hochon's Arrow: The Social Imagination of Fourteenth-Century Texts* (Princeton: Princeton University Press, 1992), 124.

66. Middleton, "The Idea of Public Poetry," 95–96.

67. Justice, *Writing and Rebellion,* 208–16; and David Aers, "Vox Populi and the Literature of 1381," in *The Cambridge History of Medieval English Literature,* ed. David Wallace (New York: Cambridge University Press, 1999), 439–44. On the relationship between the narrator's voice and the people's voice in both the *Vox Clamantis* and the *Cronica Tripertita,* see Ferster, *Fictions of Advice,* 129–32. Ferster notes the similarity between Gower's formulations and the contemporary notion of parliamentary representation as *plena potestas,* a concept I have connected to the *Franklin's Tale* in my previous chapter. The connections between these works of Gower are strengthened by the fact that the *Traitié* is included with the *Vox Clamantis* in All Souls MS 98 and in the manuscripts owned by the Hunterian Museum, Glasgow.

68. As Siân Echard has argued, we need not see Gower's use of Latin as necessarily socially conservative, since in works such as the *Vox Clamantis,* Gower's Latin
commentary is directed against social elites as well as against the peasantry. See Siân
Echard, "Gower's 'bokes of Latin': Language, Politics, and Poetry," *SAC* 25 (2003):
123–56. The *Traitié* provides further evidence for Echard's challenge to the conventional view that Gower's career is a progression toward an English poetic voice.

69. My thanks to Frank Grady for drawing my attention to this parallel.

70. Watt, *Amoral Gower,* 4. Janet Coleman has made a broader claim than mine
(or Watt's), arguing for Gower's primary audience as the "expanded middle estate."
See *Medieval Readers and Writers, 1350–1400* (New York: Columbia University Press,
1981), 156. Although different from the question of Gower's intended audience, recent manuscript studies suggest that Gower's works, and the *Confessio* in particular,
may have reached a broad audience that included members of the middle strata of
society as well as aristocratic and royal readers. In "Reading Gower in a Manuscript
Culture," Emmerson argues that two of the three recension manuscripts of the
Confessio (in which the dedication had been changed from Richard II to the future
Henry IV and written "for Engelondes sake"), Fairfax 3 and Harley 3869 (both of
which also contained the *Traitié*), may have been designed for public reading either
at court or other public gatherings, suggesting a possible link between public reading and Gower's understanding of himself as speaking in "public voice." Furthermore, Emmerson notes that many later fifteenth-century manuscripts of the *Confessio*
were geared to merchant-class readers. Derek Pearsall describes a blending of early
manuscripts associated with the Lancastrian royal family with those made for and
owned by richer merchants in the fifteenth century. See Derek Pearsall, "The Manuscripts and Illustrations of Gower's Works," in *A Companion to Gower,* 73–97.

Chapter Three.   *Performing Reform*

1. See R. W. Pfaff, *New Liturgical Feasts in Later Medieval England* (Oxford: Clarendon Press, 1970), 40–61, 97–115. New feasts of the Virgin added in the late Middle
Ages include: the Visitation (1389), the Compassion of the Virgin (1497), and the Presentation of the Virgin (1372).

2. A date of 1468 written on the manuscript gives a *terminus ad quem* for the
cycle, but the play may have been performed or written down earlier. See *The N-Town
Play: Cotton MS Vespasian D. 8,* ed. Stephen Spector, EETS, s.s. 11 (Oxford: Oxford
University Press, 1991), xxxviii. On the uniqueness of the attention devoted to Mary
and Joseph in the N-Town plays, see Rosemary Woolf, *The English Mystery Plays*
(Berkeley and Los Angeles: University of California Press, 1972), 161. For other late
medieval English texts recounting the life of the Virgin, see John Lydgate, *A Critical*

Edition of John Lydgate's Life of Our Lady, ed. Joseph A. Lauritis, Ralph A. Klinefelter, and Vernon F. Gallagher, Duquesne Philological Series, no. 2 (Pittsburgh: Duquesne University Press, 1961), 18–40; *The Middle English Stanzaic Versions of the Life of Saint Anne,* ed. Roscoe E. Parker, EETS, o.s. 174 (London: Oxford University Press, 1928); Nicholas Love, *Nicholas Love's Mirror of the Blessed Life of Jesus Christ,* ed. Michael G. Sargent (New York: Garland, 1992). Earlier versions of the life of the Virgin also give little attention to the subject of her marriage, including the acknowledged sources for the N-Town Mary plays, most notably the *Legenda Aurea.* See Jacobus de Voragine, *The Golden Legend,* trans. William Granger Ryan (Princeton: Princeton University Press, 1993), 149–58.

3. Cases have been put forward for Coventry, Lincoln, Norwich, Bury St. Edmunds, and Thetford. For a summary of the long history of critical dispute about the origin of the N-Town plays, see Stephen Spector, "Introduction," *The N-Town Play,* xiii–xviii; Alan Fletcher, "The N-Town Plays," in *Cambridge Companion to Medieval English Theatre,* ed. Richard Beadle (Cambridge: Cambridge University Press, 1994), 163–88; and Gail McMurray Gibson, "Bury St. Edmunds, Lydgate, and the N-Town Cycle," *Speculum* 56 (1981): 56–90. For the more recent theory for a Thetford origin, also see Douglas Sugano, "'This game wel pleyd': The N-Town Playbooks and East Anglian Games," *Comparative Drama* 28, no. 2 (1994): 221–34.

4. See Alan Fletcher, "The N-Town Plays," 168 and 178. On place and scaffold production, also see Meg Twycross, "The Theatricality of Medieval English Plays," in *Cambridge Companion to Medieval English Theatre,* ed. Beadle, 56.

5. Stephen Spector, "The Composition and Development of an Eclectic Manuscript: Cotton Vespasian D. VIII," *Leeds Studies in English* n.s. 9 (1977): 62–83, esp. 71; and Spector, ed., *The N-Town Play,* 2:537–43. Spector analyzed the meter of "The Marriage of Mary and Joseph" and other parts of the N-Town manuscript, concluding that the play combines material from the "original" cycle and the "Mary Play." He demonstrates that the marriage play contains both thirteeners (a meter found in pageants that were part of the original cycle and correspond to the plays described in the Proclamation) and long-lined octaves (the meter found in the "Mary Play"). In addition, he notes that in the "Marriage of Mary and Joseph" section of the manuscript, the scribe-compiler dotted in red the lobes of paragraph marks before material taken from the "Mary Play" and left the ones taken from the Proclamation plays blank. On this last point, also see *The N-Town Plays: A Facsimile of British Library MS Cotton Vespasian D. VIII,* ed. Peter Meredith and Stanley J. Kahrl (Leeds: University of Leeds, School of English, 1976), xvii. Also see *The Mary Play from the N. Town Manuscript,* ed. Peter Meredith (New York: Longman, 1987), 1–3.

6. Fletcher, "N-Town Plays," 177; and Sugano, "This game wel pleyd," 223. On *compilatio,* see Malcolm B. Parkes, "The Influence of the Concepts of *Ordinatio* and *Compilatio* on the Development of the Book," in *Medieval Learning and Literature:*

Essays Presented to R. W. Hunt, ed. J. J. G. Alexander and M. T. Gibson (Oxford: Clarendon Press, 1976), 115–41.

7. Peter Meredith has reconstructed and edited the original "Mary Play" from the N-Town manuscript, a designation adopted by a number of recent critics. See *The Mary Play from the N. Town Manuscript.* Instead, I use the designation "Mary plays" to indicate the plays from the manuscript on the subject of the life of the Virgin. On the importance of making the manuscript itself the subject of study, rather than a reconstructed version of one of its sources, see note 8 below.

8. Fletcher notes the problems of previous criticism on the N-Town manuscript, some of which has relied on an anachronistically modern notion of authorial integrity by emphasizing the thematic unity of the manuscript and failing to acknowledge its disparate character. On the other hand, attempts to isolate the individual layers of this composite text are similarly problematic, according to Fletcher, because they also search for an originary purity of authorship. See Fletcher, "The N-Town Plays," 171, 177–78. The scribe-compiler's own acknowledgment of the hybridity of the N-Town manuscript is aptly illustrated by his revelation of the seams between the Mary and the Proclamation material at the edges of "Marriage of Mary and Joseph." See note 5 above. In focusing on the N-Town manuscript, I join a number of recent critics who have emphasized the textual nature of medieval drama and its engagement with nondramatic literature and hermeneutics. See, for example, Theresa Coletti, *Mary Magdalene and the Drama of Saints: Theater, Gender and Religion in Late Medieval England* (Philadelphia: University of Pennsylvania Press, 2004), esp. 15; Ruth Nisse, *Defining Acts: Drama and the Politics of Interpretation in Late Medieval England* (Notre Dame, IN: University of Notre Dame Press, 2005); and Maura Nolan, *John Lydgate and the Making of Public Culture* (New York: Cambridge University Press, 2005), 71–83.

9. I have adapted Douglas Sugano's useful distinction between what he terms "narrative and theological integrity" and "dramatic and theatrical continuity." See "'This game wel pleyd.'"

10. On the use of the manuscript for performance, see commentary on "reviser B" in *The N-Town Plays: A Facsimile,* vii.

11. Gibson, *The Theater of Devotion,* 127.

12. Ibid., 133 and 135.

13. Ibid., 108. In this book, Gibson notes the "striking thematic links" between the N-Town Mary plays and the devotional works of John Lydgate, 126. For a stronger case suggesting Lydgate as a possible author of the text, see Gibson, "Bury St. Edmunds, Lydgate, and the N-Town Cycle." Since no link to a specific origin can be definitely proved on manuscript evidence, and since records prove that late medieval East Anglian drama might sometimes be written down in places without cultural or dramatic centers, most recent critics have chosen, as I have, to analyze the

N-Town plays in the broad context of East Anglian culture. On the problems of seeking a specific origin for the N-Town manuscript, see Fletcher, "The N-Town Plays," 164–67.

14. Nisse, *Defining Acts,* 65–74, esp. 66; and Coletti, *Mary Magdalene and the Drama of Saints,* 90–99, 105.

15. See Kathleen Ashley, "Image and Ideology: Saint Anne in Late Medieval Drama and Narrative," in *Interpreting Cultural Symbols: Saint Anne in Late Medieval Society,* ed. Kathleen Ashley and Pamela Sheingorn (Athens: University of Georgia Press, 1990), 117.

16. *The Mary Play from the N. Town Manuscript,* 9–12; and for a reading of the "Mary Play" as "ideally suited to lay piety," also see Peter Meredith, "Performance, Verse and Occasion in the N-Town *Mary Play,*" in *Individuality and Achievement in Middle English Poetry,* ed. O. S. Pickering (Cambridge: D. S. Brewer, 1997), 205–21. Robert Reynes was a church reeve of Acle, a village near Norwich; his commonplace book contains a series of texts that appear to be for public recitation at guild festivities, including notes on Anne's parentage, genealogies of Mary, and a poem in honor of Saint Anne. In his introduction to *Middle English Stanzaic Versions of the Life of Saint Anne,* xxx and xxxiv–liii, Parker argues that one of the three extant manuscripts of the *Life of Saint Anne* shows evidence of being written for the feast of Anne (xxx), and he claims this text as a source for the N-Town Mary plays. The emphasis on Saint Anne and Mary led E. K. Chambers to suggest that the N-Town plays were performed on Saint Anne's Day rather than on Corpus Christi Day. See Chambers, *Medieval Stage* (London: Oxford University Press, 1903; rpt. Mineola, NY: Dover, 1996), ii, 126–27, 421. The evidence that a Saint Anne guild in Lincoln sponsored plays also played a role in the (now discounted) theory that the N-Town plays were from that town.

17. On the presence and persecution of Lollards in East Anglia, see John A. F. Thomson, *The Later Lollards, 1414–1520* (London: Oxford University Press, 1967), 117–38; and Anne Hudson, *The Premature Reformation: Wycliffite Texts and Lollard History* (Oxford: Clarendon Press, 1988).

18. Norman P. Tanner, ed., *Heresy Trials in the Diocese of Norwich 1428–31,* Camden 4th ser., vol. 20 (London: Royal Historical Society, 1977).

19. Gibson, *Theater of Devotion,* 31; and Norman P. Tanner, *The Church in Late Medieval Norwich, 1370–1532* (Toronto: Pontifical Institute of Mediaeval Studies, 1984), 166.

20. Hudson, *Premature Reformation,* 429 and 411. Hudson and H. L. Spencer have shown that there was considerable textual exchange between orthodox and Wycliffite writers: Lollards revised orthodox works, and Wycliffite sermons were integrated into ostensibly orthodox vernacular sermon collections. See Hudson, 390–45; and H. Leith Spencer, *English Preaching in the Late Middle Ages* (Oxford: Oxford University

Press, 1993), esp. 278–20. Sarah Beckwith, "Sacrum Signum: Sacramentality and Dissent in York's Theatre of Corpus Christi," in *Criticism and Dissent in the Middle Ages,* ed. Rita Copeland (New York: Cambridge University Press, 1996), 265. In this same passage, Beckwith notes that attempting to treat sacramental culture as either orthodox or dissentient "might be termed the inquisitorial fallacy, in which complex practices are deformed through the constricting filter of the ecclesiastical tribunal," arguing that the York plays "might rather be understood as a component part of a vigorous lay and vernacular religiosity" (278).

21. Coletti, *Mary Magdalene and the Drama of Saints,* 5. Also see Kathleen Ashley, "Sponsorship, Reflexity and Resistance: Cultural Readings of the York Cycle Plays," in *The Performance of Middle English Culture: Essays on Chaucer and the Drama in Honor of Martin Stevens,* ed. James J. Paxson, Lawrence M. Clopper, and Sylvia Tomasch (Cambridge: D. S. Brewer, 1998), 9–24, in which she argues for seeing medieval plays as both social performances and verbal artifacts "riven with mixed messages, incompatible world views and multiple voices."

22. All citations from the plays are from *The N-Town Play,* ed. Spector, and will be included in the text.

23. In *De bono coniugali,* Augustine argued that sex in marriage is not merely excusable but actually a positive good if it is for procreation rather than recreation. *Saint Augustin: On the Holy Trinity,* 400 and 404.

24. On the cult of Saint Anne, see Kathleen Ashley and Pamela Sheingorn, "Introduction," *Interpreting Cultural Symbols,* 1–68; Ashley, "Image and Ideology," in *Interpreting Cultural Symbols,* 111–30; Gail McMurray Gibson, "Saint Anne and the Religion of Childbed: Some East Anglian Texts and Talismans," in *Interpreting Cultural Symbols,* 95–110; Ann W. Astell, "Chaucer's 'St. Anne Trinity': Devotion, Dynasty, Dogma and Debate," *Studies in Philology* 94 (1997): 395–416; Ton Brandenbarg, "Saint Anne: A Holy Grandmother and Her Children," in *Sanctity and Motherhood: Essays on Holy Mothers in the Middle Ages,* ed. Anneke B. Mulder-Bakker (New York: Garland, 1995), 31–65, and "St. Anne and Her Family: The Veneration of St. Anne in Connection with Concepts of Marriage and the Family in the Early Modern Period," in *Saints and She-Devils: Images of Women in the Fifteenth and Sixteenth Centuries,* ed. Lène Dresen-Coenders (London: Rubicon Press, 1987), 101–27; and Theresa Coletti, "Genealogy, Sexuality and Sacred Power: The Saint Anne Dedication of the *Digby Candlemas Day* and the *Killing of the Children of Israel," JMEMS* 29 (1999): 25–59.

25. Bridget of Sweden, *The Liber Celestis of St Bridget of Sweden,* ed. Roger Ellis, vol. 1, EETS, o.s. 291 (Oxford: Oxford University Press, 1987), 467.

26. See John Mirk, *Mirk's Festial,* ed. Theodor Erbe, part 1, EETS, e.s. 96 (London: Kegan Paul, Trench and Trübner, 1905. Repr., Millwood, NY: Kraus Reprint, 1987), 216.

27. On the Immaculate Conception as tied to the promotion of marriage, see Astell, "Chaucer's 'St. Anne Trinity.'"

28. On the Holy Kinship and Anne's *trinubium,* see Ashley and Sheingorn, "Introduction," *Interpreting Cultural Symbols,* 13–43, and their sources.

29. Brandenbarg, "St. Anne and Her Family," 101–27. On Anne as a "polysemic" symbol that could express dynastic as well as civic impulses, see Ashley and Sheingorn, "Introduction," *Interpreting Cultural Symbols,* esp. 4–5 and 51–52.

30. Brandenbarg, "St. Anne and Her Family," 121–22.

31. See Brandenbarg, "Saint Anne: A Holy Grandmother and Her Children," 38. On Saint Anne as a trigger for "a set of genealogical associations that were particularly important to the Ricardian lay nobility and the urban merchant class" of Chaucer's London, see Astell, "Chaucer's 'St. Anne Trinity.'" In "Genealogy, Sexuality and Sacred Power," Coletti situates the Saint Anne dedication of the *Digby Candlemas Day* and the *Killing of the Children* in similar social context.

32. Parker, ed., *Stanzaic Life of Saint Anne,* ix–xi.

33. Gibson, "Saint Anne and the Religion of Childbed," 101. The Acle poem repeats that assertion later in the poem, claiming that they "haddyn worldly ryches ful gret plente." *The Commonplace Book of Robert Reynes of Acle: An Edition of Tanner MS 407,* ed. Cameron Louis (New York: Garland, 1980), 197 and 201.

34. A passage similar to the one in the Acle manuscript occurs in the Trinity College manuscripts of the *Stanzaic Life of Saint Anne,* which says that Anne "of worldly goods lackyd none doubtless" (98). Osbern Bokenham's legend of Saint Anne not only describes Joachim as "a ryche man and of gret dignyte," but explicitly depicts him as a merchant, describing him going to the temple to make his sacrifice "wyth other burgeys of hys cyte." Osbern Bokenham, *Legendys of Hooly Wummen,* ed. Mary S. Serjeantson, EETS, o.s. 206 (London: Oxford University Press, 1938), 45–46. The fact that Bokenham gives Anne her own legend instead of telling the story in the context of Mary's birth is symptomatic of the growing popularity of the cult of Saint Anne in the fifteenth century. On this point, see Brandenbarg, "Saint Anne: A Holy Grandmother and Her Children."

35. These parish churches and their works of art are material testimony to the power that lay wealth could potentially wield over clerical authority. Surviving artists' contracts showed that wealthy lay patrons exerted considerable control over the works of art in churches. See Gibson, *Theater of Devotion,* 19–46, 67–106.

36. R. N. Swanson, *Religion and Devotion in Europe c. 1215–c. 1515* (New York: Cambridge University Press, 1995), 235–56. In *People of the Parish* (Philadelphia: University of Pennsylvania Press, 2001), Katherine French shows that laypeople played a significant role in the administration of the parish. Not only did they pay tithes and attend the liturgy, they also maintained the nave and the churchyard, supplied liturgical items, and participated in the administrative structure that raised and spent money (20). On this topic, also see Virginia R. Bainbridge, *Guilds in the Medieval Countryside: Social and Religious Change in Cambridgeshire c. 1350–1558* (Woodbridge: Boydell Press, 1996), 54–60.

37. This dialogue is found neither in the recognized sources for this N-Town play, such as Jacobus de Voragine, *The Golden Legend*, 131, nor in other contemporary versions of the story, such as John Lydgate's *Life of Our Lady* and the *Stanzaic Life of Saint Anne* (which says merely "Joachim went to hys herdsmen," 114). Similarly, Bokenham's legend of Anne gives the shepherds only passing mention. See Bokenham, *Legendys of Hooly Wummen*, 47.

38. Nicholas Love, *Mirror of the Blessed Life of Jesus Christ*, 39.

39. *Lollard Sermons*, ed. Gloria Cigman, EETS, o.s. 294 (Oxford: Oxford University Press, 1989), 62. For an example of a Lollard sermon on the Nativity that closely resembles Love's discussion of the poverty of the shepherds, see *English Wycliffite Sermons*, vol. 2, ed. Pamela Gradon (Oxford: Clarendon Press, 1988), 206–14.

40. The seventh of the "Sixteen Points on which the Bishops accuse Lollards," for example, was "þat þer schulde be bot oo degre aloone of prestehod in þe chirche of God, and euery good man is a prest and haþ power to preche þe word of God." For the text of this early fifteenth-century manuscript see *Selections from English Wycliffite Writings*, ed. Anne Hudson (New York: Cambridge University Press, 1978), 19–24. Similarly, in the records of the Lollard trials in Norwich by Bishop Alnwich in 1428–31, one of the defendants allegedly made this characteristic claim: "Every good Cristen man that hath noon ordre is a good prest, and hath as moche poar to do and mynystre alle the sacraments in the Churche as ony other prest ordred." See *Heresy Trials in the Diocese of Norwich 1428-31*, ed. Tanner, 153.

41. Compare Osbern Bokenham's *Legendys of Hooly Wummen*, 47.

42. On the spiritual equality of Joachim and Anne, see Carroll Anne Hilles, "'Double Birth and Double Lineage': Individual and Social Identity in Fifteenth-Century Devotional Literature" (Ph.D. diss., Duke University, 1994), 153–63.

43. Hugh of Saint Victor, *Hugh of Saint Victor on the Sacraments of the Christian Faith*, trans. Roy J. Deferrari (Cambridge: Medieval Academy of America, 1951), 326. For the full quotation, see my introduction.

44. Gibson, *Theater of Devotion*, 6.

45. "Holy Maidenhood," *Anchoritic Spirituality*, trans. and ed. Anne Savage and Nicholas Watson (New York: Paulist Press, 1991), 234 and 239. Also see *Hali Meidenhad*, ed. F. J. Furnivall, revised by Oswald Cockayne, EETS, o.s. 18 (London: Oxford University Press, 1922), 33 and 53, for another modernization. Lydgate makes this connection between Mary's vow and the choice of the religious life even more explicit: "Now Marie, hath founde an ordre newe / To kepe hir clene and inviolate." See *John Lydgate's Life of Our Lady*, 292.

46. See, for example, *John Lydgate's Life of Our Lady*, 290, and *The Middle English Stanzaic Versions of the Life of Saint Anne*, 11. The source of this law is apocryphal and does not refer to Jewish custom.

47. Compare, for example, *John Lydgate's Life of Our Lady*, 289–90, in which the law is not treated as problematic, and Mary's resistance meets with a unified front

in support of the law. No solicitation of God's advice or the intervention of an angel appears necessary:

> And whan they sawe hir hert not mutable
> But ay stedfaste, of oon affection
> And euere Ilyche, as any centre stable
> Thay haue made, a conuocacion
> Of all the kynrede as in conclusion
> The viii day forto come in fere
> By one assent, to trete of this matier
> This is to say, þat of the olde usage
> Of Custome kept . . .

In this version, the test of the rods is presented as Ysakar's idea, in order to reveal God's opinion on who Mary's partner should be, not on whether or not she should marry, as in N-Town. The marriage law is given similarly unproblematic status in *The Middle English Stanzaic Versions of the Life of Saint Anne,* 13. Jacobus de Voragine's *The Golden Legend,* 153, on the other hand, echoes N-Town in its account of the prayer as directed to God about whether Mary should be made to marry at all rather than as a question of whom it is that she is to marry; this dilemma is very briefly discussed, but it is given much more emphasis in the N-Town version.

48. Jerome, *St. Jerome: Letters and Select Works,* trans. W. H. Fremantle, 2nd ser., vol. 6, *A Select Library of the Nicene and Post-Nicene Fathers,* ed. Philip Schaff and Henry Wace (New York: Christian Literature Co., 1893), 335.

49. *Works of St. Jerome,* 366.

50. *Saint Augustin: Sermon on the Mount, Harmony of the Gospels, Homilies on the Gospels,* ed. Philip Schaff, 1st ser., vol. 6, *A Select Library of the Nicene and Post-Nicene Fathers of the Christian Church* (Grand Rapids: Eerdmans, 1956), 102–3.

51. On the role of the holy couple's marriage in the development of sacramental marriage, see Penny S. Gold, "The Marriage of Mary and Joseph in the Twelfth-Century Ideology of Marriage," in *Sexual Practices and the Medieval Church,* ed. Vern L. Bullough and James Brundage (Buffalo: Prometheus Books, 1982), 102–17. On the development of the marriage sacrament, see introduction, note 9.

52. *Hugh of Saint Victor on the Sacraments of the Christian Faith,* 332. See also Hugh of St. Victor, "De B. Mariae Virginitate," in PL 176: 837–76.

53. *Hugh of Saint Victor on the Sacraments of the Christian Faith,* 326.

54. For marriage sermons, see D. L. d'Avray, *Medieval Marriage Sermons: Mass Communication in a Culture Without Print* (New York: Oxford University Press, 2001); D. L. d'Avray and M. Tausche, "Marriage Sermons in *Ad Status* Collections of the Central Middle Ages," *Archives d'histoire doctrinale et littéraire du moyen âge* 47 (1981): 71–119; John Mirk, *Mirk's Festial,* 289–93; B. Hauréau, *Notices et extraits de quelques manuscrits latins de la Bibliothèque Nationale* (Paris: Librairie Klincksieck, 1890),

1:189–202; and David d'Avray, "The Gospel of the Marriage Feast of Cana and Marriage Preaching in France," in *The Bible in the Medieval World: Essays in Memory of Beryl Smalley,* ed. Katherine Walsh and Diana Wood (Oxford: Basil Blackwell, 1985), 207–24.

55. See note 1.

56. On the tensions surrounding the issue of chaste marriage in the work of Augustine and others, see Dyan Elliott, *Spiritual Marriage: Sexual Abstinence in Medieval Wedlock* (Princeton: Princeton University Press, 1993), 55–63.

57. Hugh of Saint Victor, "De B. Mariae Virginitate," PL 176:863–64, and *On the Sacraments,* 326.

58. See Elizabeth Frances Rogers, *Peter Lombard and the Sacramental System* (Merrick, NY: Richwood, 1976), 243–46.

59. "Marriage is begun by betrothal and completed by mixing. Hence between the bethrothed there is a marriage, but only a beginning; between the coupled there is a ratified marriage" (c. 27, q. 2, xxxiv). Gratian, "Marriage Canons from the Decretum," trans. John T. Noonan, Jr. (unpublished, 1967), 12. On Gratian's definition of marriage, see James Brundage, *Law, Sex and Christian Society in Medieval Europe* (Chicago: University of Chicago Press, 1987), 235–42.

60. C. 27, q. 2, c. 3. See "Marriage Canons from the Decretum," 2. For a discussion of this passage see Gold, "The Marriage of Mary and Joseph," 102–17; and Elliott, *Spiritual Marriage,* 178.

61. Peter Lombard, Raymond of Penafort, and John of Freiburg all adopted the passage. See Elliott, *Spiritual Marriage,* 178. Although Mary and Joseph's marriage was key to the development of two of Augustine's goods of marriage, *sacramentum* and *fides,* it is with difficulty that he integrates the example of Mary and Joseph's marriage with the third good of *proles.* The contorted logic of the following passage from *De Nuptiis et Concupiscentia* testifies to the complexity of this reconciliation:

> The entire good, therefore, of nuptial institution was effected in the case of these parents of Christ: there was offspring, there was faithfulness, there was the bond. As offspring, we recognize the Lord Jesus Christ Himself; the fidelity, in that there was no adultery; the bond, because there was no divorce. Only there was no nuptial cohabitation; because He who was to be without sin, and was sent not in sinful flesh, but in the likeness of sinful flesh, could not possibly have been made in sinful flesh itself without that shameful lust of the flesh which comes from sin, and without which He willed to be born, in order that He might teach us, that every one who is born of sexual intercourse is in fact sinful flesh. Nevertheless conjugal intercourse is not in itself a sin, when it is had for the intention of producing children; because the mind's good-will leads the ensuing bodily pleasure, instead of following

its lead; and the human choice is not distracted by the yoke of sin pressing down upon it, inasmuch as the blow of the sin is rightly brought back to the purposes of procreation. (2.1.13)

Saint Augustin: Anti-Pelagian Writings, trans. Peter Holmes and Robert Ernest Wallis, 1st ser., vol. 5, *A Select Library of the Nicene and Post-Nicene Fathers of the Christian Church,* ed. Philip Schaff (Grand Rapids: Eerdmans, 1956), 269. The rhetorical structure of this passage is permeated with double negatives and words like *only* and *nevertheless* marking logical shifts in argument, which are the syntactical equivalent of the N-Town bishop's anxiety over the Virgin's marriage. In the end Augustine can only achieve a synthesis of spiritual and physical marriage models through an allusion to the Incarnation, the central event that combines physical and spiritual, earthly and divine, but a quintessentially exceptional event that is inimitable by ordinary people.

62. *Le Ménagier de Paris,* translated by Eileen Power as *The Goodman of Paris* (London: Routledge, 1928), 140. For discussion, see Elliott, *Spiritual Marriage,* 179 ff.

63. On the cult of Joseph, see Francis Filas, *Joseph: The Man Closest to Jesus: The Complete Life, Theology and Devotional History of St. Joseph* (Boston: St. Paul Editions, 1962).

64. The inclusion of the marriage liturgy in the story of Mary and Joseph is unique to the N-Town play. For the liturgy, see *Monumenta Ritualia Ecclesiae Anglicanae,* ed. William Maskell (Oxford: Clarendon Press, 1882), 1:5–77; or *The Sarum Missal in English,* trans. Frederick E. Warren (London: De La More Press, 1911), 143–50. For a comparison between the liturgy and the lines in N-Town, see *The Mary Play,* 103–4.

65. *The Sarum Missal in English,* 147–48.

66. "The Twelve Conclusions of the Lollards," which were nailed to the doors of Westminster Hall during the session of Parliament in 1395, included a critique of clerical celibacy on the grounds that it led to vice: "sorwful to here is þat þe lawe of continence annexyd to presthod, þat in preiudys of wimmen was first ordeynid, inducith sodomie in al holy chirche . . . Þe correlary of þis conclusiun is þat þe priuat religions, begynneris of þis synne, were most worthi to ben anullid." See *Selections from English Wycliffite Writings,* 25. On Lollards and marriage, see Alcuin Blamires, "The Wife of Bath and Lollardy," *Medium Aevum* 58 (1989): 224–42; and Shannon McSheffrey, *Gender and Heresy: Women and Men in Lollard Communities* (Philadelphia: University of Pennsylvania Press, 1995), 82–87.

67. "Et sic phariseice colamus culicem et deglutimus camelum, horrentes in sacerdotibus corporale coniugium ut venenum, sed negociacionem eciam simoniacam cum quantumque seculari conversacione tamquam tyriacum sanativam ac defensivam ecclesie approbamus"; and "Michi autem videtur, quod omnis sacerdos coniugatus debet abstinere a carnali connublic nec presbiterari, antequam deobligetur

quoad reddicionem debiti, sicut episopus coniugatus debet seiungi a plaga cristian-
ismi occidua quoad cohabitacionem cum sua uxore, si inded occasione data scan-
dalum generetur." Quoted in H. Hargraves, "Sir John Oldcastle and Wycliffite Views
on Clerical Marriage," *Medium Aevum* 42 (1973): 144.

68. *English Works of Wyclif,* ed. F. D. Mathews, EETS, o.s. 74 (London: Kegan
Paul, Trübner & Co., 1880), 100.

69. *Select English Works of John Wyclif,* ed. Thomas Arnold (Oxford: Clarendon
Press, 1896), 3:190. Wyclif's authorship of this tract is uncertain. Arnold attributes it
(with qualifications) to Wyclif; he says "it is not mentioned even by Bale, and the only
reason for ascribing it to Wyclif is that it is found in a volume which Archbishop
Parker, in the sixteenth century, believed to contain only tracts of Wyclif's composition, and under that belief bequeathed to the college. St. Augustine's being called
here 'Seynt Austyn,' instead of simply 'Austyn,' as in the Homilies, appears a suspi-
cious circumstance, yet capable of explanation, if we suppose the tract to have been
composed by Wyclif in his younger days" (3:188). Another edition of this text can be
found in *The Trials and Joys of Marriage,* ed. Eve Salisbury (Kalamazoo: Medieval Institute Publications, 2002), 191–201. See 19–20 and 202–4 for commentary and bibli-
ography on the tract. For a similar claim that clerical marriage is not based on old law,
the Gospel, or the epistles but only the law of the Church, see *An Apology for Lollard
Doctrines,* ed. James Henthorn Todd (London: Camden Society, 1842), 70–71.

70. See *Heresy Trials in the Diocese of Norwich 1428-31.* On the presence and persecution of Lollards in East Anglia, see Thomson, *The Later Lollards, 1414-1520* (London: Oxford University Press, 1967), 117–38; and Hudson, *The Premature Reformation.*

71. *Heresy Trials,* 160, and Tanner's commentary, 17. A similar position was taken
by the priest William White, thought to have been the teacher of the heretics accused in the Norwich trials. According to Netter's account of his trial, White ad-
mitted teaching that the law of Christ called for the marriage of all three estates,
including the clergy, and rejected priestly celibacy, claiming it was an invention of
the Antichrist and asserting that it led to vice among the priesthood. Even after ab-
juring heresy, White himself married, which clearly scandalized Netter, since he
colorfully describes this arrangement as living "in fornicariis et illicitis amplexibus,
sub colore matrimonii." For Netter's account of the trial, see *Fasciculi Zizaniorum,*
ed. W. W. Shirley (London: Longman, Brown, Green, Longmans and Roberts, 1858),
417–32. For a discussion of White's views and for an argument that White was the
most important teacher of those accused in the Norwich heresy trials, see Margaret
Aston, *Lollards and Reformers: Images and Literacy in Late Medieval Religion* (London:
Hambledon Press, 1984), 71–100.

72. *Lollard Sermons,* ed. Cigman, 57.

73. Ibid., 58.

74. "Lex continencie a beata Uirgine, Dei genitrice, inter Dei cultores originem
sumpsit, et Christus ac eius apostoli uiris ecclesiasticis exemplarunt perpetue con-

tinencie puritatem." *Rogeri Dymmok: Liber Contra XII Errores et Hereses Lollardorum,* ed. H. S. Cronin (London: Kegan Paul, Trench and Trübner, 1922), 72. My translation.

75. "[I]deo Uirgo gloriosa uotum condicionaliter emisit uirginitatis, antequam esset desponsata, scilicet, si Deo placeret, set post matrimonium inter ipsam at Ioseph celebratum ex diuina inspiracione, marito consenciente, expresse castitatem est professa cum eodum." Dymmok, *Liber Contra XII Errores et Hereses Lollardorum,* 72. My translation.

76. R. H. Helmholz, *Marriage Litigation in Medieval England* (London: Cambridge University Press, 1974).

77. Marriage cases seeking to establish that a marriage had taken place were the most common form of marriage litigation. See Charles Donahue, Jr., "The Canon Law on the Formation of Marriage and Social Practice in the Later Middle Ages," *Journal of Family History* 8 (1983): 144–58; Helmholz, *Marriage Litigation;* Richard M. Wunderli, *London Church Courts and Society on the Eve of the Reformation* (Cambridge: Medieval Academy of America, 1981); and Michael Sheehan, "The Formation and Stability of Marriage in Fourteenth Century England: Evidence of an Ely Register," *Mediaeval Studies* 33 (1971): 228–63, and "Marriage Theory and Practice in the Conciliar Legislation and Diocesan Statutes of Medieval England," *Mediaeval Studies* 40 (1978): 408–60 (reprinted in Michael M. Sheehan, *Marriage, Family and Law in Medieval Europe: Collected Studies,* ed. James K. Farge [Toronto: University of Toronto Press, 1996], 38–76 and 118–76). For examples of these local laws, see *Lynwood's Provinciale,* ed. J. V. Bullard and H. Chamber Bell (London: Faith Press, 1929), 116–18.

78. Quoted in Michael Sheehan, "Choice of Marriage Partner in the Middle Ages: Development and Mode of Application of a Theory of Marriage," *Studies in Medieval and Renaissance History* n.s. 1 (1978): 22–23 (reprinted in Michael M. Sheehan, *Marriage, Family and Law in Medieval Europe,* 87–117).

79. *Robert of Brunne's* Handlying Synne, ed. Frederick J. Furnivall, EETS, o.s. 119 (London: Kegan Paul, Trench, Trübner & Co., 1903), 2:346.

80. "Sermon de Nupcijs," in *Mirk's Festial,* 289 and 291.

81. *Heresy Trials,* 153.

82. Ibid., 111, and elsewhere in the depositions.

83. ". . . dicendum, quod verba quibus consensus matrimonalis exprimitur sunt forma huius sacramenti . . . Et ideo, sicut poenitentia non habet aliam materiam nisi ipsos actus sensui subiectos, qui sunt loco materialis elementi, ita est de matrimonio." Quoted in Seamus P. Heaney, *Development of Sacramentality of Marriage from Anselm of Laon to Thomas Aquinas* (Washington, DC: Catholic University of America Press, 1963), 67 n. 276 and 68 n. 277.

84. For an example of the use of these Augustinian quotations by a later theologian, see Peter Lombard, book 4 of the Distinctions in Rogers, *Peter Lombard and the Sacramental System,* 79.

85. Hugh of Saint Victor, *On the Sacraments,* 331.

86. On the staging of medieval plays, see Robert Weimann, *Shakespeare and the Popular Tradition in the Theater* (Baltimore: Johns Hopkins University Press, 1978), 49–97; and Twycross, "The Theatricality of Medieval English Plays," 37–84.

87. J. L. Austin, *How to Do Things with Words* (Cambridge: Harvard University Press, 1962), 6. For a discussion of the antisacramentality of Austin's description of the performative utterance, see Timothy Gould, "The Unhappy Performative," in *Performativity and Performance,* ed. Andrew Parker and Eve Kosofsky Sedgwick (New York: Routledge, 1995), 21. Austin insists that in the performative the act is accomplished in the words, and is not an act occurring otherwise than in the words themselves. As Gould notes, Austin insisted that the utterance does not refer to some inward, invisible act, for which the words would then be taken as the outward and visible but still descriptive sign. See Austin, *How to Do Things with Words,* 9.

88. Austin, *How to Do Things with Words,* 22. Despite Austin's assertion, a growing number of critics have seen Austin's work as useful not only to studying theatricality but also specifically to studying the relationship between performativity of social life and the stage. For a useful introduction to and overview of this material, see Parker and Sedgwick, eds., *Performativity and Performance,* esp. 56–75. On the application of Austin's theory to the drama, see especially W. B. Worthen, "Drama, Performativity and Performance," *PMLA* 113, no. 5 (1998): 1093–1107.

89. Pierre Bourdieu, *Language and Symbolic Power,* ed. John B. Thompson (Cambridge: Harvard University Press, 1994), 111.

90. See "The Life of Saint Anne" from ms. University of Minnesota Z.822, N.81, in *Middle English Stanzaic Version of the Life of Saint Anne,* ed. Parker, 21–22, and Lydgate's *Life of Our Lady,* 405–8. I have discussed the play's engagement with legal procedures in "Language on Trial: Performing the Law in the N-Town Trial Play," in *The Letter of the Law: Legal Practice and Literary Production in Medieval England,* ed. Emily Steiner and Candace Barrington (Ithaca: Cornell University Press, 2002), 115–35. On the law in the N-Town trial play, also see Lynn Squires, "Law and Disorder in Ludus Coventriae," in *The Drama of the Middle Ages,* ed. Clifford Davidson, C. J. Gianakaris, and John H. Stroupe (New York: AMS Press, 1982), 272–85; Theresa Coletti, "Purity and Danger: The Paradox of Mary's Body and the Engendering of the Infancy Narrative in the English Mystery Cycles," in *Approaches to the Body in Medieval Literature,* ed. Linda Lomperis and Sarah Stanbury (Philadelphia: University of Pennsylvania Press, 1993), 65–95; Alison M. Hunt, "Maculating Mary: The Detractors of the N-Town Cycle's 'Trial of Joseph and Mary,'" *Philological Quarterly* 73 (1994): 11–29; Cindy L. Carlson, "Mary's Obedience and Power in the Trial of Mary and Joseph," *Comparative Drama* 29 (1995): 348–62.

91. As opposed to the consistory court in which each step was written down. See Wunderli, *London Church Courts and Society,* 25–62; and Ralph Houlbrooke,

Church Courts and the People During the English Reformation, 1520-1570 (Oxford: Oxford University Press, 1979), 21–54.

92. For an eleventh-century Latin version of this lai from the Cambridge Songs, and a twelfth-century version by Matthew of Vendôme, see F. J. E. Raby, *A History of Secular Latin Poetry in the Middle Ages* (Oxford: Clarendon Press, 1934), 1:295–97, 2:34. For a later medieval French version, see *Recueil général et complet des fabliaux des XIIIe et XIVe siècles,* ed. M. Anatole de Montaiglon (Paris: Librairie des Bibliophiles, 1872), 1:162–67, trans. in Robert L. Harrison, *Gallic Salt; Eighteen Fabliaux Translated from the Old French* (Berkeley: University of California Press, 1974), 380–89. For commentary, see Woolf, *English Mystery Plays,* 176.

93. Harrison, *Gallic Salt,* 380–81. On lying and the fabliau, see Carl Lindahl, *Earnest Games* (Bloomington: Indiana University Press, 1987), 124–55.

94. This association of women and carnality is familiar from Chaucer's Wife of Bath, who famously asserts, "My joly body shall tell a tale." A particularly colorful example is the fabliau "Du Chevalier qui fist les cons parler," in Harrison, *Gallic Salt,* 218–55. For a discussion of the association of speech with the female body in French fabliaux, see E. Jane Burns, *Bodytalk: When Women Speak in Old French Literature* (Philadelphia: University of Pennsylvania Press, 1993).

95. The detractors' idolatry is linked to the sin of lust, invoking a standard iconography of visual representation, in which sexual vices were often identified with false representation. Michael Camille, *The Gothic Idol: Ideology and Image-Making in Medieval Art* (Cambridge: Cambridge University Press, 1989), 61.

96. Quoted in Aston, *Lollards and Reformers,* 139. Wyclif's criticism of images was moderate in comparison with that of later Lollards, although they shared his concerns about images.

97. Sarah Stanbury, "The Vivacity of Images: St. Katherine, Knighton's Lollards, and the Breaking of Idols," in *Images, Idolatry and Iconoclasm in Late Medieval England: Textuality and the Visual Image,* ed. Jeremy Dimmick, James Simpson, and Nicolette Zeeman (New York: Oxford University Press, 2002), 141.

98. As William R. Jones has shown, in "Lollards and Images: The Defense of Religious Art in Later Medieval England," *Journal of the History of Ideas* 34, no. 1 (1973): 27–50, there is a body of commentary on images in the period which belongs to neither the Lollard iconoclasts nor the orthodox defenders of images. This group denounced the corruptions of images but accepted their proper use for spiritual purposes.

99. "Images and Pilgrimages," *Selections from English Wycliffite Writings,* 87. The "Tretise of Miraclis Pleyinge" applied a similar logic to its antitheatrical polemic when it refuted the orthodox claim that images and plays were useful for educating the illiterate, by claiming that "myraclis pleyinge . . . ben made more to deliten men bodily þan to ben bokis to lewid men" (*Selections from English Wycliffite Writings,* 104).

100. Barbara G. Lane, *The Altar and the Altarpiece: Sacramental Themes in Netherlandish Painting* (New York: Harper and Row, 1984), esp. 13–39.

101. Gibson, *Theater of Devotion*, 7–13. This logic was behind the "Incarnational Aesthetic," which Gibson has deemed central to fifteenth-century East Anglian culture and religious drama.

102. Sarah Beckwith, *Signifying God: Social Relation and Symbolic Act in the York Corpus Christi Plays* (Chicago: University of Chicago Press, 2001), 59.

103. Some influential accounts of the Mass as *ludus* include Richard Axton, *European Drama of the Early Middle Ages* (London: Hutchinson, 1974), chap. 4; O. B. Hardison, *Christian Rite and Christian Drama in the Middle Ages: Essays in the Origin and Early History of Modern Drama* (Baltimore: Johns Hopkins University Press, 1965), 77–79, 187–92; Karl Young, *The Drama of the Medieval Church* (Oxford: Clarendon Press, 1933).

104. Paul Hymans, "Trial by Ordeal: The Key to Proof in the Early Common Law," in *On the Laws and Customs of England: Essays in Honor of Samuel E. Thorne*, ed. Morris S. Arnold et al. (Chapel Hill: University of North Carolina Press, 1981), 92.

105. "When therefore Joseph had drunk and had walked around the altar, no sign of sin appeared in him." The relevant section of the text of the Apocrypha is reprinted in *John Lydgate's Life of Our Lady*, 78–79, from *Evangelia Apocrypha*, ed. Constantine Tischendorf (Lipsiae: H. Mendelssohn, 1876).

106. Notably, Lydgate's version does not give the same emphasis to language:

> And al at onys, fell dovne afore
> This holy mayde, with humble Reuerence
> And wold hir fete, haue kyssed ther anone
> Axyng mercy, of thayre grete offence
> And she forgaf it, to hem euerycheone.

See *Life of Our Lady*, 422.

107. Ibid., 420–21.

108. This use of Mary as the ideal speaker in the N-Town play is consistent with the role often given Mary in the Bible and vernacular literature as quiet and saying little. For example, in Lydgate's version, Mary's completion of the test is described as follows: "Al be that she, speke but wordes fewe / Withoutyn speche, shall the dede shewe" (*John Lydgate's Life of Our Lady*, 78). As Edwin D. Craun observes in *Lies, Slander, and Obscenity in Medieval English Literature* (New York: Cambridge University Press, 1997), 52, the Virgin is often a figure for judicious speech, and she speaks only seven words in the Gospels.

109. Internal manuscript evidence suggests that this prose treatise was written between 1405 and about 1410. See *Dives and Pauper*, ed. Priscilla Heath Barnum, EETS, o.s. 275, vol. 1, part 1 (London: Oxford University Press, 1976), ix.

110. The discussion of images is part of his exposition of the practical meaning of the first commandment. See *Dives and Pauper,* 82.

111. *Dives and Pauper,* vol. 1, part 1, 82.

112. The three "goods" of marriage—sacrament (*sacramentum*), faith, and off-spring (*fides et proles*)—all referred not to the precise moment of the wedding but to the married state. For Augustine's three goods, see *De Bono Coniugali* in *Saint Augustin: On the Holy Trinity,* 397–413.

113. See the introduction in *A Tretise of Miraclis Pleyinge,* ed. Clifford Davidson (Kalamazoo: Medieval Institute Publications, 1993), 1–52.

114. Ritchie D. Kendall, *The Drama of Dissent: The Radical Poetics of Nonconformity, 1380-1590* (Chapel Hill: University of North Carolina Press, 1986), 50–89. On the reforming drama of the Protestants, see Huston Diehl, *Staging Reform, Reforming the Stage* (Ithaca: Cornell University Press, 1997).

115. See Weimann, *Shakespeare and the Popular Tradition in the Theater,* 92–94; Sarah Beckwith, *Signifying God,* 90–117; and Ruth Nisse, *Defining Acts,* 23–45.

Chapter 4.   The Marriage of Love and Sex

1. These documents are printed in appendix 3 in *The Book of Margery Kempe,* ed. Sanford Brown Meech and Hope Emily Allen, EETS, o.s. 212 (New York: Oxford University Press, 1940). All references will be to this edition and will be included in the text. On Margery and her family, also see Anthony Goodman, *Margery Kempe and Her World* (New York: Longman, 2002), esp. 15–55.

2. Sheila Delany, "Sexual Economics, Chaucer's Wife of Bath and *The Book of Margery Kempe,*" *Minnesota Review* 5 (1975): 110–11.

3. David Aers, *Community, Gender, and Individual Identity: English Writing 1360-1430* (New York: Routledge, 1988), 80.

4. Sarah Beckwith, *Christ's Body: Identity, Culture and Society in Late Medieval Writing* (New York: Routledge, 1993), 102.

5. Kathleen Ashley, "Historicizing Margery: *The Book of Margery Kempe* as Social Text," *JMEMS* 28 (1998): 374. On Margery and bourgeois identity, also see Clarissa W. Atkinson, *Mystic and Pilgrim: The Book and the World of Margery Kempe* (Ithaca: Cornell University Press, 1983), 67–101; and Deborah S. Ellis, "The Merchant's Wife's Tale: Language, Sex and Commerce in Margery Kempe and in Chaucer," *Exemplaria* 2 (1990): 595–626.

6. Lynn Staley, *Margery Kempe's Dissenting Fictions* (University Park: Pennsylvania State University Press, 1994), 1–38. On sacred biography as social criticism, also see Thomas J. Heffernan, *Sacred Biography: Saints and Their Biographers in the Middle Ages* (New York: Oxford University Press, 1988).

7. Gail McMurray Gibson, *The Theater of Devotion: East Anglian Drama and Society in the Late Middle Ages* (Chicago: University of Chicago Press, 1989), 47–65; and Sarah Beckwith, *Christ's Body*, 78–111.

8. Katherine J. Lewis, "Margery Kempe and Saint Making in Later Medieval England," in *A Companion to the Book of Margery Kempe*, ed. John H. Arnold and Katherine J. Lewis (Rochester, NY, and Woodbridge, Suffolk: D. S. Brewer, 2004), 195–215.

9. Referring to his patron, Bokenham prays "That I may translate in wurdys pleyne / In-to oure langwage oute of latyn / The lyf of blyssyd Mare Mawdelyn, / To hyr goostly confourth in especyal, / And of them generally wych it redyn shal." See Osbern Bokenham, *Legendys of Hooly Wummen*, ed. Mary S. Serjeantson, EETS, o.s. 206 (London: Oxford University Press, 1938), 144.

10. Susan Dickerman, "Margery Kempe and the Continental Tradition of the Pious Woman," in *The Medieval Mystical Tradition in England: Papers Read at Dartington Hall, July 1984*, ed. Marion Glasscoe (Cambridge: D. S. Brewer, 1984), 157. On Continental holy women and Margery Kempe, see especially Atkinson, *Mystic and Pilgrim*, 157–94; Karma Lochrie, *Margery Kempe and the Translations of the Flesh* (Philadelphia: University of Pennsylvania Press, 1991), 76–88 and 118–20; Julia Bolton Holloway, "Bride, Margery, Julian and Alice: Bridget of Sweden's Textual Community in Medieval England," in *Margery Kempe: A Book of Essays*, ed. Sandra J. McEntire (New York: Garland, 1992), 203–21; David Wallace, "Mystics and Followers in Siena and East Anglia: A Study in Taxonomy, Class and Cultural Mediation," in *The Medieval Mystical Tradition in England*, ed. Glasscoe, 169–91; Ute Stargardt, "The Beguines of Belgium, the Dominican Nuns of Germany, and Margery Kempe," in *The Popular Literature of Medieval England*, ed. Thomas J. Heffernan, vol. 28, Tennessee Studies in Literature (Knoxville: University of Tennessee Press, 1985), 277–313; and Staley, *Margery Kempe's Dissenting Fictions*, 39–82.

11. Bridget of Sweden, *The Liber Celestis of St. Bridget of Sweden*, ed. Roger Ellis, vol. 1, EETS, o.s. 291 (New York: Oxford University Press, 1987), 8. For references to Bridget and her book in *The Book of Margery Kempe*, see 39, 47, 95, and 143. On the popularity of Saint Bridget in fifteenth-century England, see F. R. Johnston, "The English Cult of St. Bridget of Sweden," *Analecta Bollandiana* 103 (1985): 75–93; and Roger Ellis, "'Flores ad Fabricandam . . . Coronam': An Investigation into the Uses of the Revelations of St. Bridget of Sweden in Fifteenth-Century England," *MAE* 51 (1982): 163–86.

12. Jacques de Vitry, *The Life of Marie d'Oignies*, trans. Margot H. King (Saskatoon: Peregrina, 1986), 102.

13. Margery also seeks the company of Mary Magdalene, who had ceased her sexual activity prior to sainthood. Goodman notes the popularity of Saints Katherine and Margaret in East Anglia, observing that statues of the two saints flanked

the shrine of Our Lady of Walsingham and that these two were depicted more often in Norwich stained glass windows than any other early female martyrs. See Goodman, *Margery Kempe and Her World,* 122; Eamon Duffy, *The Stripping of the Altars: Traditional Religion in England 1400–1580* (New Haven: Yale University Press, 1992), 171; and Christopher Woodforde, *The Norwich School of Glass Painting in the Fifteenth Century* (London: Oxford University Press, 1950), 177.

14. Sarah Salih, *Versions of Virginity in Late Medieval England* (Woodbridge, Suffolk, and Rochester, NY: D. S. Brewer, 2001), 195–201; Katherine J. Lewis, *The Cult of St. Katherine of Alexandria in Late Medieval England* (Rochester, NY, and Woodbridge, Suffolk: Boydell Press, 2000), 244–56.

15. For the popularity of Saint Katherine narratives among married women, and the uses of Saint Katherine in conduct books to promote marital rather than virginal chastity, see Lewis, *The Cult of St. Katherine,* 227–42.

16. *Legendys of Hooly Wummen.* Furthermore, one of the three married saints included in the collection, Saint Cecelia, had a chaste marriage, and another, Saint Elizabeth, refuses remarriage after her husband's death, insisting instead on remaining a widow.

17. Ibid., 22.

18. Marc Glasser, "Marriage in Medieval Hagiography," *Studies in Medieval and Renaissance History* n.s. 4 (1981): 6.

19. Ibid., 7.

20. *Legendys of Hooly Wummen,* 263.

21. See Aers, *Community, Gender, and Individual Identity,* 90. Delany, "Sexual Economics, Chaucer's Wife of Bath and *The Book of Margery Kempe,*" 112. Delany's materialist feminist argument continues to be widely influential, as does her emphasis on understanding Margery's earthly marriage to her husband, John, in the context of the social conditions of late medieval women and marriage practices. Delany's article has since been reprinted in her own essay collection *Writing Woman: Women Writers and Women in Literature, Medieval to Modern* (New York: Schocken Books, 1983), 76–92, and in *Feminist Readings in Middle English Literature: The Wife of Bath and All her Sect,* ed. Ruth Evans and Lesley Johnson (New York: Routledge, 1994), 72–87.

22. See, for example, Barbara A. Hanawalt, *The Ties That Bound: Peasant Families in Medieval England* (New York: Oxford University Press, 1986), and *Growing Up in Medieval London: The Experience of Childhood in History* (New York: Oxford University Press, 1993); Judith M. Bennett, *Women in the Medieval English Countryside: Gender and Household in Brigstock Before the Plague* (New York: Oxford University Press, 1987), 188; and Sylvia L. Thrupp, *The Merchant Class of Medieval London* (Chicago: University of Chicago Press, 1948), 170.

23. For Salih, this scene is "a competition between Margery and John Kempe as to which of them is the more creative reader of virgin martyr legends." She argues

that John "first positions himself as the virgin martyr, given the choice of sex or decapitation," while Margery is "placed as the vengeful suitor," and subsequently that Margery "regains the advantage by her readiness to sacrifice John's life for the sake of mutual celibacy, effectively recasting herself as the martyr." See *Versions of Virginity,* 199–200.

24. Aers, *Community, Gender, and Individual Identity,* 93.

25. Bokenham's *Legendys of Hooly Wummen,* 204.

26. See Ellis, "The Merchant's Wife's Tale," 609; and Staley, *Dissenting Fictions,* 63.

27. On *couverture,* see *The Treatise on the Laws and Customs of the Realm of England Commonly Called Glanvill,* ed. G. D. G. Hall (London: Nelson and Sons, 1965), bk. 6: 58–60; Sir Frederick Pollock and Frederic William Maitland, *The History of English Law Before the Time of Edward I* (Cambridge: Cambridge University Press, 1968), 2:399–414, esp. 404–7; Kay E. Lacey, "Women and Work in Fourteenth- and Fifteenth-Century England," in *Women and Work in Pre-Industrial England,* ed. Lindsey Charles and Lorna Duffin (London: Croom Helm, 1985), 26–42; Bennett, *Women in the Medieval English Countryside,* 104–14. For an analysis of the meanings of *couverture* in late medieval England and in *The Book of Margery Kempe,* see Karma Lochrie, *Covert Operations: The Medieval Uses of Secrecy* (Philadelphia: University of Pennsylvania Press, 1999), 135–64.

28. On *femme sole,* see Lacey, "Women and Work," 41–57. As Brian W. Gastle has recently argued, this legal category not only "legitimized women's economic role" but also granted them an autonomy that disrupted medieval ideas of the mutual obligation of the marital debt. See " 'As if she were single'; Working Wives and the Late Medieval English *Femme Sole,*" in *The Middle Ages at Work: Practicing Labor in Late Medieval England,* ed. Kellie Robertson and Michael Ubel (New York: Palgrave Macmillan, 2004), 41–64.

29. In this case, the husband and wife own in joint tenancy, and the assent of both parties was required for any transaction. Unlike dower, the wife could inherit all the lands when the husband died. This arrangement was most often obtained by women like Margery Kempe who were of a higher social status than their husbands. See Pollock and Maitland, *History of English Law,* 2:20, 245–46; Sue Sheridan Walker, "Litigation as Personal Quest: Suing for Dower in the Royal Courts, circa 1272–1350," in *Wife and Widow in Medieval England,* ed. Sue Sheridan Walker (Ann Arbor: University of Michigan Press, 1993), 96; Andrea Dianne Maxeiner, "Dower and Jointure: A Legal and Statistical Analysis of the Property Rights of Married Women in Late Medieval England" (Ph.D. diss., Catholic University of America, 1990), 2–3, 59–66, 112–17. Evidence that women of means were aware of jointure as an option can be found in the Paston letters. See *Paston Letters and Papers of the Fifteenth Century,* ed. Norman Davis (Oxford: Clarendon Press, 1971), part 1, 206, letter no. 121.

30. After her husband's death, a wife could file a writ to regain her dowry if alienated during her lifetime or to collect her dower, which was a third of the property in which her husband had been *seised,* or legally possessed, during his lifetime. One can easily imagine that a woman as feisty and vocal as Margery Kempe might have effectively discouraged any prospective property buyer by making it clear that, in the event of her husband's death, she planned to file a writ of *cui in vita.* See Lacey, "Women and Work," 27–29; *The Treatise on the Laws and Customs of the Realm of England Commonly Called Glanvill,* 58–65, 134–35; Pollock and Maitland, *The History of English Law,* 404–29; Walker, "Litigation as Personal Quest"; Robert C. Palmer, "Contexts of Marriage in Medieval England: Evidence from the King's Court circa 1300," *Speculum* 59 (1984): 42–67; and Maxeiner, "Dower and Jointure," 36–42, 56–58. The only way to secure property against a subsequent claim of the wife was to use a "fine," in which the wife was examined separately from her husband, but these were expensive and uncommon. A thirteenth-century poem complains of the difficulties of dealing with the property of a married woman:

> Jesu as thou art heaven's king
> Send us grace to have knowing
> Who will beware in purchasing
> Consider the points here following;
> First see that the land be clear
> In any title of the seller;
> And that it stand in no danger
> Of any woman's dower

Quoted in Maxeiner, "Dower and Jointure," 40.

31. In *Margery Kempe and Her World,* Goodman gives a less legalistic explanation, arguing that "John allowed her to control her possessions and to treat her acquisitions as her own" (70), also noting that burgesses "are likely to have been generally inclined to allow their wives control over at least some of their own assets" since wealthy women in Lynn often played a crucial partnership role in both business and social life (60).

32. George Duby's influential *Medieval Marriage: Two Models from Twelfth-Century France,* trans. Elborg Forster (Baltimore: Johns Hopkins University Press, 1978), has played a significant role in perpetuating the view that consensual theory was overshadowed by concerns of money and family alliances in the formation of medieval marriage. While the book is widely cited, Duby was in fact discussing only the highest levels of medieval society. For a discussion of how marriage was affected by class, see Michael M. Sheehan, "The Wife of Bath and Her Four Sisters: Reflections on a Woman's Life in the Age of Chaucer," *Medievalia et Humanistica* n.s. 13 (1985): 23–42 (reprinted in *Marriage, Family and Law in Medieval Europe,* ed. James K. Farge [Toronto: University of Toronto Press, 1996], 177–98).

33. 3if any man bidde þe worschipe, and will wedde the,
    Auysely answere hym; scorne hym noght, what he be.
    Schewe it to þin frendis, and fohele it noght.
    Sitte bi hym, ne stnde þer synne may be wroght.

The Good Wife Taught Her Daughter, the Good Wyfe Wold a Pylgremage, the Thewis of Gud Women, ed. Tauno F. Mustanoja (Helsinki: Suomalaisen Kirjallisuuden Scuran, 1948), 159.

34. See *The Book of Margery Kempe,* 6. On urban marriage patterns, see P. J. P. Goldberg, *Women, Work and Life Cycle in a Medieval Economy: Women in York and Yorkshire c. 1300-1520* (Oxford: Clarendon Press, 1992), 201–79. On the relevance of this paradigm to Margery Kempe, see Goldberg, 231.

35. On this scene as an instance of the couple's "long-lasting mutual affection," also see Goodman, *Margery Kempe and Her World,* 73. Goodman also points to current ideas that sexual pleasure should not be indulged as central to the "marital tension" between John and Margery. See *Margery Kempe and Her World,* 75, 103.

36. On the marital debt, see Pierre J. Payer, *The Bridling of Desire: Views of Sex in the Later Middle Ages* (Toronto: University of Toronto Press, 1993), 89–97; James A. Brundage, *Law, Sex and Christian Society in Medieval Europe* (Chicago: University of Chicago Press, 1987), esp. 241–42, 358–60, 505–7; Thomas N. Tentler, *Sin and Confession on the Eve of the Reformation* (Princeton: Princeton University Press, 1977), 170–74; Elizabeth M. Makowski, "The Conjugal Debt and Medieval Canon Law," in *Equally in God's Image,* ed. Julia Bolton Holloway, Joan Bechtold, and Constance S. Wright (New York: Peter Lang, 1990). Although potentially an area of theoretical equality between the sexes, the interpretation and practice of the theory of the marital debt did not support this equality. See especially Elliott, *Spiritual Marriage,* 148–55.

37. My italics. First portion translated and quoted from the Vulgate by Payer, *The Bridling of Desire,* 90, and second portion translated and quoted by Makowski, "Conjugal Debt," 129.

38. On the gap between spiritual life and material sexuality in marriage theology see especially Eleanor McLaughlin, "Equality of Souls, Inequality of Sexes: Woman in Medieval Theology," in *Religion and Sexism: Images of Woman in the Jewish and Christian Traditions,* ed. Rosemary Radford Ruether (New York: Simon and Schuster, 1974), esp. 228–30. As McLaughlin puts it, "Physical sex was always suspect, and could never be the vehicle of love, which was defined in wholly spiritual terms" (229).

39. See Tentler, *Sin and Confession*; D. L. d'Avray and M. Tausche, "Marriage Sermons in *Ad Status* Collections of the Central Middle Ages," *Archives d'histoire doctrinale et littéraire du moyen âge* 47 (1981): 71–119; and D. L. d'Avray, *Medieval Marriage Sermons: Mass Communication in a Culture Without Print* (New York: Oxford University Press, 2001).

40. Payer, *The Bridling of Desire,* 14.

41. James A. Brundage, "The Problem of Impotence," in *Sexual Practices and the Medieval Church,* ed. Vern L. Bullough and James Brundage (Buffalo: Prometheus Books, 1982), 135–40; and Brundage, *Law, Sex and Christian Society,* 201–2, 290–92, esp. 456–58 and plate 14; Makowski, "Conjugal Debt," 134–35; Payer, *The Bridling of Desire,* 73–75.

42. Brundage, *Law, Sex and Christian Society,* 236; Makowski, "Conjugal Debt," 136–37; and Payer, *Bridling of Desire,* 90–91.

43. Wolfgang Riehle, *The Middle English Mystics* (London: Routledge & Kegan Paul, 1981), 38.

44. Anthony Goodman, "The Piety of John Brunham's Daughter, of Lynn," in *Medieval Women,* ed. Derek Baker (Oxford: Basil Blackwell, 1978), 347–58.

45. On the "unabashed sexuality" (159) of what she terms "la mystique courtoise" of the thirteenth-century Beguines, see Barbara Newman, *From Virile Woman to WomanChrist* (Philadelphia: University of Pennsylvania Press, 1995), 137–67. As Newman has observed, the "so-called bridal spirituality of the Middle Ages does not always evoke the refinements of mystical union; it could appeal to very earthly motives" (32). On Margery Kempe and this tradition, see Stargardt, "The Beguines of Belgium," 295–97.

46. Dickerman, "Margery Kempe and the Continental Tradition of the Pious Woman," 161.

47. On the babysitting episode, see Ashley, "Historicizing Margery," 380.

48. Quoted in Beckwith, *Christ's Body,* 145 n. 17.

49. One example of Bernard's meticulously drawn distinctions among the kinds of love and his hierarchical ranking of them is in Sermon 50:

> [T]here is an affection which the flesh begets, and one which reason controls, and one which wisdom seasons. The first is that which the apostle says is not subject to the law of God, nor can be (Rom 8:7); the second, on the contrary, he shows to [*sic*] in agreement with the law of God because it is good (Rom 7:16)—one cannot doubt that the insubordinate and the agreeable differ from each other. The third, however, is far from either of them, because it tastes and experiences that the Lord is sweet (Ps 33:9); it banishes the first and rewards the second. The first is pleasant, of course, but shameful; the second is emotionless but strong; the last is rich and delightful.

Bernard of Clairvaux, *On the Song of Songs,* trans. Kilian Walsh and Irene M. Edmonds (Kalamazoo: Cistercian Publications, 1979), 3:32–33. In Sermon 1, Bernard clearly identified his audience as monastic, indicating that his sermons were not intended for those "of the world" who he evidently believed were not able to understand clearly his distinctions. See Bernard of Clairvaux, *On the Song of Songs,* trans. Kilian Walsh (Kalamazoo: Cistercian Publications, 1971), 1:1; and discussion in

E. Ann Matter, *The Voice of My Beloved: The Song of Songs in Western Medieval Christianity* (Philadelphia: University of Pennsylvania Press, 1990), 125.

50. Sermon 85 in *On the Song of Songs,* trans. Irene Edmonds, Cistercian Fathers Series 40 (Kalamazoo: Cistercian Publications, 1980), 4:209.

51. *Anchoritic Spirituality:* Ancrene Wisse *and Associated Works,* trans. and ed. Anne Savage and Nicholas Watson (New York: Paulist Press, 1991), 239.

52. "Si vis nubere terrestri marito propter divitias, considera quod terrenae divitiae fallaces sunt et transitoriae, quia aut in praesenti vita transeunt, aut saltem in morte recedunt. Nube ergo illi, apud quem thesauri sunt incomparabiles, et divitiae immutables; quas nec furatur, nec tinea demolitur." Alan de Lille, *Summa de arte praedicatoria* 47, PL 210:195bc; quoted and translated by Newman, *From Virile Woman to WomanChrist,* 32.

53. On the application of Bernard's bridal motifs to women, see John Bugge, *Virginitas: An Essay in the History of a Medieval Ideal* (The Hague: Martinus Nijhoff, 1975), 91. On the history of the Song of Songs tradition, also see Ann W. Astell, *The Song of Songs in the Middle Ages* (Ithaca: Cornell University Press, 1990); and Matter, *The Voice of My Beloved.*

54. Sermon 1, in *On the Song of Songs,* trans. Kilian Walsh, 1:1.

55. For a discussion of this passage, and Bernard's intended audience, see Matter, *The Voice of My Beloved,* 125.

56. Richard Rolle, *The Fire of Love and the Mending of Life or The Rule of Living,* trans. Richard Misyn, ed. Ralph Harvey, EETS, o.s. 106 (London: Kegan Paul, Trench & Trübner, 1896), 2.

57. The fragility of this and other distinctions was a subject of concern to Church authorities who believed religious materials should be limited to clerics and sought to regulate vernacular religious material directed to a lay audience. On this subject, see especially Nicholas Watson, "Censorship and Cultural Change in Late-Medieval England: Vernacular Theology, the Oxford Translation Debate, and Arundel's Constitutions of 1409," *Speculum* 70 (1995): 822–64. For a discussion of the politics of the affective tradition, and the ways it invited a blurring of the boundaries between the active and contemplative life which was threatening to clerical authority, see Beckwith, *Christ's Body,* 45–77.

58. See *The Life of Catherine of Siena by Raymond of Capua,* trans. Conleth Kearns (Wilmington: Michael Glazier, 1980), 106–9. In a similar vein, in *The Cult of St. Katherine of Alexandria,* Lewis notes that Katherine of Alexandria's life also includes a marriage ceremony that is similar to Margery's in its depiction of a heavenly assembly of witnesses, but she notes that Kempe's imagery is more overtly sexual (199–204).

59. The "Sermon de Nupcijs," *Mirk's Festial,* 291.

60. Hugh of Saint Victor, *Hugh of Saint Victor on the Sacraments of the Christian Faith,* trans. Roy J. Deferrari (Cambridge: Medieval Academy of America, 1951), 151.

This was consistent with Origin's reading of the *sponsa christi* metaphor as applying to the individual soul, in contrast to the other tradition of seeing it as the ecclesiological union of Christ and the Church. See Bugge, *Virginitas,* 86–87.

61. See introduction, note 31.

62. *The Goodman of Paris (Le Ménagier de Paris),* trans. Eileen Power (London: Routledge, 1928), 94.

63. *The Goodman of Paris,* 95. An almost identical passage occurs in Caxton's *The Book of the Knight of the Tower,* ed. M. Y. Offord, EETS, s.s. 2 (New York: Oxford University Press, 1971), 156–57. He too specifies that the parable of the precious stone should be understood to apply equally to wives, widows, and virgins.

64. *Early English Meals and Manners,* ed. Frederick J. Furnivall, EETS, o.s. 32 (London: Oxford University Press, 1868), 263.

65. Ibid., 265.

66. Majorie K. McIntosh, "Finding Language for Misconduct: Jurors in Fifteenth-Century Local Courts," in *Bodies and Disciplines: Intersections of Literature and History in Fifteenth-Century England,* ed. Barbara A. Hanawalt and David Wallace (Minneapolis: University of Minnesota Press, 1996), 87–122, and *Controlling Misbehavior in England, 1370–1600* (Cambridge: Cambridge University Press, 1998).

67. Quoted in William R. Jones, "English Religious Brotherhoods and Medieval Lay Piety: The Inquiry of 1388–89," *The Historian* 36 (1973–74): 651. On this subject, also see Barbara A. Hanawalt, "Keepers of the Lights: Late Medieval English Parish Gilds," *JMRS* 14 (1984): 21–37; and Ben R. McRee, "Religious Guilds and Regulation of Behavior in Late Medieval Towns," in *People, Politics and Community in the Later Middle Ages,* ed. Joel Rosenthal and Colin Richmond (New York: St. Martin's Press, 1987), 108–22.

68. Lee Patterson, *Chaucer and the Subject of History* (Madison: University of Wisconsin Press, 1991), 322.

69. Clarissa W. Atkinson, "'Precious Balsam in a Fragile Glass': The Ideology of Virginity in the Later Middle Ages," *Journal of Family History* 8 (1983): 131–43.

70. Compare *Catherine of Siena: The Dialogue* with Raymond of Capua, *The Life of Catherine of Siena by Raymond of Capua.*

71. On the narrative as structured by marriage, see Nancy Partner, "'And Most of All for Inordinate Love': Desire and Denial in the Book of Margery Kempe," *Thought* 64 (1989): 254–67.

72. As Sarah Beckwith has observed, Christ's "love is likened to the way a bourgeois husband might clothe his wife to give her a status which would make her and him the envy of his neighbors, here placed in the position of competitors" (*Christ's Body,* 86).

73. See Susan Crane, *The Performance of Self: Ritual, Clothing and Identity During the Hundred Years War* (Philadelphia: University of Pennsylvania Press, 2002), 11–20;

and Claire Sponsler, *Drama and Resistance: Bodies, Goods and Theatricality in Late Medieval England* (Minneapolis: University of Minnesota Press, 1997), 1–23.

74. See *The Book of the Knight of La Tour-Landry,* ed. Thomas Wright, EETS, o.s.33 (London: Trübner, 1868), 10 and 38.

75. Crane, *The Performance of Self,* 4.

76. In a section entitled, "The Bourgeois Family and the Institutionalization of a Privateness Oriented to an Audience," Jürgen Habermas has linked this audience-oriented subjectivity not only to the bourgeois but also to the rise of the letter and of the domestic novel in the eighteenth century, the latter of which he calls "the psychological description in autobiographical form" (49), a category of obvious relevance to the *Book of Margery Kempe.* See *The Structural Transformation of the Public Sphere: An Inquiry into a Category of Bourgeois Society,* trans. Thomas Burger, with the assistance of Frederick Lawrence (Cambridge: MIT Press, 1991), 43–53.

77. Staley, *Dissenting Fictions,* 54.

78. For Margery's engagement with Lollardy as part of Margery's "queer touch" that participates in the "breaking up of the comfortable unities of gender, desire, and the body on which her community, its sexual norms, and its family structure are founded" (152), see Carolyn Dinshaw, *Getting Medieval: Sexualities and Communities, Pre- and Postmodern* (Durham: Duke University Press, 1999). For Margery's engagement with Lollardy as a "strategy of dissent" that interrogates contemporary ideas of national community, see Staley, *Margery Kempe's Dissenting Fictions.* On Kempe's engagement with Lollardy as a "critique of the prevailing discourses that would define heresy," see Ruth Shklar [now Nisse], "Cobham's Daughter: *The Book of Margery Kempe* and the Power of Heterodox Thinking," *MLQ* 56 (1995): 277–304. On the resemblance between Kempe's preaching and Lollardy, see Lochrie, *Margery Kempe and Translations of the Flesh,* 107–13. David Aers emphasizes the relationship between Margery's subversion of gender hierarchy and the accusations of Lollardy she provokes, noting elements of her behavior as "Lollard-like" (84). See Aers, *Community, Gender and Individual Identity,* 108–16. Similarly, Nancy Partner has argued that Margery's "style was Lollard." See "Reading the Book of Margery Kempe," *Exemplaria* 3 (1991): 33. Atkinson comments on the difficulties of defining Lollardy since it was never an organized movement, and claims that "Margery Kempe was no Lollard" (105), but identifies aspects of her behavior as "heterodox." See Atkinson, *Mystic and Pilgrim,* 103–12.

79. In "Cobham's Daughter," Nisse demonstrates that Lollards were associated with deviant sexuality and accused others of the same and also suggests that "'Lollardy' is in fact an all purpose term for social and sexual transgression" (294).

80. On this distinction, see Mary Erler, "Margery Kempe's White Clothes," *Medium Aevum* 62 (1993): 78–83. Erler sees Margery as "a woman vowed to chastity, but wearing the garments of symbolic virginity" (79). For Gunnel Cleve, "Seman-

tic Dimensions in Margery Kempe's 'Whyght Clothys,'" *Mystics Quarterly* 12 (1986): 162–70, "the very colour [of Margery's white clothes] suggests purity and virginity" (163). Sarah Salih has recently challenged the certainty of this ascription, arguing that "white clothing is associated with liminality" and only associated with virginity and holiness in certain contexts (223). See *Versions of Virginity in Late Medieval England*, 217–24. On Margery's white clothes as marking sexual deviance, heresy, and socio-political disruption, see Dinshaw, *Getting Medieval*, 143–52.

81. Although accusations of preaching may invoke contemporary fears of Lol-lard women preachers, as Katherine Lewis has demonstrated, Margery's role in this scene has another (more orthodox) model for nonconformity: the virgin-martyr Saint Katherine of Alexandria, another woman who spoke publicly about doctrine while being crossexamined by religious and social male authorities. See Lewis, *The Cult of St. Katherine of Alexandria*, 242–56.

82. Translated by C. W. Marx in Blamires, *Women Defamed and Women Defended: An Anthology of Medieval Texts* (Oxford: Clarendon Press, 1992), 252. For the Latin text, see Alcuin Blamires and C. W. Marx, "Woman Not to Preach: A Disputation in British Library MS Harley 31," *Journal of Medieval Latin* 3 (1993): 34–63. On *The Book of Margery Kempe* and the figure of the Lollard woman preacher, see especially Lochrie, *Margery Kempe and the Translations of the Flesh*, 107–13.

83. Shannon McSheffrey, *Gender and Heresy: Women and Men in Lollard Commu-nities* (Philadelphia: University of Pennsylvania Press, 1995). As Rebecca Krug has noted, the Norwich court records suggest that the extent to which women were involved in Lollardy at all may have been exaggerated: in the Norwich heresy tri-als of 1428–31, only nine of the sixty defendants were women. See *Reading Families: Women's Literate Practice in Late Medieval England* (Ithaca: Cornell University Press, 2002), 115. On Lollards and women, also see Margaret Aston, *Lollards and Reform-ers: Images and Literacy in Late Medieval Religion* (London: Hambledon Press, 1984), 49–70; and Claire Cross, "'Great Reasoners in Scripture': The Activities of Women Lollards, 1380–1530," in *Medieval Women*, ed. Derek Baker (Oxford: Basil Black-well, 1978), 359–80.

84. Staley, *Dissenting Fictions*, 54. As Dyan Elliott has shown, the archbishop's as-sociation of Margery's white garb with domestic disruption should be understood as part of a broader phenomenon, whereby the husband's control of his wife's dress was seen as more important than her ability to use her dress for pious goals: "The Church ultimately collaborated with husbands in controlling or even suppressing outward dis-plays of female piety, thus depriving women of the freedom to imitate a saintly model openly." See Dyan Elliott, "Dress as Mediator Between Inner and Outer Self: The Pious Matron of the High and Later Middle Ages," *Mediaeval Studies* 53 (1991): 302.

85. Translated by Marx in Blamires, *Women Defamed and Women Defended*, 253. For the Latin text, see Blamires and Marx, "Woman Not to Preach," 34–63.

86. See *The Book of Margery Kempe,* 115 and note 79.

87. Shklar [Nisse], "Cobham's Daughter," 299.

88. John H. Arnold, "Margery's Trials: Heresy, Lollardy and Dissent," in *A Companion to* The Book of Margery Kempe, ed. John H. Arnold and Katherine J. Lewis (Cambridge: D. S. Brewer, 2004), 92. On the ways in which Kempe's account especially reveals the "vagueness of the popular concept of Lollardy" and "obscure[s] the line between reform and dissent," see Shklar [Nisse], "Cobham's Daughter," 290–91.

BIBLIOGRAPHY

Primary Sources

Aelred of Rievaulx. *Aelred of Rievaulx, Spiritual Friendship.* Trans. Mary Eugenia Laker. Cistercian Fathers Series 5. Kalamazoo: Cistercian Publications, 1974.

Anchoritic Spirituality. Trans. and ed. Anne Savage and Nicholas Watson. New York: Paulist Press, 1991.

Andreas Capellanus. *Andreas Capellanus on Love.* Trans. P. G. Walsh. London: Duckworth, 1982.

———. *The Art of Courtly Love.* Trans. John Jay Parry. New York: Columbia University Press, 1990.

An Apology for Lollard Doctrines. Ed. James Henthorn Todd. London: Camden Society, 1842.

Aquinas, Thomas. *Commentary on Aristotle's* Nicomachean Ethics. 2 vols. Trans. C. I. Litzinger. Chicago: Henry Regnery, 1964. Reprint, Notre Dame, IN: Dumb Ox Books, 1993.

Augustine. *Saint Augustin: Anti-Pelagian Writings.* Trans. Peter Holmes and Robert Ernest Wallis. 1st ser., vol. 5. *A Select Library of the Nicene and Post-Nicene Fathers of the Christian Church.* Ed. Philip Schaff. Grand Rapids: Eerdmans, 1956.

———. *Saint Augustin: On the Holy Trinity, Doctrinal Treatises, Moral Treatises.* Ed. Philip Schaff. 1st ser., vol. 3. *A Select Library of the Nicene and Post-Nicene Fathers of the Christian Church.* Buffalo: Christian Literature Co., 1956.

———. *Saint Augustin: Sermon on the Mount, Harmony of the Gospels, Homilies on the Gospels.* Trans. William Findlay. 1st ser., vol. 6. *A Select Library of the Nicene and Post-Nicene Fathers of the Christian Church.* Ed. Philip Schaff. Grand Rapids: Eerdmans, 1956.

Benoît de Sainte-More. *Le Roman de Troie.* 6 vols. Ed. Léopold Constans. Paris: Firmin Didot, 1904–12.

Bernard of Clairvaux. "In Assumptione Beatae Mariae Virginis." PL 184:1001–10.

———. *On the Song of Songs.* Vols. 1–4. Trans. Kilian Walsh and Irene Edmonds. Kalamazoo: Cistercian Publications, 1971–80.

Boccaccio, Giovanni. *De Casibus Virorum Illustrium, a Facsimile of the c. 1520 Paris Edition.* Ed. Lewis Brewer Hall. Gainesville: University of Florida Press, 1962.

———. *The Fates of Illustrious Men.* Trans. Louis Brewer Hall. New York: Frederick Ungar, 1965.

———. *Il Filocolo.* Trans. Donald Cheney. New York: Garland, 1985.

Bokenham, Osbern. *Legendys of Hooly Wummen.* Ed. Mary S. Serjeantson. EETS, o.s. 206. London: Oxford University Press, 1938.

The Book of the Knight of La Tour-Landry. Ed. Thomas Wright. EETS, o.s. 33. London: Trübner, 1868.

The Book of the Knight of the Tower. Trans. William Caxton. Ed. M. Y. Offord. EETS, s.s. 2. New York: Oxford University Press, 1971.

Bouicicault, Mareschal. *Livre des faits du Mareschal de Bouicicault.* In *Collection complète des mémoirs relatifs à l'histoire de France.* Ed. Claude B. Petitot. Paris: Foucault, 1825.

Bridget of Sweden. *The Liber Celestis of St. Bridget of Sweden.* Vol. 1. Ed. Roger Ellis. EETS, o.s. 291. New York: Oxford University Press, 1987.

Catherine of Siena. *Catherine of Siena: The Dialogue.* Trans. Suzanne Noffke. New York: Paulist Press, 1980.

Chaucer, Geoffrey. *The Riverside Chaucer.* 3rd ed. Ed. Larry D. Benson. Boston: Houghton Mifflin, 1987.

Chrétien de Troyes. *Chrétien de Troyes: Arthurian Romances.* Ed. William W. Kibler. New York: Penguin Books, 1991.

Christine de Pizan. *The Book of the City of Ladies.* Trans. Earl Jeffrey Richards. New York: Persea Books, 1982.

Cicero. *De Senectute, De Amicitia, De Divinatione.* Trans. William Armstead Falconer. 1923. Reprint, Cambridge: Harvard University Press, 1996.

The Commonplace Book of Robert Reynes of Acle: An Edition of Tanner MS 407. Ed. Cameron Louis. New York: Garland, 1980.

de Montaiglon, M. Anatole. *Recueil général et complet des fabliaux des XIIIe et XIVe siècles.* Vol. 1. Paris: Librairie des bibliophiles, 1872.

Deschamps, Eustache. *Oeuvres complètes de Eustache Deschamps.* Ed. Auguste H. E. Queux de Saint-Hilaire and Gaston Raynaud. Paris: Firmin Didot, 1878–1903; rpt. New York: Johnson Reprint Corp., 1966.

Dives and Pauper. Vol. 1. Parts 1 and 2. Ed. Priscilla Heath Barnum. EETS, o.s. 275 and 280. London: Oxford University Press, 1976 and 1980.

Dymmok, Roger. *Rogeri Dymmok: Liber Contra XII Errores et Hereses Lollardorum.* Ed. H. S. Cronin. London: Kegan Paul, Trench and Trübner, 1922.

Early English Meals and Manners. Ed. Frederick J. Furnivall. EETS, o.s. 32. London: Oxford University Press, 1868.

English Guilds. Ed. Joshua Toulmin Smith. EETS, o.s. 40. London: Trübner, 1870.

English Wycliffite Sermons. 2 vols. Ed. Pamela Gradon. Oxford: Clarendon Press, 1988.

English Works of Wycliffe. Ed. F. D. Matthew. EETS, o.s. 74. London: Kegan Paul, Trübner & Co., 1880.

Evangelia Apocrypha. Ed. Constantine Tischendorf. Lipsiae: H. Mendelssohn, 1876.

Fasciculi Zizaniorum. Ed. W. W. Shirley. London: Longman, Brown, Green, Longmans and Roberts, 1858.

Fasciculus Morum: A Fourteenth-Century Preacher's Handbook. Ed. and trans. Siegfried Wenzel. University Park: Pennsylvania State University Press, 1989.

Gawain on Marriage: The Textual Tradition of the De Coniuge Non Ducenda with Critical Edition and Translation. Ed. A. G. Rigg. Toronto: Pontifical Institute of Mediaeval Studies, 1986.

Geoffroi de Charny. *The Book of Chivalry.* Trans. Elspeth Kennedy. In *The* Book of Chivalry *of Geoffroi de Charny: Text, Context and Translation.* Ed. and trans. Richard E. Kaeuper and Elspeth Kennedy. Philadelphia: University of Pennsylvania Press, 1996.

The Good Wife Taught Her Daughter, the Good Wyfe Wold a Pylgremage, the Thewis of Gud Women. Ed. Tauno F. Mustanoja. Helsinki: Suomalaisen Kirjallisuuden Scuran, 1948.

Gower, John. *The Complete Works of John Gower.* 4 vols. Ed. G. C. Macaulay. Oxford: Clarendon Press, 1899–1902.

Gratian. "Canon Law: Gratian, Marriage Canons from the *Decretum.*" Trans. John T. Noonan, Jr. Unpublished, 1967.

Guillaume de Lorris, and Jean de Meun. *Le Roman de la Rose.* Ed. Félix Lecoy. Paris: Editions Champion, 1966.

———. *The Romance of the Rose.* Trans. Charles Dahlberg. Hanover, NH: University Press of New England, 1983.

Hali Meidenhad. Ed. F. J. Furnivall. Revised by Oswald Cockayne. EETS, o.s. 18. London: Oxford University Press, 1922.

Hauréau, B. *Notices et extraits de quelques manuscrits latin de la Bibliothèque Nationale.* Vol. 1. Paris: Librairie Klincksieck, 1890.

Heresy Trials in the Diocese of Norwich 1428-31. Ed. Norman P. Tanner. Camden 4th Series 20. London: Royal Historical Society, 1977.

Hugh of Saint Victor. "De B. Mariae Virginitate." PL 176:837–76.

———. *Hugh of Saint Victor on the Sacraments of the Christian Faith.* Trans. Roy J. Deferrari. Cambridge: Medieval Academy of America, 1951.

Jacobus de Voragine. *The Golden Legend.* Trans. William Granger Ryan. Princeton: Princeton University Press, 1993.

Jacques de Vitry. *The Life of Marie d'Oignies.* Trans. Margot H. King. Saskatoon: Peregrina, 1986.

Jerome. *St. Jerome: Letters and Select Works.* Trans. W. H. Fremantle. 2nd ser. vol. 6. *A Select Library of the Nicene and Post-Nicene Fathers of the Christian Church.* Ed.

Philip Schaff and Henry Wace. New York: Christian Literature Co., 1893. Reprint, Grand Rapids: Eerdmans, 1954.

John of Salisbury. *Policraticus.* Ed. Cary J. Nederman. New York: Cambridge University Press, 1990.

Kempe, Margery. *The Book of Margery Kempe.* Ed. Sanford Brown Meech and Hope Emily Allen. EETS, o.s. 212. New York: Oxford University Press, 1940.

Lollard Sermons. Ed. Gloria Cigman. EETS, o.s. 294. Oxford: Oxford University Press, 1989.

Love, Nicholas. *Nicholas Love's Mirror of the Blessed Life of Jesus Christ.* Ed. Michael G. Sargent. New York: Garland, 1992.

Lydgate, John. *A Critical Edition of John Lydgate's Life of Our Lady.* Ed. Joseph A. Lauritis, Ralph A. Klinefelter, and Vernon F. Gallagher. Duquesne Philological Series, no. 2. Pittsburgh: Duquesne University Press, 1961.

Lynwood's Provincial. Ed. J. V. Bullard and H. Chamber Bell. London: Faith Press, 1929.

Machaut, Guillaume de. *Guillaume de Machaut:* The Fountain of Love (La Fonteinne Amoureuse) *and Two Other Love Vision Poems.* Ed. and trans. R. Barton Palmer. New York: Garland, 1993.

Marie de France. *The Lais of Marie de France.* Trans. Robert Hanning and Joan Ferrante. Durham: Labyrinth Press, 1978.

Map, Walter. *De Nugis Curialium, Courtiers' Trifles.* Ed. and trans. M. R. James. Oxford: Clarendon Press, 1983.

The Mary Play from the N. Town Manuscript. Ed. Peter Meredith. New York: Longman, 1987.

Le Ménagier de Paris. Trans. Eileen Power as *The Goodman of Paris.* London: Routledge, 1928.

The Middle English Stanzaic Versions of the Life of Saint Anne. Ed. Roscoe E. Parker. EETS, o.s. 174. London: Oxford University Press, 1928.

Migne, J. P. *Patrologia Cursus Completus: Series Latina.* 221 vols. Paris: Migne, 1844–91.

Mirk, John. *Mirk's Festial: A Collection of Homilies by Johannes Mirkus.* Ed. Theodor Erbe. Part 1. EETS, e.s. 96. London: Kegan Paul, Trench and Trübner, 1905. Reprint, Millwood, NY: Kraus Reprint, 1987.

Monumenta Ritualia Ecclesiae Anglicanae. Vol. 1. 2nd ed. Ed. William Maskell. Oxford: Clarendon Press, 1882.

The N-Town Play: Cotton MS Vespasian D. 8. Ed. Stephen Spector. EETS, s.s. 11. Oxford: Oxford University Press, 1991.

The N-Town Plays: A Facsimile of British Library MS Cotton Vespasian D. VIII. Ed. Peter Meredith and Stanley J. Kahrl. Leeds: University of Leeds, School of English, 1976.

"Of Weddid Men and Wifis and of Here Children Also." In *The Trials and Joys of Marriage.* Ed. Eve Salisbury. Kalamazoo: Medieval Institute Publications, 2002. 191–210.

Ovid. *Ovid: Heroides and Amores.* Trans. Grant Showerman. Cambridge: Harvard University Press, 1914.

———. *Ovid: Metamorphoses.* Trans. Rolfe Humphries. Bloomington: Indiana University Press, 1955.

Paston Letters and Papers of the Fifteenth Century. Ed. Norman Davis. Oxford: Clarendon Press, 1971.

Raymond of Capua. *The Life of Catherine of Siena by Raymond of Capua.* Trans. Conleth Kearns. Wilmington: Michael Glazier, 1980.

Robert of Brunne. *Robert of Brunne's* Handlying Synne. Parts 1 and 2. Ed. Frederick J. Furnivall. EETS, o.s. 119 and 123. London: Kegan Paul, Trench, Trübner & Co., 1901 and 1903.

Rolle, Richard. *The Fire of Love and the Mending of Life or The Rule of Living.* Trans. Richard Misyn. Ed. Ralph Harvey. EETS, o.s. 106. London: Kegan Paul, Trench and Trübner, 1896.

Rotuli Parliamentorum. Ed. John Strachey. London, 1767–77.

Sainte-Maure, Benoît de. *Le Roman de Troie.* 6 vols. Ed. Leopold Constans. Paris: Firmin Didot, 1904–12.

The Sarum Missal in English. Trans. Frederick E. Warren. London: De La More Press, 1911.

Select English Works of John Wyclif. Vol. 3. Ed. Thomas Arnold. Oxford: Clarendon Press, 1896.

Selections from English Wycliffite Writings. Ed. Anne Hudson. New York: Cambridge University Press, 1978.

"Sir Launfal." In *The Middle English Breton Lays.* Ed. Anne Laskaya and Eve Salisbury. Kalamazoo: Medieval Institute Publications, 2001. 201–62.

The South English Legendary. Vol 1. Ed. Charlotte D'Evelyn and Anna J. Mill. EETS, o.s. 235. London: Oxford University Press, 1956.

Statutes of the Realm. Vol. 1. London: Eyre and Strahan, 1810–28.

The Treatise on the Laws and Customs of the Realm of England Commonly Called Glanvill. Ed. G. D. G. Hall. London: Nelson, 1965.

A Tretise of Miraclis Pleyinge. Ed. Clifford Davidson. Kalamazoo: Medieval Institute Publications, 1993.

Secondary Sources

Aers, David. *Chaucer, Langland and the Creative Imagination.* Boston: Routledge and Kegan Paul, 1980.

———. *Community, Gender and Individual Identity: English Writing 1360–1430.* New York: Routledge, 1988.

———. "Vox Populi and the Literature of 1381." In *The Cambridge History of Medieval English Literature*. Ed. David Wallace. New York: Cambridge University Press, 1999. 432–53.

Amos, Mark Addison. "'For Manners Make Man': Bourdieu, de Certeau, and the Common Appropriation of Noble Manners in the *Book of Courtesy*." In *Medieval Conduct*. Ed. Kathleen Ashley and Robert L. A. Clark. Minneapolis: University of Minnesota Press, 2001. 23–48.

Arnold, John T. "Margery's Trials: Heresy, Lollardy and Dissent." In *A Companion to* The Book of Margery Kempe. Ed. John H. Arnold and Katherine J. Lewis. Cambridge: D. S. Brewer, 2004. 75–94.

Ashley, Kathleen. "Historicizing Margery: *The Book of Margery Kempe* as Social Text." *JMEMS* 28 (1998): 374–404.

———. "The Miroir des Bonnes Femmes: Not for Women Only?" In *Medieval Conduct*. Ed. Kathleen Ashley and Robert L. A. Clark. Minneapolis: University of Minnesota Press, 2001. 86–105.

———. "Sponsorship, Reflexity and Resistance: Cultural Readings of the York Cycle Plays." In *The Performance of Middle English Culture: Essays on Chaucer and the Drama in Honor of Martin Stevens*. Ed. James J. Paxon, Lawrence M. Clopper, and Sylvia Tomasch. Cambridge: D. S. Brewer, 1998. 9–24.

Ashley, Kathleen, and Pamela Sheingorn, eds. *Interpreting Cultural Symbols: Saint Anne in Late Medieval Society*. Athens: University of Georgia Press, 1990.

Astell, Ann W. "Chaucer's 'St. Anne Trinity': Devotion, Dynasty, Dogma and Debate." *Studies in Philology* 94 (1997): 395–416.

———. *The Song of Songs in the Middle Ages*. Ithaca: Cornell University Press, 1990.

Aston, Margaret. *Lollards and Reformers: Images and Literacy in Late Medieval Religion*. London: Hambledon Press, 1984.

Atkinson, Clarissa W. *Mystic and Pilgrim: The Book and the World of Margery Kempe*. Ithaca: Cornell University Press, 1983.

———. "'Precious Balsam in a Fragile Glass': The Ideology of Virginity in the Later Middle Ages." *Journal of Family History* 8 (1983): 131–43.

Auerbach, Erich. *Mimesis: The Representation of Reality in Western Literature*. Trans. Willard R. Trask. Princeton: Princeton University Press, 1953.

Austin, J. L. *How to Do Things with Words*. Cambridge: Harvard University Press, 1962.

Axton, Richard. *European Drama of the Early Middle Ages*. London: Hutchinson, 1974.

Bainbridge, Virginia R. *Guilds in the Medieval Countryside: Social and Religious Change in Cambridgeshire c. 1350-1558*. Woodbridge: Boydell Press, 1996.

Beckwith, Sarah. *Christ's Body: Identity, Culture and Society in Late Medieval Writing*. New York: Routledge, 1993.

———. "Making the World in York and the York Cycle." In *Framing Medieval Bodies*. Ed. Sarah Kay and Miri Ruben. New York: Manchester University Press, 1994. 254–76.

———. "Sacrum Signum: Sacramentality and Dissent in York's Theatre of Corpus Christi." In *Criticism and Dissent in the Middle Ages.* Ed. Rita Copeland. New York: Cambridge University Press, 1996. 264–88.

———. *Signifying God: Social Relation and Symbolic Act in the York Corpus Christi Plays.* Chicago: University of Chicago Press, 2001.

Bedier, Joseph. *Les fabliaux: Etudes de littérature populaire et d'histoire littéraire du moyen âge.* Geneva: Slatkine, 1982.

Bennett, J. A. W. "Gower's 'Honeste Love.' " In *Patterns of Love and Courtesy: Essays in Memory of C. S. Lewis.* Ed. John Lawlor. Evanston: Northwestern University Press, 1966. 107–21.

Bennett, Judith M. *Women in the Medieval English Countryside: Gender and Household in Brigstock Before the Plague.* New York: Oxford University Press, 1987.

Bennett, Michael. "Careerism in Late Medieval England." In *People, Politics and Community in the Later Middle Ages.* Ed. Joel Rosenthal and Colin Richmond. New York: St. Martin's Press, 1987.

Benson, Larry D. "Courtly Love and Chivalry in the Later Middle Ages." In *Fifteenth-Century Studies: Recent Essays.* Ed. Robert. F. Yeager. Hamden, CT: Archon Press, 1984. 237–57.

Black, Antony. *Guilds and Civil Society in European Political Thought from the Twelfth Century to the Present.* Ithaca: Cornell University Press, 1984.

Blamires, Alcuin. "The Wife of Bath and Lollardy." *Medium Aevum* 58 (1989): 224–42.

———. *Women Defamed and Women Defended: An Anthology of Medieval Texts.* Oxford: Clarendon Press, 1992.

Blamires, Alcuin, and C. W. Marx. "Woman Not to Preach: A Disputation in British Library MS Harley 31." *Journal of Medieval Latin* 3 (1993): 34–63.

Bloch, R. Howard. *Medieval Misogyny and the Invention of Western Romantic Love.* Chicago: University of Chicago Press, 1991.

Bolton, J. L. *The Medieval English Economy, 1150–1500.* 2nd ed. London: Dent, 1980.

Boswell, John. *Christianity, Social Tolerance and Homosexuality: Gay People in Western Europe from the Beginning of the Christian Era to the Fourteenth Century.* Chicago: University of Chicago Press, 1980.

Bourdieu, Pierre. *Language and Symbolic Power.* Ed. John B. Thompson. Cambridge: Harvard University Press, 1994.

Brandenbarg, Ton. "Saint Anne: A Holy Grandmother and Her Children." In *Sanctity and Motherhood: Essays on Holy Mothers in the Middle Ages.* Ed. Anneke B. Mulder-Bakker. New York: Garland, 1995. 31–65.

———. "St. Anne and Her Family: The Veneration of St. Anne in Connection with Concepts of Marriage and the Family in the Early Modern Period." In *Saints and She-Devils: Images of Women in the Fifteenth and Sixteenth Centuries.* Ed. Lène Dresen-Coenders. London: Rubicon Press, 1987. 101–27.

Brewer, Derek S. "Honour in Chaucer." *Essays and Studies* 26 (1973): 1–19.

Brown, A. L. *The Governance of Late Medieval England 1272-1461.* Stanford: Stanford University Press, 1989.

Brundage, James A. *Law, Sex and Christian Society in Medieval Europe.* Chicago: University of Chicago Press, 1987.

———. "The Problem of Impotence." *Sexual Practices and the Medieval Church.* Ed. Vern L. Bullough and James Brundage. Buffalo: Prometheus Books, 1982. 135–40.

Bryan, W. F., and Germaine Dempster, eds. *Sources and Analogues of Chaucer's Canterbury Tales.* New York: Humanities Press, 1958.

Bugge, John. *Virginitas: An Essay in the History of a Medieval Ideal.* The Hague: Martinus Nijhoff, 1975.

Burger, Glenn. *Chaucer's Queer Nation.* Minneapolis: University of Minnesota Press, 2003.

Burke, Linda Barney. "Women in John Gower's *Confessio Amantis.*" *Mediaevalia* 3 (1977): 238–59.

Burns, Jane E. *Bodytalk: When Women Speak in Old French Literature.* Philadelphia: University of Pennsylvania Press, 1993.

Bynum, Caroline Walker. *Fragmentation and Redemption: Essays on Gender and the Human Body in Medieval Religion.* New York: Zone Books, 1991.

Calin, William. "John Gower's Continuity in the Tradition of French *Fin Amor.*" *Mediaevalia* 16 (1993): 91–111.

Cam, H. M. "The Theory and Practice of Representation in Medieval England." *Historical Studies of the English Parliament.* Vol. 1. Ed. E. B. Fryde and Edward Miller. Cambridge: Cambridge University Press, 1970. 262–78.

Camille, Michael. *The Gothic Idol: Ideology and Image-Making in Medieval Art.* Cambridge: Cambridge University Press, 1989.

Carlson, Cindy L. "Mary's Obedience and Power in the Trial of Mary and Joseph." *Comparative Drama* 29 (1995): 348–62.

Cartlidge, Neil. *Medieval Marriage: Literary Approaches, 1100-1300.* Cambridge: D. S. Brewer, 1997.

Certeau, Michel de. *The Practice of Everyday Life.* Trans. Steven Rendall. Berkeley: University of California Press, 1984.

Chambers, E. K. *Medieval Stage.* London: Oxford University Press, 1903. Reprint, Mineola, NY: Dover, 1996.

Chatman, Seymour. *Story and Discourse: Narrative Structure in Fiction and Film.* Ithaca: Cornell University Press, 1978.

Clarke, M. V. *Medieval Representation and Consent.* New York: Russell and Russell, 1964.

Cleve, Gunnel. "Semantic Dimensions in Margery Kempe's 'Whyght Clothys.'" *Mystics Quarterly* 12 (1986): 162–70.

Coffman, George R. "John Gower in His Most Significant Role." *Elizabethan Studies and Other Essays in Honor of George F. Reynolds.* Ed. George Fulmer Reynolds. Boulder: University of Colorado Press, 1945. 52–61.

————. "John Gower, Mentor for Royalty: Richard II." *PMLA* 9 (1954): 953–64.

Coleman, Janet. *Medieval Readers and Writers, 1350–1400.* New York: Columbia University Press, 1981.

Coletti, Theresa. "Genealogy, Sexuality and Sacred Power: The Saint Anne Dedication of the *Digby Candlemas Day* and the *Killing of the Children of Israel.*" *JMEMS* 29 (1999): 25–59.

————. *Mary Magdalene and the Drama of Saints: Theater, Gender and Religion in Late Medieval England.* Philadelphia: University of Pennsylvania Press, 2004.

————. "Purity and Danger: The Paradox of Mary's Body and the Engendering of the Infancy Narrative in the English Mystery Cycles." In *Approaches to the Body in Medieval Literature.* Ed. Linda Lomperis and Sarah Stanbury. Philadelphia: University of Pennsylvania Press, 1993. 65–95.

Cooper, John M. "Political Animals and Civic Friendship." In *Friendship: A Philosophical Reader.* Ed. Neera Kapur Badhwar. Ithaca: Cornell University Press, 1993. 303–26.

Copeland, Rita. *Rhetoric, Hermeneutics and Translation in the Middle Ages.* Cambridge: Cambridge University Press, 1991.

Correale, Robert M., and Mary Hamel, eds. *Sources and Analogues of the* Canterbury Tales. Vol. 1. Woodbridge, Suffolk, and Rochester, NY: D. S. Brewer, 2002.

Crane, Susan. *Gender and Romance in Chaucer's* Canterbury Tales. Princeton: Princeton University Press, 1994.

————. *The Performance of Self: Ritual, Clothing and Identity During the Hundred Years War.* Philadelphia: University of Pennsylvania Press, 2002.

Craun, Edwin D. *Lies, Slander, and Obscenity in Medieval English Literature.* New York: Cambridge University Press, 1997.

Cross, Claire. "'Great Reasoners in Scripture': The Activities of Women Lollards, 1380–1530." In *Medieval Women.* Ed. Derek Baker. Oxford: Basil Blackwell, 1978. 359–80.

D'Avray, D. L. *Medieval Marriage Sermons: Mass Communication in a Culture Without Print.* New York: Oxford University Press, 2001.

D'Avray, D. L., and M. Tausche. "Marriage Sermons in *Ad Status* Collections of the Central Middle Ages." *Archives d'histoire doctrinale et littéraire du moyen âge* 47 (1980): 71–119.

D'Avray, David. "The Gospel of the Marriage Feast of Cana and Marriage Preaching in France." In *The Bible in the Medieval World: Essays in Memory of Beryl Smalley.* Ed. Katherine Walsh and Diana Wood. Oxford: Basil Blackwell, 1985. 207–24.

Delany, Sheila. "Sexual Economics, Chaucer's Wife of Bath and *The Book of Margery Kempe.*" *Minnesota Review* 5 (1975): 104–15. Reprinted in *Feminist Readings in Middle English Literature: The Wife of Bath and All her Sect.* Ed. Ruth Evans and Lesley Johnson. New York: Routledge, 1994. 72–87.

———. *Writing Woman: Women Writers and Women in Literature, Medieval to Modern.* New York: Schocken Books, 1983.

Denholm-Young, N. *The Country Gentry in the Fourteenth Century.* Oxford: Clarendon Press, 1969.

Dickerman, Susan. "Margery Kempe and the Continental Tradition of the Pious Woman." In *The Medieval Mystical Tradition in England: Papers Read at Dartington Hall, July 1984.* Ed. Marion Glasscoe. Cambridge: D. S. Brewer, 1984. 150–68.

Diehl, Huston. *Staging Reform, Reforming the Stage.* Ithaca: Cornell University Press, 1997.

Dinshaw, Carolyn. *Getting Medieval: Sexualities and Communities, Pre- and Postmodern.* Durham: Duke University Press, 1999.

———. "Rivalry, Rape and Manhood: Gower and Chaucer." In *Chaucer and Gower: Difference, Mutuality and Exchange.* Ed. R. F. Yeager. Victoria: English Literary Studies, 1991. 130–52.

Donahue, Charles, Jr. "The Canon Law on the Formation of Marriage and Social Practice in the Later Middle Ages." *Journal of Family History* 8 (1983): 144–58.

———. "The Policy of Alexander the Third's Consent Theory of Marriage." In *Proceedings of the Fourth International Conference of Medieval Canon Law, Toronto, 21–25 August 1972.* Ed. Stephen Kuttner. Monumenta Iuris Canonici. Ser. C: Subsidia, vol. 5. Vatican City: Biblioteca Apostolica Vaticana, 1976. 251–81.

Drake, Peter. *Medieval Latin and the Rise of the European Love-Lyric.* Oxford: Clarendon Press, 1965.

Dronzek, Anna. "Gendered Theories of Education in Fifteenth-Century Conduct Books." In *Medieval Conduct.* Ed. Kathleen Ashley and Robert L. A. Clark. Minneapolis: University of Minnesota Press, 2001. 135–59.

Duby, Georges. *Medieval Marriage: Two Models from Twelfth-Century France.* Trans. Elborg Forster. Baltimore: Johns Hopkins University Press, 1978.

Duffy, Eamon. *The Stripping of the Altars: Traditional Religion in England 1400–1580.* New Haven: Yale University Press, 1992.

Dyer, Christopher. *Standards of Living in the Later Middle Ages: Social Change in England c. 1200–1520.* Cambridge: Cambridge University Press, 1989.

Echard, Siân. "Gower's 'Bokes of Latin': Language, Politics, and Poetry." *SAC* 25 (2003): 123–56.

Edwards, A. S. G. "Gower's Women in the *Confessio.*" *Mediaevalia* 16 (1993): 223–38.

Edwards, J. G. "*Plena Potestas* of English Parliamentary Representatives." In *Historical Studies of the English Parliament.* Ed. E. B. Fryde and Edward Miller. Cambridge: Cambridge University Press, 1970. 136–49.

Edwards, Robert R. "The Franklin's Tale." In *Sources and Analogues of* The Canterbury Tales. Ed. Robert M. Correale and Mary Hamel. Cambridge: D. S. Brewer, 2002. 1:211–65.

Elliott, Dyan. "Dress as Mediator Between Inner and Outer Self: The Pious Matron of the High and Later Middle Ages." *Mediaeval Studies* 53 (1991): 279–308.

———. *Spiritual Marriage: Sexual Abstinence in Medieval Wedlock.* Princeton: Princeton University Press, 1993.

Ellis, Deborah S. "The Merchant's Wife's Tale: Language, Sex and Commerce in Margery Kempe and in Chaucer." *Exemplaria* 2 (1990): 595–626.

Ellis, Roger. "'Flores ad Fabricandum . . . Coronam': An Investigation into the Uses of the Revelations of St. Bridget of Sweden in Fifteenth-Century England." *MAE* 51 (1982): 163–86.

Emmerson, Richard. "Reading Gower in a Manuscript Culture: Latin and English in Illustrated Manuscripts of the *Confessio Amantis.*" *SAC* 21 (1999): 143–86.

Erler, Mary. "Margery Kempe's White Clothes." *Medium Aevum* 62 (1993): 78–83.

Farnham, William. *The Medieval Heritage of Elizabethan Tragedy.* Berkeley: University of California Press, 1936.

Ferster, Judith. *Fictions of Advice: The Literature and Politics of Counsel in Late Medieval England.* Philadelphia: University of Pennsylvania Press, 1996.

———. "Interpretation and Imitation in Chaucer's *Franklin's Tale.*" *Medieval Literature: Criticism, Ideology and History.* Ed. David Aers. New York: St. Martin's Press, 1986. 148–68.

Filas, Francis. *Joseph: The Man Closest to Jesus: The Complete Life, Theology and Devotional History of St. Joseph.* Boston: St. Paul Editions, 1962.

Fisher, John H. "A Calendar of Documents Relating to the Life of John Gower the Poet." *JEGP* 52 (1959): 1–23.

———. *John Gower: Moral Philosopher and Friend of Chaucer.* New York: New York University Press, 1964.

Fiske, Adele. "Paradisus Homo Amicus." *Speculum* 40 (1965): 436–59.

Fletcher, Alan. "The N-Town Plays." In *The Cambridge Companion to Medieval English Theatre.* Ed. Richard Beadle. Cambridge: Cambridge University Press, 1994. 163–88.

Fradenburg, Louise Olga. *City, Marriage, Tournament: Arts of Rule in Late Medieval Scotland.* Madison: University of Wisconsin Press, 1991.

French, Katharine. *People of the Parish.* Philadelphia: University of Pennsylvania Press, 2001.

Friedman, Lionel J. "Jean de Meun and Ethelred of Rievaulx." *L'Esprit Createur* 2 (1962): 135–41.

Galloway, Andrew. "Gower in His Most Learned Role and the Peasants' Revolt of 1381." *Mediaevalia* 16 (1993): 329–47.

———. "The Politics of Pity in Gower's *Confessio Amantis.*" In *The Letter of the Law: Legal Practice and Literary Production in Medieval England.* Ed. Emily Steiner and Candice Barrington. Ithaca: Cornell University Press, 2002. 67–104.

Gastle, Brian W. "'As if she were single': Working Wives and the Late Medieval English *Femme Sole.*" In *The Middle Ages at Work: Practicing Labor in Late Medieval England.* Ed. Kellie Robertson and Michael Ubel. New York: Palgrave Macmillan, 2004. 41–64.

Gaylord, Alan T. "The Promises in the *Franklin's Tale.*" *ELH* 31 (1964): 331–65.

Gerould, Gordon Hall. "The Social Status of Chaucer's Franklin." *PMLA* 41 (1926): 262–79.

Gibson, Gail McMurray. "Bury St. Edmunds, Lydgate, and the N-Town Cycle." *Speculum* 56 (1981): 56–90.

———. *The Theater of Devotion: East Anglian Drama and Society in the Late Middle Ages.* Chicago: University of Chicago Press, 1989.

Gist, Margaret Adlum. *Love and War in the Middle English Romances.* Philadelphia: University of Pennsylvania Press, 1947.

Given-Wilson, Chris. *The English Nobility in the Late Middle Ages: The Fourteenth-Century Political Community.* New York: Routledge and Kegan Paul, 1987.

Glasser, Marc. "Marriage in Medieval Hagiography." *Studies in Medieval and Renaissance History* n.s. 4 (1981): 3–34.

Gold, Penny S. "The Marriage of Mary and Joseph in the Twelfth-Century Ideology of Marriage." In *Sexual Practices and the Medieval Church.* Ed. Vern L. Bullough and James Brundage. Buffalo: Prometheus Books, 1982. 102–28.

Goldberg, P. J. P. *Women, Work and Life Cycle in a Medieval Economy: Women in York and Yorkshire c. 1300–1520.* Oxford: Clarendon Press, 1992.

Goodich, Michael. *The Unmentionable Vice: Homosexuality in the Later Medieval Period.* New York: Dorset Press, 1979.

Goodman, Anthony. *Margery Kempe and Her World.* New York: Longman, 2002.

———. "The Piety of John Brunham's Daughter, of Lynn." In *Medieval Women.* Ed. Derek Baker. Oxford: Basil Blackwell, 1978. 347–58.

Gould, Timothy. "The Unhappy Performative." In *Performativity and Performance.* Ed. Andrew Parker and Eve Kosofsky Sedgwick. New York: Routledge, 1995. 19–44.

Grady, Frank. "The Generation of 1399." In *The Letter of the Law: Legal Practice and Literary Production in Medieval England.* Ed. Emily Steiner and Candace Barrington. Ithaca: Cornell University Press, 2002. 202–29.

———. "The Lancastrian Gower and the Limits of Exemplarity." *Speculum* 70 (1995): 552–75.

Gravdal, Kathryn. *Ravishing Maidens: Writing Rape in Medieval French Literature and Law.* Philadelphia: University of Pennsylvania Press, 1991.

Green, Richard Firth. *A Crisis of Truth: Literature and Law in Richardian England.* Philadelphia: University of Pennsylvania Press, 1999.

———. *Poets and Princepleasers: Literature in the English Court in the Late Middle Ages.* Toronto: University of Toronto Press, 1980.

Habermas, Jürgen. *The Structural Transformation of the Public Sphere: An Inquiry into a Category of Bourgeois Society.* Trans. Thomas Burger, with the assistance of Frederick Lawrence. Cambridge: MIT Press, 1991.

Hanawalt, Barbara A. "'The Childe of Bristowe' and the Making of Middle-Class Adolescence." In *Bodies and Disciplines: Intersections of Literature and History in Fifteenth-Century England.* Ed. Barbara A. Hanawalt and David Wallace. Minneapolis: University of Minnesota Press, 1996. 155–78.

———. *Growing Up in Medieval London: The Experience of Childhood in History.* New York: Oxford University Press, 1993.

———. "Keepers of the Lights: Late Medieval English Parish Gilds." *JMRS* 14 (1984): 19–37.

———. *"Of Good and Ill Repute": Gender and Social Control in Medieval England.* Oxford: Oxford University Press, 1998.

———. *The Ties That Bound: Peasant Families in Medieval England.* New York: Oxford University Press, 1986.

Hardison, O. B. *Christian Rite and Christian Drama in the Middle Ages: Essays in the Origin and Early History of Modern Drama.* Baltimore: Johns Hopkins University Press, 1965.

Hargraves, H. "Sir John Oldcastle and Wycliffite Views on Clerical Marriage." *Medium Aevum* 42 (1973): 141–46.

Harrison, Robert L. *Gallic Salt: Eighteen Fabliaux Translated from the Old French.* Berkeley: University of California Press, 1974.

Harriss, G. L. "The Formation of Parliament, 1272–1377." In *The English Parliament in the Middle Ages.* Ed. H. G. Richardson and G. O. Sayles. Manchester: Manchester University Press, 1981. 29–60.

Harriss, Gerald. "Political Society and the Growth of Government in Late Medieval England." *Past and Present* 138 (1993): 28–57.

Heaney, Seamus P. *The Development of the Sacramentality of Marriage from Anselm of Laon to Thomas Aquinas.* Washington, DC: Catholic University of America Press, 1963.

Heffernan, Thomas J. *Sacred Biography: Saints and Their Biographers in the Middle Ages.* New York: Oxford University Press, 1988.

Helmholz, R. H. *Marriage Litigation in Medieval England.* London: Cambridge University Press, 1974.

Hilles, Carroll Anne. "'Double Birth and Double Lineage': Individual and Social Identity in Fifteenth-Century Devotional Literature." Ph.D. diss., Duke University, 1994.

Hilton, Rodney. H. *The English Peasantry in the Later Middle Ages.* Oxford: Clarendon Press, 1975.

———, ed. *The Transition from Feudalism to Capitalism.* London: New Left Books, 1976.

———. "Warriors and Peasants." *New Left Review* 83 (1974): 83–94.

Hines, John, Nathalie Cohen, and Simon Roffy. "Iohannes Gower, Armiger, Poeta: Records and Memorials of His Life and Death." In *A Companion to Gower*. Ed. Siân Echard. Cambridge: D. S. Brewer, 2004. 23–41.

Holloway, Julia Bolton. "Bride, Margery, Julian and Alice: Bridget of Sweden's Textual Community in Medieval England." In *Margery Kempe: A Book of Essays*. Ed. Sandra J. McEntire. New York: Garland, 1992. 203–21.

Houlbrooke, Ralph. *Church Courts and the People During the English Reformation, 1520–1570*. Oxford: Oxford University Press, 1979.

Hudson, Anne. *The Premature Reformation: Wycliffite Texts and Lollard History*. Oxford: Clarendon Press, 1988.

Hunt, Alison M. "Maculating Mary: The Detractors of the N-Town Cycle's 'Trial of Joseph and Mary.'" *Philological Quarterly* 73 (1994): 11–29.

Huot, Sylvia. "The *Miroir de Mariage*: Deschamps Responds to the *Roman de la Rose*." In *Eustache Deschamps, French Courtier-Poet*. Ed. Deborah M. Sinnreich-Levi. New York: AMS Press, 1998. 131–44.

Hyatte, Reginald. *The Arts of Friendship: The Idealization of Friendship in Medieval and Early Renaissance Literature*. New York: E. J. Brill, 1994.

Hymans, Paul. "Trial by Ordeal: The Key to Proof in the Early Common Law." In *On the Laws and Customs of England: Essays in Honor of Samuel E. Thorne*. Ed. Morris S. Arnold et al. Chapel Hill: University of North Carolina Press, 1981.

Ingram, Martin. "Spousal Litigation in the English Ecclesiastical Courts c. 1350–c. 1640." In *Marriage and Society: Studies in the Social History of Marriage*. Ed. R. B. Outhwaite. London: Europa, 1982. 35–57.

Ives, E. W. *The Common Lawyers of Pre-Reformation England*. New York: Cambridge University Press, 1983.

Jacobs, Kathryn. "The Marriage Contract of the *Franklin's Tale*: The Remaking of Society." *Chaucer Review* 20 (1985): 132–43.

———. *Marriage Contracts from Chaucer to the Renaissance Stage*. Gainesville: University Press of Florida, 2001.

Jaeger, C. Stephen. *Ennobling Love: In Search of a Lost Sensibility*. Philadelphia: University of Pennsylvania Press, 1999.

———. *The Origins of Courtliness: Civilizing Trends and the Formation of Courtly Ideals 939–1210*. Philadelphia: University of Pennsylvania Press, 1985.

Jameson, Fredric. *The Political Unconscious: Narrative as a Socially Symbolic Act*. Ithaca: Cornell University Press, 1981.

Jones, William R. "English Religious Brotherhoods and Medieval Lay Piety: The Inquiry of 1388–89." *The Historian* 36 (1973–74): 646–59.

———. "Lollards and Images: The Defense of Religious Art in Later Medieval England." *Journal of the History of Ideas* 34, no. 1 (1973): 27–50.

Johnston, F. R. "The English Cult of St. Bridget of Sweden." *Analecta Bollandiana* 103 (1985): 75–93.

Justice, Steven. *Writing and Rebellion: England in 1381.* Berkeley and Los Angeles: University of California Press, 1994.

Kantorowicz, Ernst H. *The King's Two Bodies: A Study in Medieval Political Theology.* Princeton: Princeton University Press, 1957.

Keen, Maurice. *Chivalry.* New Haven: Yale University Press, 1984.

Kelly, Henry Ansgar. *Chaucerian Tragedy.* Cambridge: D. S. Brewer, 1997.

———. *Ideas and Forms of Tragedy from Aristotle to the Middle Ages.* Cambridge: Cambridge University Press, 1993.

———. *Love and Marriage in the Age of Chaucer.* Ithaca: Cornell University Press, 1975.

Kendall, Ritchie D. *The Drama of Dissent: The Radical Poetics of Nonconformity, 1380–1590.* Chapel Hill: University of North Carolina Press, 1986.

Kennedy, Edward Donald. "Gower, Chaucer, and French Prose Arthurian Romance." *Mediaevalia* 16 (1993): 55–90.

Kittredge, George Lyman. *Chaucer and His Poetry.* Cambridge: Harvard University Press, 1915.

———. "Chaucer's Discussion of Marriage." *Modern Philology* 9 (1911–12): 435–67. Reprinted in *Chaucer and His Poetry.* Cambridge: Harvard University Press, 1915.

Knight, Stephen. "The Social Function of Middle English Romances." In *Medieval Literature: Criticism, Ideology and History.* Ed. David Aers. New York: St. Martin's Press, 1986. 99–122.

Kooper, Eric. "Loving the Unequal Equal: Medieval Theologians and Marital Affection." In *The Olde Daunce: Love, Friendship, Sex and Marriage in the Medieval World.* Ed. Robert R. Edwards and Stephen Spector. Albany: State University of New York Press, 1991. 44–56.

Krug, Rebecca. *Reading Families: Women's Literate Practice in Late Medieval England.* Ithaca: Cornell University Press, 2002.

Kurath, Hans, ed. *The Middle English Dictionary.* Ann Arbor: University of Michigan Press, 1952–65.

Lacey, Kay E. "Women and Work in Fourteenth- and Fifteenth-Century London." In *Women and Work in Pre-Industrial England.* Ed. Lindsey Charles and Lorna Duffin. London: Croom Helm, 1985. 26–42.

Lane, Barbara G. *The Altar and the Altarpiece: Sacramental Themes in Early Netherlandish Painting.* New York: Harper and Row, 1984.

Lane, Robert. "The Franklin's Tale: Of Marriage and Meaning." In *Portraits of Marriage in Literature.* Ed. Anne C. Hargrove and Maurine Magliocco. Macomb: Western Illinois University Press, 1984. 107–24.

Le Bras, G. "La doctrine du mariage chez les théologiens et les canonistes depuis l'an mille." *Dictionnaire de Théologie Catholique.* Ed. A. Vacant et al. Vol. 9. II. Cols. 2123–2317.

Leclerq, Jean. *Monks and Love in Twelfth-Century France.* Oxford: Clarendon Press, 1979.

Legge, M. Dominica. *Anglo-Norman Literature and Its Background.* Oxford: Clarendon Press, 1963.

Lerer, Seth. *Chaucer and His Readers: Imagining the Author in Late-Medieval England.* Princeton: Princeton University Press, 1993.

Lewis, C. S. *The Allegory of Love: A Study in Medieval Tradition.* New York: Oxford University Press, 1936.

Lewis, Katherine J. *The Cult of St. Katherine of Alexandria in Late Medieval England.* Rochester, NY, and Woodbridge, Suffolk: Boydell Press, 2000.

———. "Margery Kempe and Saint Making in Later Medieval England." In *A Companion to the Book of Margery Kempe.* Ed. John H. Arnold and Katherine J. Lewis. Rochester, NY, and Woodbridge, Suffolk: D. S. Brewer, 2004. 195–215.

Lindahl, Carl. *Earnest Games.* Bloomington: Indiana University Press, 1987.

Lipton, Emma. "Language on Trial: Performing the Law in the N-Town Trial Play." In *The Letter of the Law: Legal Practice and Literary Production in Medieval England.* Ed. Emily Steiner and Candace Barrington. Ithaca: Cornell University Press, 2002. 115–35.

Lochrie, Karma. *Covert Operations: The Medieval Uses of Secrecy.* Philadelphia: University of Pennsylvania Press, 1999.

———. *Margery Kempe and the Translations of the Flesh.* Philadelphia: University of Pennsylvania Press, 1991.

Lumiansky, R. M. *Of Sondry Folk: The Dramatic Principle in the* Canterbury Tales. Austin: University of Texas Press, 1955.

Maddicott, J. R. "Parliament and the Constituencies." In *The English Parliament in the Middle Ages.* Ed. R. G. Davies and J. H. Denton. Philadelphia: University of Pennsylvania Press, 1981. 61–87.

Makowski, Elizabeth M. "The Conjugal Debt and Medieval Canon Law." In *Equally in God's Image.* Ed. Julia Bolton Holloway, Joan Bechtold, and Constance S. Wright. New York: Peter Lang, 1990. 129–43. Reprinted from *Journal of Medieval History* 3 (1977): 99–114.

Mathew, Gervase. *The Court of Richard II.* London: John Murray, 1968.

———. "Ideals of Friendship." In *Patterns of Love and Courtesy.* Ed. John Lawlor. Evanston: Northwestern University Press, 1966. 45–53.

———. "Marriage and *Amour Courtois* in Late Fourteenth-Century England." In *Essays Presented to Charles Williams.* London: Oxford University Press, 1947. 128–35.

Matter, E. Ann. *The Voice of My Beloved: The Song of Songs in Western Medieval Christianity.* Philadelphia: University of Pennsylvania Press, 1990.

Maxeiner, Andrea Dianne. "Dower and Jointure: A Legal and Statistical Analysis of the Property Rights of Married Women in Late Medieval England." Ph.D. diss., Catholic University of America, 1990.

McCarthy, Conor. *Marriage in Medieval England: Law, Literature and Practice.* Rochester, NY, and Woodbridge, Suffolk: Boydell Press, 2004.

McGlynn, Margaret, and Richard J. Moll. "Chaste Marriage in the Middle Ages: 'It Were to Hire a Great Merite.'" In *Handbook of Medieval Sexuality.* Ed. Vern L. Bullough and James A. Brundage. New York: Garland, 1996. 103–22.

McGuire, Brian Patrick. *Friendship and Community: The Monastic Experience 350-1250.* Kalamazoo: Cisterian Publications, 1988.

McIntosh, Marjorie Keniston. *Controlling Misbehavior in England 1370-1600.* Cambridge: Cambridge University Press, 1998.

———. "Finding Language for Misconduct: Jurors in Fifteenth-Century Local Courts." In *Bodies and Disciplines: Intersections of Literature and History in Fifteenth-Century England.* Ed. Barbara A. Hanawalt and David Wallace. Minneapolis: University of Minnesota Press, 1996. 87–122.

McLaughlin, Eleanor. "Equality of Souls, Inequality of Sexes: Woman in Medieval Theology." In *Religion and Sexism: Images of Woman in the Jewish and Christian Traditions.* Ed. Rosemary Radford Ruether. New York: Simon and Schuster, 1974. 213–65.

McNally, John J. "The Penitential and Courtly Traditions in Gower's *Confessio Amantis.*" In *Studies in Medieval Culture.* Ed. John R. Sommerfeldt. Kalamazoo: Western Michigan University Press, 1964. 74–94.

McNamara, Jo Ann. "Chaste Marriage and Clerical Celibacy." In *Sexual Practices and the Medieval Church.* Ed. Vern L. Bullough and James Brundage. Buffalo: Prometheus Books, 1982. 22–33.

McRee, Ben R. "Religious Guilds and Regulation of Behavior in Late Medieval Towns." In *People, Politics and Community in the Later Middle Ages.* Ed. Joel Rosenthal and Colin Richmond. New York: St. Martin's Press, 1987. 108–22.

McSheffrey, Shannon. *Gender and Heresy: Women and Men in Lollard Communities.* Philadelphia: University of Pennsylvania Press, 1995.

Meredith, Peter. "Performance, Verse and Occasion in the N-Town *Mary Play.*" In *Individuality and Achievement in Middle English Poetry.* Ed. O. S. Pickering. Cambridge: D. S. Brewer, 1997. 205–21.

Middleton, Anne. "The Idea of Public Poetry in the Reign of Richard II." *Speculum* 53 (1978): 94–114.

Miller, Robert P. "The Epicurean Homily on Marriage by Chaucer's Franklin." *Mediaevalia* 6 (1980): 151–86.

Murphy, James J. *Rhetoric in the Middle Ages: A History of Rhetorical Theory from Saint Augustine to the Renaissance.* Berkeley: University of California Press, 1974.

Newman, Barbara. *From Virile Woman to WomanChrist.* Philadelphia: University of Pennsylvania Press, 1995.

Nicholls, Jonathan. *The Matter of Courtesy: Medieval Courtesy Books and the Gawain-Poet.* Woodbridge, Suffolk: Brewer, 1985.

Nichols, Ann Eljenholm. *Seeable Signs: The Iconography of the Seven Sacraments 1350–1544.* Rochester: Boydell Press, 1994.

Nisse, Ruth. *Defining Acts: Drama and the Politics of Interpretation in Late Medieval England.* Notre Dame, IN: University of Notre Dame Press, 2005.

Nolan, Maura. *John Lydgate and the Making of Public Culture.* New York: Cambridge University Press, 2005.

Noonan, John T. "Marital Affection in the Canonists." *Studia Gratiana* 12 (1967): 479–509.

———. "Power to Choose." *Viator* 4 (1973): 419–34.

Owst, G. R. *Literature and Pulpit in Mediaeval England: A Neglected Chapter in the History of English Letters and of the English People.* Oxford: Blackwell, 1966.

Pakaluk, Michael. "Political Friendship." In *The Changing Face of Friendship.* Ed. Leroy S. Rouner. Notre Dame, IN: University of Notre Dame Press, 1994. 197–213.

Palmer, Robert C. "Contexts of Marriage in Medieval England: Evidence from the King's Court Circa 1300." *Speculum* 59 (1984): 42–67.

Parker, Andrew, and Eve Kosofsky Sedgwick, eds. *Performativity and Performance.* New York: Routledge, 1995.

Parkes, Malcolm B. "The Influence of the Concepts of *Ordinatio* and *Compilatio* on the Development of the Book." In *Medieval Learning and Literature: Essays Presented to R. W. Hunt.* Ed. J. J. G. Alexander and M. T. Gibson. Oxford: Clarendon Press, 1976. 115–41.

Partner, Nancy F. "'And Most of All for Inordinate Love': Desire and Denial in the Book of Margery Kempe." *Thought* 64 (1989): 254–67.

———. "Reading the Book of Margery Kempe." *Exemplaria* 3 (1991): 29–66.

Patterson, Lee. *Chaucer and the Subject of History.* Madison: University of Wisconsin Press, 1991.

———. "Court Politics and the Invention of Literature: The Case of Sir John Clanvowe." In *Culture and History 1350–1600: Essays on English Communities, Identities and Writing.* Ed. David Aers. Detroit: Wayne State University Press, 1992. 7–41.

———. *Negotiating the Past: The Historical Understanding of Medieval Literature.* Madison: University of Wisconsin Press, 1987.

Payer, Pierre J. *The Bridling of Desire: Views of Sex in the Later Middle Ages.* Toronto: University of Toronto Press, 1993.

Pearsall, Derek. "Gower's Narrative Art." *PMLA* 81 (1966): 475–84.

———. "The Manuscripts and Illustrations of Gower's Works." In *A Companion to Gower.* Ed. Siân Echard. Cambridge: D. S. Brewer, 2004. 73–97.

Peck, Russell A. *Kingship and Common Profit in Gower's* Confessio Amantis. Carbondale: Southern Illinois University Press, 1978.

———. "Sovereignty and the Two Worlds of the *Franklin's Tale.*" *Chaucer Review* 1 (1967): 253–71.

Pedersen, Frederik. "Did the Medieval Laity Know the Canon Law Rules on Marriage? Some Evidence from Fourteenth-Century York Cause Papers." *Mediaeval Studies* 56 (1994): 111–52.

———. *Marriage Disputes in Medieval England.* London: Hambledon Press, 2000.

Pfaff, R. W. *New Liturgical Feasts in Later Medieval England.* Oxford: Clarendon Press, 1970.

Pocock, J. G. A. *The Machiavellian Moment: Florentine Political Thought and the Atlantic Republican Tradition.* Princeton: Princeton University Press, 1975.

Pollock, Sir Frederick, and Frederic William Maitland. *The History of English Law Before the Time of Edward I.* 2 vols. 2nd ed. Cambridge: Cambridge University Press, 1968.

Poovey, Mary. *Uneven Developments: The Ideological Work of Gender in Mid-Victorian England.* Chicago: University of Chicago Press, 1988.

Porter, Elizabeth. "Gower's Ethical Microcosm and Political Macrocosm." In *Gower's* Confessio Amantis: *Responses and Reassessments.* Ed. A. J. Minnis. Cambridge: D. S. Brewer, 1983. 135–62.

Postan, M. M. *Essays on Medieval Agriculture and General Problems of the Medieval Economy.* New York: Cambridge University Press, 1973.

Pratt, Robert A. "Jankeyn's Book of Wikked Wyves: Medieval Antimatrimonial Propaganda in the Universities." *Annuale Medievale* 3 (1962): 5–27.

Quillet, Jeannine. "Community, Counsel and Representation." In *The Cambridge History of Medieval Political Thought c. 350-1450.* Ed. J. H. Burns. New York: Cambridge University Press, 1988.

Raby, F. J. E. *A History of Secular Latin Poetry in the Middle Ages.* 2 vols. Oxford: Clarendon Press, 1934.

Riddy, Felicity. "Mother Knows Best: Reading Social Change in a Courtesy Text." *Speculum* (1996): 66–86.

Riehle, Wolfgang. *The Middle English Mystics.* London: Routledge & Kegan Paul, 1981.

Robertson, D. W., Jr. "Chaucerian Tragedy." In *Chaucer Criticism.* Vol. 2. Ed. Richard J. Schoeck and Jerome Taylor. Notre Dame, IN: University of Notre Dame Press, 1961.

Rogers, Elizabeth Frances. *Peter Lombard and the Sacramental System.* Merrick, NY: Richwood, 1976.

Rousseau, Constance M., and Joel T. Rosenthal, eds. *Women, Marriage, and Family in Medieval Christendom: Essays in Memory of Michael M. Sheehan.* Kalamazoo: Medieval Institute Publications, 1998.

Rubin, Miri. *Corpus Christi: The Eucharist in Medieval Culture.* New York: Cambridge University Press, 1991.

Ruether, Rosemary Radford. "Misogynism and Virginal Feminism in the Fathers of the Church." In *Religion and Sexism: Images of Women in the Jewish and Christian*

Traditions. Ed. Rosemary Radford Ruether. New York: Simon and Schuster, 1974. 150–83.

Salih, Sarah. *Versions of Virginity in Late Medieval England.* Woodbridge, Suffolk, and Rochester, NY: D. S. Brewer, 2001.

Sargent, Michael G., ed. *Nicholas Love's Mirror of the Blessed Life of Jesus Christ.* New York: Garland, 1992.

Saul, Nigel. *Knights and Esquires: The Gloucestershire Gentry in the Fourteenth Century.* Oxford: Oxford University Press, 1981.

———. "The Social Status of Chaucer's Franklin: A Reconsideration." *Medium Aevum* 52 (1983): 10–26.

Scanlon, Larry. *Narrative, Authority, and Power: The Medieval Exemplum and the Chaucerian Tradition.* Cambridge: Cambridge University Press, 1994.

Schillebeeckx, Edward. *Marriage: Human Reality and Saving Mystery.* Trans. N. D. Smith. New York: Sheed and Ward, 1965.

Schmidt, Gary D. "The Marriage Irony in the Tales of the Merchant and Franklin." In *Portraits of Marriage in Literature.* Ed. Anne C. Hargrove and Maurine Magliocco. Macomb: Western Illinois University Press, 1984. 97–106.

Schollmeier, Paul. *Other Selves: Aristotle on Personal and Political Friendship.* Albany: State University of New York Press, 1994.

Sedgwick, Eve Kosofsky. *Between Men: English Literature and Male Homosexual Desire.* New York: Columbia University Press, 1985.

Sheehan, Michael M. "Maritalis Affecto Revisited." In *The Olde Daunce: Love, Friendship, Sex and Marriage in the Medieval World.* Ed. Robert R. Edwards and Stephen Spector. Albany: State University of New York Press, 1991. 32–43.

———. *Marriage, Family and Law in Medieval Europe: Collected Studies.* Ed. James K. Farge. Toronto: University of Toronto Press, 1996.

———. "The Wife of Bath and Her Four Sisters: Reflections on a Woman's Life in the Age of Chaucer." *Marriage, Family and Law in Medieval Europe: Collected Studies.* Ed. James K. Farge. Toronto: University of Toronto Press, 1996. 177–98.

Shklar [now Nisse], Ruth. "Cobham's Daughter: *The Book of Margery Kempe* and the Power of Heterodox Thinking." *MLQ* 56 (1995): 277–304.

Skinner, Quentin. *The Foundations of Modern Political Thought.* Vol. 1. Cambridge: Cambridge University Press, 1978.

Specht, Henrik. *Chaucer's Franklin in the* Canterbury Tales*: The Social and Literary Background of a Chaucerian Character.* Copenhagen: Akademik Forlag, 1981.

Spector, Stephen. "The Composition and Development of an Eclectic Manuscript: Cotton Vespasion D. VIII." *Leeds Studies in English* n.s. 9 (1977): 62–83.

———. "Introduction." In *The N-Town Play, Cotton MS Vespasian D. 8.* Ed. Stephen Spector. EETS, s.s. 11. Oxford: Oxford University Press, 1991. vii–xlv.

Spencer, H. Leith. *English Preaching in the Late Middle Ages.* Oxford: Oxford University Press, 1993.

Sponsler, Claire. *Drama and Resistance: Bodies, Goods and Theatricality in Late Medieval England.* Minneapolis: University of Minnesota Press, 1997.

Squires, Lynn. "Law and Disorder in Ludus Coventriae." In *The Drama of the Middle Ages: Comparative and Critical Essays.* Ed. Clifford Davidson, C. J. Gianakaris, and John H. Stroupe. New York: AMS Press, 1982. 272–85.

Staley, Lynn. *Languages of Power in the Age of Richard II.* University Park: Pennsylvania State University Press, 2005.

——. *Margery Kempe's Dissenting Fictions.* University Park: Pennsylvania State University Press, 1994.

Stanbury, Sarah. "The Vivacity of Images: St. Katherine, Knighton's Lollards, and the Breaking of Idols." In *Images, Idolatry and Iconoclasm in Late Medieval England: Textuality and the Visual Image.* Ed. Jeremy Dimmick, James Simpson, and Nicolette Zeeman. New York: Oxford University Press, 2002. 131–50.

Stargardt, Ute. "The Beguines of Belgium, the Dominican Nuns of Germany, and Margery Kempe." In *The Popular Literature of Medieval England.* Ed. Thomas J. Heffernan. Knoxville: University of Tennessee Press, 1985. 277–313.

Stern-Gillet, Suzanne. *Aristotle's Philosophy of Friendship.* Albany: State University of New York Press, 1995.

Storey, R. L. "Gentleman-bureaucrats." In *Profession, Vocation and Culture in Later Medieval England: Essays in Memory of A. R. Myers.* Ed. Cecil H. Clough. Liverpool: University of Liverpool Press, 1982. 90–129.

Strohm, Paul. *Hochon's Arrow: The Social Imagination of Fourteenth-Century Texts.* Princeton: Princeton University Press, 1992.

——. "Politics and Poetics: Usk and Chaucer in the 1380s." In *Literary Practice and Social Change in Britain, 1380-1530.* Ed. Lee Patterson. Berkeley: University of California Press, 1990. 83–112.

——. *Social Chaucer.* Cambridge: Harvard University Press, 1989.

Sugano, Douglas. "'This game wel pleyd': The N-Town Playbooks and East Anglian Games." *Comparative Drama* 28, no. 2 (1994): 221–34.

Swanson, R. N. *Religion and Devotion in Europe c. 1215-c. 1515.* New York: Cambridge University Press, 1995.

Tanner, Norman P. *The Church in Late Medieval Norwich, 1370-1532.* Toronto: Pontifical Institute of Mediaeval Studies, 1984.

——, ed. *Heresy Trials in the Diocese of Norwich 1428-31.* Camden 4th ser., vol. 20. London: Royal Historical Society, 1977.

Tavormina, M. Teresa. *Kindly Similitude: Marriage and Family in Piers Plowman.* Cambridge: D. S. Brewer, 1995.

Teetaert, Amédeé, O.C. *Les confessions au laiques dans l'église latine depuis le VIIIe jusqu'au XIVe siècles.* Paris: J. Gabalda, 1926.

Tentler, Thomas N. *Sin and Confession on the Eve of the Reformation.* Princeton: Princeton University Press, 1977.

Thomson, John A. F. *The Later Lollards, 1414-1520.* London: Oxford University Press, 1967.

Thrupp, Sylvia L. *The Merchant Class of Medieval London.* Chicago: University of Chicago Press, 1948.

Trexler, Richard C. *Public Life in Renaissance Florence.* New York: Academic Press, 1980.

Twycross, Meg. "The Theatricality of Medieval English Plays." In *Cambridge Companion to Medieval English Theatre.* Ed. Richard Beadle. New York: Cambridge University Press, 1994. 37–84.

Utley, Frances Lee. *The Crooked Rib.* Columbus: Ohio State University Press, 1944.

Wack, Mary Frances. *Lovesickness in the Middle Ages: The* Viaticum *and Its Commentaries.* Philadelphia: University of Pennsylvania Press, 1990.

Walker, Sue Sheridan. "Litigation as Personal Quest: Suing for Dower in the Royal Courts, Circa 1272–1350." In *Wife and Widow in Medieval England.* Ed. Sue Sheridan Walker. Ann Arbor: University of Michigan Press, 1993. 81–108.

Wallace, David. *Chaucerian Polity: Absolutist Lineages and Associational Forms in England and Italy.* Stanford: Stanford University Press, 1997.

———. "Mystics and Followers in Siena and East Anglia: A Study in Taxonomy, Class and Cultural Mediation." In *The Medieval Tradition in England: Papers Read at Dartington Hall, July 1984.* Ed. Marion Glasscoe. Cambridge: D. S. Brewer, 1984. 169–91.

Watson, Nicholas. "Censorship and Cultural Change in Late-Medieval England: Vernacular Theology, the Oxford Translation Debate, and Arundel's Constitutions of 1409." *Speculum* 70 (1995): 822–64.

Watt, Diane. *Amoral Gower: Language, Sex and Politics.* Minneapolis: University of Minnesota Press, 2003.

Weimann, Robert. *Shakespeare and the Popular Tradition in the Theater.* Baltimore: Johns Hopkins University Press, 1978.

Weinstein, Donald, and Rudolph M. Bell. *Saints and Society: The Two Worlds of Western Christendom, 1000-1700.* Chicago: University of Chicago Press, 1982.

Weisl, Angela Jane. *Conquering the Reign of Femeny: Gender and Genre in Chaucer's Romance.* Cambridge: D. S. Brewer, 1995.

Wieck, Roger S. *Time Sanctified: The Book of Hours in Medieval Art and Life.* New York: Braziller, 1988.

Wilson, Katharina M., and Elizabeth Makowski. *Wykked Wyves and the Woes of Marriage: Misogamous Literature from Juvenal to Chaucer.* Albany: State University of New York Press, 1990.

Wimsatt, James I. *Chaucer and His French Contemporaries: Natural Music in the Fourteenth Century.* Toronto: University of Toronto Press, 1991.

———. "Reason, Machaut, and the Franklin." In *The Olde Daunce: Love, Friendship, Sex and Marriage in the Medieval World.* Ed. Robert R. Edwards and Stephen Spector. Albany: State University of New York Press, 1991. 201–10.

Winstead, Karen A. *Virgin Martyrs: Legends of Sainthood in Late Medieval England.* Ithaca: Cornell University Press, 1997.

Wood, Chaucey. "Of Time and Tide in the *Franklin's Tale.*" *Philological Quarterly* 45 (1966): 688–711.

Woodforde, Christopher. *The Norwich School of Glass Painting in the Fifteenth Century.* London: Oxford University Press, 1950.

Woolf, Rosemary. *The English Mystery Plays.* Berkeley and Los Angeles: University of California Press, 1972.

Worthen, W. B. "Drama, Performativity and Performance." *PMLA* 113, no. 5 (1998): 1093–1107.

Wunderli, Richard M. *London Church Courts and Society on the Eve of the Reformation.* Cambridge: Medieval Academy of America, 1981.

Yeager, Robert F. "John Gower's Audience: The Ballades." *Chaucer Review* 40 (2005): 81–105.

———. "John Gower's French." In *A Companion to Gower.* Ed. Siân Echard. Cambridge: D. S. Brewer, 2004. 137–51.

———. *John Gower's Poetic: The Search for a New Arion.* Cambridge: D. S. Brewer, 1990.

Young, Karl. *The Drama of the Medieval Church.* Vol. 1. Oxford: Clarendon Press, 1933.

INDEX

Adam, 30–31, 36, 76, 85, 106
adultery, 37, 52, 57, 59, 63, 74, 76, 80–81
    alleged of Mary and Joseph, 19, 90,
        118–19, 121, 123
Aelred of Rievaulx, *De Spirituali*
    Amicitia, 35–37, 41
Aers, David, 32, 86, 129, 135–36
affection
    in friendship, 39, 41, 45
    marital, 1, 6, 39, 64, 93, 100, 105, 110,
        114, 127, 130, 139–40, 142, 144
    —in marriage of Anne and
        Joachim, 99–100, 120, 130
"Against Marrying," 44
Agamemnon, 63, 79, 84
Alan de Lille, 74, 145
Alboin, 59–60, 80
Alexander III, Pope, 6, 113
Ambrose, Saint, 41
Amis and Amiloun, 41
Amos, Mark, 10
Ancrene Wisse, 73
Andreas Capellanus, *De Amore,* 27, 44, 66
Anne, Saint, 8, 95
    guild of, 92, 95
    Immaculate Conception, 95
    Life of Saint Anne, 118
    See also N-Town plays, "Joachim
        and Anna"

Anselm, Saint, 41
antimatrimonial, 15, 34, 65–67, 70,
    77, 119
Aquinas, Saint Thomas
    commentary on Aristotle's
        Nicomachean Ethics, 36
    on marriage, 34, 114
Aristotle, *Nicomachean Ethics,* 35–36, 45.
    See also Aquinas, Saint Thomas
Arnold, John H., 159
Ashley, Kathleen, 8, 92, 130
Atkinson, Clarissa W., 153
Augustine, Saint, 1, 3, 5, 94, 101, 104–6,
    111, 114, 127, 140, 150
    De Bono Coniugali, 5, 76, 94
    De Consensu Evangelistarum, 105
    De Nuptiis et Concupiscentia, 5, 196n61
Austin, J. L., 117

Bakhtin, Mikhail, 16
baptism, 7, 115
Bathsheba, 65, 72–74, 83
Beckwith, Sarah, 16, 93, 123–24,
    128–30, 132, 211n72
behavioral manuals. *See* conduct books
Bennett, J. A. W., 55
Benoît de Sainte-More, *Roman de Troie,*
    55, 62–64
Bernard, Saint, 35, 97, 145–46, 209n49

EMMA LIPTON

is assistant professor of English

at the University of Missouri, Columbia.